PHANTOM

'They were wonderful days which I would not have
missed for anything.'

DAVID NIVEN

ABOUT THE AUTHOR

Philip Warner (1914-2000) enlisted in the Royal Corps of Signals after graduating from St Catharine's, Cambridge in 1939. He fought in Malaya and spent 1,100 days as 'a guest of the Emperor' in Changi, on the Railway of Death and in the mines of Japan, an experience he never discussed. A legendary figure to generations of cadets during his thirty years as a Senior Lecturer at the Royal Military Academy, Sandhurst, he will also be long remembered for his contribution of more than 2,000 obituaries of prominent army figures to *The Daily Telegraph*.

In addition he wrote fifty-four books on all aspects of military history, ranging from castles and battlefields in Britain, to biographies of prominent military figures (such as *Kitchener: The Man Behind The Legend, Field Marshal Earl Haig, Horrocks: The General Who Led From The Front* and *Auchinleck: The Lonely Soldier*) to major histories of the SAS, the Special Boat Services and the Royal Corps of Signals.

The D-Day Landings was republished by Pen & Sword Books to mark the 60th Anniversary of this historic event and was adopted by *The Daily Telegraph* as its official commemorative book.

*　*　*

PHANTOM

PHILIP WARNER

Pen & Sword
MILITARY

First published in 1982 by William Kimber & Co Ltd
and reprinted in this format in 2005 by

PEN & SWORD MILITARY
an imprint of
Pen & Sword Books Limited
47 Church Street
Barnsley
S. Yorkshire
S70 2AS

ISBN 1 84415 218 9

A CIP catalogue record for this book
is available from the British Library.

Printed and bound in Great Britain by
CPI UK

Pen & Sword Books Ltd incorporates the imprints of
Pen & Sword Aviation, Pen & Sword Maritime, Pen & Sword Military,
Wharncliffe Local History, Pen & Sword Select,
Pen & Sword Military Classics and Leo Cooper.

For a complete list of Pen & Sword titles please contact:
PEN & SWORD BOOKS LIMITED
47 Church Street, Barnsley, South Yorkshire, S70 2AS, England.
E-mail: enquiries@pen-and-sword.co.uk
Website: www.pen-and-sword.co.uk

Contents

Amazon
july 2009

List of Maps

Acknowledgements

This account of Phantom is in two parts. The first part is a narrative of events as they occurred, in chronological sequence whenever possible. This part enables the reader to appreciate the detail given in the second part which consists entirely of personal experiences and recollections.

It will be obvious that I have had magnificently generous help from many people to enable me to write this book. I interviewed as many people as I could, and all were unreservedly helpful. I have no doubts that those members of the regiment whom I did not manage to see would have been just as cooperative.

My thanks are especially due to Lady Wallinger who kindly lent me photographs and gave me permission to quote from the late Christopher Cadogan's diary and to the librarians of the Staff College, Camberley and the Royal Military Academy Sandhurst. As always, the staff at the Public Record Office at Kew were extremely helpful.

In thanking the following members of the regiment I am well aware that I may have omitted some names which should be on it. To them I offer my apologies for any unintended discourtesy. There are many other names which I would have liked to have been able to put on it but it seemed to me that fifty would give an adequate sample of views and experiences. In the event I wished I had had time to make it a hundred as I found almost everyone I interviewed recommended someone else.

W. Adam, Esq.; Dr J. P. Astbury, Major the Hon Sir John Astor, MBE, DL; I. Balfour-Paul, Esq., MC; G. F. K. Bell, Esq.; G. Brain, Esq., T.D.; Lord Bridge of Harwich, P.C., D. Brook-Hart, Esq., MC; Major A. Crawley-Boevey, MBE; Lord Cullen of Ashbourne, MBE; F. M. Cumberledge, Esq.; F. A. de Marwicz, Esq.; Colonel J. P. Fane, MC; Colonel B. Franks, MC; M. Felgate-Catt, Esq.; J. B. L. Fitzwilliam, Esq.; The Right Hon Sir Hugh Fraser, PC, MBE, MP; Colonel J. D. Hignett; P. Hincks, Esq.; B. E. Hutton-Williams, Esq. MBE; H. L. Light, Esq.; The Right Hon Maurice Macmillan, PC, MP; Lord Mayhew, PC; A. A. Maclaren, Esq.; John Morgan, Esq.; C. R. Moore, Esq. MC; David Niven, Esq.; P. S. Newall, Esq.; Professor M. J. Oakeshott, FBA; E. F. Oliver, Esq.; P. D. Pattrick, Esq. MBE;

G. H. Pinckney, Esq.; R. J. H. Pogucki, Esq.; G. O'B. Power, Esq.; N. Radcliffe, Esq.; J. H. Randall, Esq.; G. F. N. Reddaway, Esq., CBE; Major Miles Reid; K. V. Rose, Esq.; D. L. Russell, Esq.; Milton Schulman, Esq.; A. R. M. Sedgwick, Esq.; Professor B. Simon; P. L. Stileman, Esq.; V. A. Stump, Esq.; Major J. A. Warre, MC; J. B. Watney, Esq.; L. Whistler, Esq.; Colonel B. R. Wood, MBE, TD; W. H. Woodward, Esq.; P. G. Worsthorne, Esq.; Sir John Wrightson, Bt, TD, DL.

Part One

CHAPTER ONE

Origins

Phantom was an unorthodox, secret, highly successful regiment which was created in 1939 and ceased to exist in 1945.* Its official title was GHQ Liaison Regiment, but official titles of secret regiments do not give much away to the curious and it would not have been an easy task to discover exactly what Phantom was up to – unless, of course, you were entitled to know. 'Phantom', as we see later, was originally a code-name but soon became adopted as an appropriate designation for this regiment which would suddenly manifest itself and then disappear as mysteriously as it had come. Although Phantom was active in many different theatres its existence was not widely known, and it is not surprising that since 1945 it seems to have almost disappeared from memory. But the survivors of Phantom, an enthusiastic but inevitably dwindling band, hold annual reunions, and an even more enduring tribute to the regiment is the fact that many lessons derived from its wartime experiences have proved, and still prove, of great value to the British Army.

Unorthodox, secret regiments are usually a great adventure for those belonging to them, even though the casualty rate may be high and the fate of members, if captured, is likely to be unpleasant. Such regiments are usually regarded with extreme disfavour by the commanders of more orthodox formations who, naturally enough, resent losing some of their best officers, NCOs and men to what appear to them to be hare-brained, wasteful and ill-disciplined units. Almost invariably the men volunteering are the most enterprising, energetic and least dispensable. A regiment that has just lost, say, two first-class NCOs is not likely to be persuaded that their talents are now being more usefully employed elsewhere but generally any crumb of consolation is denied by its being almost certain that the unorthodox unit is not allowed to disclose to anyone what its achievements or failures may have been.

* Its T.A. successor continued till 1963.

World War II produced a number of unorthodox formations of varying quality. At one end of the scale were units that quickly proved their worth and then went on to enhance their reputations.

Most notable among these was the Special Air Service which began in the Western Desert by destroying enemy aircraft on the ground and continued by attacking behind-the-lines targets in Italy, France, Holland, Belgium and Germany. The SAS was disbanded in 1945 but was recreated to deal with the problems of the Malayan emergency. Recently it has received considerable publicity through its televised success in anti-terrorist operations. However, the SAS insists that it is merely a regiment of the British Army with a specialist rôle.

Other wartime creations that earned many distinctions were the Commandos, whose tradition has been continued in the Royal Marines, and the Parachute Regiment, which has cheerfully accepted many routine infantry tasks. One of the most successful, though least publicized, formations was the Long Range Desert Group, which achieved miracles in intelligence work and surveillance over vast tracts of desert. Popski's Private Army, Merrill's Marauders, and the Long Range Penetration Group all performed well against the enemy but there were also many other units which played a very useful part. Jock Columns, Camouflage teams, Deception units, the 'Y' service, and the 'J' service all had a brief but valuable existence.

A feature common to most of these units was that they owed their initial creation and impetus to the vision and driving force of one man, or sometimes a small group of men. Thus Stirling, Mayne and Lewes were the architects of the SAS, Haycock, Durnford-Slater and Young of the Commandos, Lord Lovat of Lovat's Scouts, Dudley Clarke of the Deception units, and so on.

Phantom had two guiding geniuses, neither of whom, unfortunately, survived the war. They were Fairweather of the Royal Air Force and Hopkinson of the Army.

The regiment originated as an RAF unit, named No. 3 British Air Mission,* in November 1939. Commanded by Wing Commander J. M. Fairweather, DFC, its task was liaison with the Belgian General Staff. With the development of tactical air forces it had been realised, not least by those at ground level, that it was vitally important to keep the Allied Air Forces accurately informed of the exact position of troops in forward areas. In past wars the term 'front line' had given a reasonably accurate picture of troop disposition, although in close tactical support it was by no means unknown for the artillery to range

* The name was soon changed to 'No. 3 Military and Air Mission.'

on to their own troops by accident. But if it was difficult for the Gunners, with forward observation officers, always to know precisely where everyone was, it was nearly impossible for airmen, unless some satisfactory method of transmitting up-to-date information was involved. It is bad enough to be bombed and shelled by the enemy but intolerable to be subjected to the same treatment by one's own comrades in arms. Unfortunately it happens – occasionally. Equally unfortunately friendly planes have been shot down by our own guns in moment of stress and confusion.

To avoid such disasters Fairweather was allowed seven officers and twenty-two other ranks to assist him in the task of discovering from the Belgian General Staff just where the forward British and Belgian troops were. (The term 'front line' was soon found to be no longer applicable for troops might be widely dispersed and the term 'Forward Defended Localities' – FDLs – was used instead.) The task was for the unit to ascertain from the Belgians where Allied troops were deployed and then transmit the information direct to the commander of the British Air Forces in France who was, at the time, Air Marshal Sir Arthur Barratt. From this information a 'defensive bomb line' could be made.

Clearly such a liaison unit demanded a very high degree of competence. Liaison with the Belgians was through fluent linguists, not all of whom were officers. Intelligence officers assessed the information, which was enciphered and transmitted by long-range radio sets. There was no room for failure. If the liaison officers were unable to get on with their Belgian counterparts sufficiently well to obtain all the latest information easily the mission would have little to do. Linguistic ability needed to embrace a knowledge of idiomatic French and Flemish.

In its simplest form, enciphering messages means substituting a figure, or different letter, for each letter of the original. However, as simple ciphers are easily broken by the enemy, much more complicated ones are used, perhaps using a series of numbers for each letter. The possibilities for error and thus baffling one's own friends as much as the enemy are considerable. A single error may make the entire have to be checked and re-transmitted. The error is most likely to message incomprehensible. If an error occurs, the whole message may occur when the message is being sent over radio. A figure or a group may be lost from interference by weather, instrument failure, human error, or enemy action. A unit entrusted with the task of transmitting vital information must therefore not only be skilled at the art of obtaining it but also one hundred per cent reliable in passing it on. Patience, persistence and almost superhuman conscientiousness are essential.

Fairweather's unit established itself at Valenciennes in the French, not the British zone, where it reviewed its duties and began training for them. Not least of its problems was the fact that the Belgians did not wish to co-operate with the Allies or do anything which might provoke the Germans to attack them. In mid-November 1939 Phantom was joined by Lieutenant-Colonel G. F. Hopkinson, MC, (North Staffordshire Regiment). Hopkinson had up till then been a part of the Howard-Vyse mission, a formation commanded by Major-General Sir Richard Howard-Vyse whose task was to liaise with General Gamelin in Paris. (Liaising with General Gamelin was said to be somewhat frustrating for the General spoke French very rapidly and almost inaudibly.) In any event the assignment was not one to suit the redoubtable 'Hoppy'.

Hoppy and Fairy got on very well. Both agreed that all the required information could never be acquired from the Belgian General Staff for they did not know it themselves. Ground reconnaissance must therefore be used. Hoppy was a qualified pilot and understood the airman's point of view and Fairy had a sound grasp of the problems of soldiering and warfare at ground level. Hopkinson's original title was 'Military Observer', and his staff and equipment consisted of a car, a driver, a batman and a clerk. This became the 'Hopkinson Mission'.

Hopkinson was the sort of person who would have seemed slightly improbable if he had appeared in a book of romantic, adventurous fiction. He had been in World War I, gone up to Cambridge afterwards, taken a degree in engineering, and played a very full part in university life. Then and later he became known as a dashing horseman, an intrepid sailor, and a social asset anywhere. Small, tough, cheerful, he seemed to possess unlimited energy and enterprise. But he was also a regular officer and demanded the highest standards. Discipline might appear to be relaxed but it was undoubtedly there.

Sir John Wrightson knew Hopkinson before the war: 'He was always Hoppy to almost everybody; I don't ever recall more than two or three people ever calling him George. He was absolutely ramrod, a dedicated soldier but with an enormous sense of humour. He was in the North Staffordshire Regiment and lived off his pay. He had one brother, but was a fairly lonely man.'

In 1938 Wrightson went out to Turkey where his company were building a steel works. Hoppy was working for another company as a liaison officer, having been seconded from the army for two years for this purpose; doubtless he had persuaded the War Office that he would be acquiring experience of military value. He was a successful co-ordinator and eventually negotiated a satisfactory maintenance contract; the negotiations were so long-drawn and frustrating that a less dauntless man than Hoppy would have given up.

He recruited Wrightson into Phantom in late 1940, as Intelligence Officer. Wrightson, who was in the Durham Light Infantry, had had experience on the staff of 23rd Division in France. Wrightson was given some unusual tasks: one was to explore the possibilities of signalling via the London sewage system, using ASDIC on the pipes. Wrightson was sent to discuss these underwater methods with the Navy who thought it sounded odd but were very helpful. Hopkinson then sent Wrightson to the War Office to investigate the possibilities of using carrier-pigeons in Phantom. Wrightson obtained approval and put one Lance-Corporal G. Starr in charge. Of Starr, more later. Gordon Richards, the jockey, was also a pigeon-fancier and for a time helped out with the pigeon-loft. Wrightson considered that Hopkinson's success possibly stemmed from the fact that he appeared to know all the key people in the Army and partly from his choice of subordinates. One of the latter was his second-in-command, Major the Hon Hugh Kindersley (Scots Guards). Kindersley subsequently became a General.

Soon after Hopkinson arrived at Valenciennes the mission was joined by a troop of the 12th Lancers, under Captain J. A. Warre. The 12th Lancers were Light Cavalry, and equipped with armoured cars. An armoured car troop, although small (about thirty men) can get through an enormous amount of work reconnoitring, liaising, supporting, etc. It often tests defences for strength and gets a bloody nose in the process. The value of a cavalry troop (or two) for Phantom was obvious, for the cars could move around rapidly to and from trouble spots and at the same time carry wireless sets sufficiently powerful to transmit over long distances. At this stage in the war, and for many years afterwards, wireless sets and their batteries were extremely heavy and cumbersome. But in the Guy armoured cars weight was no problem.

Hopkinson and Fairweather were both determined and dedicated to creating what they felt was an essential unit; backed by Air Marshal Barratt, they were soon harassing the War Office to agree to a proper establishment. This came through in mid-February 1940 when they had eventually made it clear to Whitehall that in the event of invasion the task of providing all the required information would be well beyond the capacity of Belgian GHQ.

The two units were now to be combined, with Fairweather in command. Fairweather himself was to be at Belgian HQ with a detachment large enough to maintain contact with Air Marshal Barratt, and with other parts of the mission. The remainder of Phantom would be with Hopkinson at what was to be known as the Advanced Report Centre. It would consist of HQ Detachment, Captain Warre's Phantom Armoured Car Squadron, a motor cycle troop, an Intelligence section and some administration personnel.

Its strength was to be 15 officers and 110 other ranks. On paper this looks a fairly orthodox unit : in practice it was quite different.

HQ consisted of four wireless detachments from the Royal Corps of Signals, but one of these was with Fairweather, another with GHQ, BEF. The Armoured Car Squadron consisted of two armoured car troops, and a motor cycle troop. The armoured cars, all fitted with No 11 wireless sets, came under the command of Captain J. A. Warre. The motor cycle troop came from Queen Victoria's Rifles and was commanded by Second-Lieutenant J. A. T. Morgan; Morgan would eventually command Phantom in 1945. The intelligence section was commanded by Captain J. S. Collings, 5th (Inniskilling) Dragoon Guards. It comprised six intelligence officers and six NCOs. All were fluent French speakers and all trained motor cyclists, of varying quality.

Although Phantom's primary task was to supply the Allied Central Air Bureau with information it took on the secondary task of supplying GHQ BEF with the same information on the basis that this might help towards obtaining much needed extra wireless equipment. Soon, however, the secondary role became of greater importance than the other. An advantage in training which Phantom enjoyed was that it could use wireless in practice as it was stationed outside the BEF area. Troops in the BEF area had to observe wireless silence as it was well known that the Germans would be listening constantly for any information of strength, disposition or intention.

Phantom was a curious mixture, and at first it seemed doubtful whether such an assortment would settle into a homogeneous unit. Some of its members had lived for long periods in Belgium or France; this made them excellent linguists but could have created a barrier. The Signals personnel were orthodox, highly-skilled but used to 'the usual channels'. Queen Victoria's Rifles, from which the motor cycle troop came, was a Territorial unit of the 60th Rifles (Greenjackets); they were Londoners. The armoured car troops had originally been

12th Lancers; the original troop had been withdrawn but Captain Warre had stayed on and formed a new squadron. The new troops were a mixture of ex-Royal Tank Regiment and drafts from other cavalry units. The unit was SECRET. Even the word 'Phantom' was not to be used, although a white P on black cloth was issued as a regimental sign.*

A problem with a mixed unit such as this is that as soon as it is formed almost everyone in it immediately becomes a stickler for the traditions of his original unit, however brief his acquaintanceship with it. Drill in Light Infantry Regiments is at 180 paces to the minute; other units prefer 130, some specialise in an even slower, more deliberate step. Nowadays, with the SLR nobody 'slopes' arms, but in the days of the 303 most units carried the rifle on the shoulder at the slope while Rifle regiments carried it in the shoulder arms position. The answer to all this has to be given firmly by the adjutant but unless the message is very clear a few people may have to learn co-operation the hard way.

There was, of course, no urgency. Poland had been overrun but apart from some occasional patrol activity the armies in the West left each other alone. The RAF were active over Germany, scattering leaflets which it was hoped would cause the Germans to remove Hitler and make peace; the Belgians hoped nothing would happen, the Dutch did not think it would, and the French, comfortably enshrouded in the ridiculous Maginot line, felt that that was a sufficient deterrent. Only at sea was there a grim battle, token of horrors to come. Most of the British Army was profoundly bored with monotonous training for static warfare which might never occur. Phantom had the advantage of training with a new purpose. But most of the excitement came from falling off motor cycles. An unexpected event was when Gracie Fields, touring the troops in France on a morale-raising expedition, visited Valenciennes. But the days of the Great Bore War were running out. On 7th May Phantom was alerted to the possibility of a German attack. On 10th May it came.

---

* This was a piece of Hopkinson buccaneering for there was no need for it to be secret. Sir John Wrightson relates that Hoppy said: 'It will be much easier to get equipment if we call it "secret".'

CHAPTER TWO

Phantom wins its spurs

News of the German advance came soon after dawn on 10th May. By 9 a.m. the unit was on the move, and by 10 a.m. over the border into Belgium, where it was rapturously welcomed by the Belgians. Fairweather's party went to Brussels and thence to Belgian GHQ at Willebroek, south of Antwerp. Hopkinson's Advanced Report Centre moved rapidly up to Mielen-sur-Aelst which is four miles east of St Trond. From here it sent patrols to Namur and the line of the Albert Canal; these gave advance information about Belgian withdrawals. At 7.30 p.m. Phantom informed GHQ BEF of the fact that the Belgians had not destroyed the Maastricht bridge and the Germans were pouring across it.

There was other sobering news of German advances too. Phantom moved its base four times in fifteen hours but it was trained for its task and was not disrupted. At this time it seemed that Phantom – and perhaps the Germans – were the only people who knew where the German penetration was going. Contact was established with the French forward units and with our own cavalry. It was clear that the Belgian Higher Command was now in a state of confusion and dismay, and that nothing further could be expected from that source. Now the reconnaissance training came into its own. Information was gathered from everywhere possible, collated, and transmitted.

Ironically Phantom's speed in reporting new disasters was the only success of the time. The German attack had not been entirely unexpected but its effectiveness certainly was. Everyone, particularly the unfortunate Belgians who received the first taste of it, was alarmed and dismayed. Blitzkrieg was undoubtedly lightning war and it made nonsense of Allied predictions and defence plans. Civilians who suddenly found themselves the target of panzer thrusts and dive-bombing attacks were thrown into confusion and panic; their reaction was to try to get away from it all by taking to the nearest road. The roads which were already congested with military traffic now became jammed tight with streams of refugees. German aircraft added to the disorder and terror by bombing and strafing the helpless columns. The only way Phantom could move around apart from its motor cyclists was by leaving the roads and going cross-country.

On 14th May it looked as if the Allies might hold a line between Givet, Namur and Antwerp but by the 18th this hope was abandoned and withdrawal began once more. As the situation seemed so desperate Hopkinson offered the services of Phantom to General Mason-Macfarlane who had created a mobile column known as 'Macforce'. Phantom's task consisted of patrol activity in the Lens-Béthune area but this did not last long and they were soon assigned to Hazebrouck.

Although there was a widespread opinion that the battle was already lost, Hopkinson and Phantom did not share that view. By promptly reporting the area and size of German penetrations they had reduced the enemy's capacity to surprise. They also provided Allied headquarters with information which would have enabled those attacks to be countered, and propaganda repudiated; however no appropriate action was taken. Instead Phantom found itself assigned to searching for missing units in the Calais area, providing an escort for the Commander-in-Chief, Viscount Gort, helping in the defence of Wormhoudt, assisting in covering various withdrawals (Second-Lieutenant Lord Banbury covered the withdrawal of part of 144 Infantry Brigade), and finally having the unwelcome task of destroying the unit's own vehicles. Hopkinson's party finally embarked for England on 31st May from La Panne, near Dunkirk.

The remainder of Phantom moved from Bruges to Ostend where two boats were waiting to evacuate survivors of the battle. One of them, the *Marquis*, took on the remainder of the military personnel, the other, an overloaded merchantman called the *Aboukir*, took on the air mission. Eight miles from the Belgian coast the *Aboukir* was torpedoed by a German E boat. Of Phantom, ten officers and twenty-two other ranks died in her.

There were very few survivors but one of them was Second Lieutenant G. F. N. Reddaway who was an exceptionally strong swimmer. He also happened to be on deck at the time. Later he became British Ambassador to Poland. Reddaway provides a good example of the adaptability of Phantom officers who were sometimes called upon to assist in tasks which were outside the function of the regiment. One such assignment fell to him in the early stages of the German attack in 1940.

Admiral Lord Keyes, who had taken a distinguished part in the

First World War, was determined to be equally to the fore in the Second. He was therefore in Belgium in May 1940 and was keeping Winston Churchill informed of his reading of the situation. He used Phantom to relay messages about the Belgian King and Commanders-in-Chief so that he could judge their possible reactions if the situation became worse. He did not mince words. One senior Belgian officer was described as a windy yes-man from whom little could be expected.

Reddaway recalls: 'I went to Antwerp with Keyes because he wanted someone who spoke French and had a motor-bike. Keyes wanted to oversee the blowing up by naval personnel of certain installations on Antwerp docks that might be useful to the Germans. I enjoyed going along and particularly the eeriness of a major town quite dead in the afternoon sunshine: Belgians all gone, Germans not yet arrived. A few cheerful naval personnel seeing to the demolitions.'

Another who was lost with the *Aboukir* was the redoubtable Wing Commander Fairweather, and Flight Lieutenant G. Zech, whose ability at obtaining vital information was only equalled by his technical skill at making wireless sets work and continue working. Others who went down with the ship were Flying Officers W. H. Humphreys and A. H. Woolcock, both of whom were cipher officers. They had been contemporaries at St Catharine's College, Cambridge. A third contemporary at the same college, Captain J. W. Jackson, was on the other boat and survived. Bill Humphreys had been an enthusiastic rugby player, Bertie Woolcock was goalkeeper and captain of the University Association Football XI.

Sad though these losses were, there was some consolation in the fact that their work for Phantom during the months had proved its value and established its claim to an expanded and continuing existence. Although many papers went down with the *Aboukir* there is a comprehensive list of Phantom messages now deposited in the Public Record Office.

When the remainder of Phantom reassembled in England, some interesting facts came up for review. It was recalled that two days after the beginning of the German attack Phantom had sent a despatch informing GHQ BEF that Belgian GHQ was 'unfit for driving a partially unwilling army'. It was noted too that time and again information had been sent in about German attacks and where those attacks could be upset. Much information had been gained from listening to German conversations between tank and unit commanders. Clearly this was something which could be exploited better in the future, as indeed it was by the 'J' and 'Y' services. There was an obvious need for official press photographers to take pictures valuable to the Allied cause – but there had been no press photographers in the forward area. Phantom found that the French were very vague about British dispositions. This suggested that the regular liaison officers were not up to the mark as the French appeared to be very willing to learn and to cooperate. It had been discovered that even with the limited resources of Phantom the entire forward area could be covered in one day.

Not least of the discoveries was that aerial photographs, admirable for many purposes, were quite inadequate for revealing the state of a battle.

Another finding was that very young liaison officers were much better at acquiring information from their French and Belgian counterparts than older and more mature officers would have been. Possibly they seemed so young and innocent; whatever the reason it was a success.

Of the equipment, it was decided that the Guy armoured vehicles were too big and cumbersome, and too lightly armed (.5 and .303 machine guns) for their purpose. The motor cycles were BSA Solos and Norton Combinations and the Nortons were felt to be good but somewhat lacking in power. The wireless sets were reasonably reliable but, as mentioned earlier, were heavy. The No 9 set had a range of 120 miles on W/T morse; the No 11 set had a range of 50 miles or morse and 20 on speech. Both used a type of collapsible aerial known as a Wyndham.

Improvisation and resource were the orders of the day. On 22nd May Trooper Hall raised his Bren at a Heinkel which was showing interest. It came down but whether solely from his contribution was never proved. Another example of improvisation was Lieutenant-Colonel Hopkinson's war diary. It was kept on the back of sheets of notepaper from the Royal Automobile Club. He wrote very clearly in spite of the circumstances. Among the messages is one from Air Marshal Barratt. It read:

Heartiest congratulations on the most valuable information with which you have kept us supplied. It has been invaluable. Please inform all concerned.

In view of the remarks which have been made subsequently about French morale it is interesting to note from these papers that initially this was high and still remained high even after heavy casualties. It appears to have deteriorated when the fighting men suspected that were not being adequately supported by their Higher Command and politicians.

So Phantom had proved itself – but at a cost. Now for the future.

CHAPTER THREE

Phantom Regroups

In the summer of 1940 the prospects of Allied victory seemed to have receded into a problematic future. There was no more talk of hanging out the washing on the Siegfried Line; rather more thought was given to what should happen if the Germans tried to cross the Channel. This they were already doing by air and it did not seem unlikely that they hoped to catch the Navy off guard and do the same by sea. Through a welter of confusion and apprehension came one steadying and inspiring voice – Churchill. He promised 'blood, toil, tears and sweat'. Somehow it was exactly the message everyone wished to hear; it was an end to false optimism and a return to reality. Of course we would win, but it would take time. None of that rubbish about the war being over by Christmas.

In the circumstances any commanding officer with a clear head and intentions was likely to get a fair hearing. Hopkinson was that and had just that. One week after returning he sent a letter to the Director of Military Operations at the War Office, describing the success of the unit in France and requesting a new and larger establishment. He asked for four units. This would have given him about 1,000 all ranks. He can hardly have expected to get all that but he did succeed in obtaining permission for half the number. And, as Hoppy knew, once you have your basic establishment it is surprising what you can add on here and there as time passes.

There were two very strong points in his favour. One was that staff officers in smaller headquarters were often too heavily involved with local problems to have the time to pass back to senior headquarters all the information which they should. This had led to conflicts on policy. If however rear formations knew exactly what was happening in forward areas co-operation would be much improved. The second point was that, though transmission of information forward worked adequately through Royal Signals providing the usual channels – from Army to Corps, Corps to Division, Division to Brigade, and Brigade to regiments – and in the process all those who should be informed were informed, the process did not work so well from the opposite direction.

There were several reasons why it was too slow. One was that in a fast moving battle situation could change within half an hour or less. Thus by the time a report was reaching Army HQ the situation report could well be out of date. Secondly, there was unlikely to be an officer in a small formation who was senior enough to give his messages an adequate priority prefix. And the 'normal channels' were in any case fully utilized by routine reports on casualty, ammunition and ration returns, among much else.

Thus Phantom was not a rival to the Royal Corps of Signals but harmoniously employed with it. Initially Phantom drew the majority of its operators from Signals and its liaison and reconnaissance members from other sources. As time passed the characteristics of the two elements became blurred. Signals personnel adapted themselves very easily to non-technical tasks and members from infantry or cavalry regiments became wise old birds in operating and maintaining wireless links.

The regiment was reborn but at this moment it almost lost the name with which it had won its spurs. Phantom seemed rather a nebulous title for a unit which must for the moment be engaged in a 'backs to the wall' policy. The title 'Ironsiders' was considered; General Sir Edmund Ironside was till the 27th May Chief of the Imperial General Staff and was now C-in-C Home Forces. (CIGS – the 'Imperial' had now been dropped – is effectively the Commander-in-Chief of the British Army; until World War I he commanded Dominion and Colonial forces as well.) The regiment at this time was billeted at Lechdale, Gloucestershire, where the war seemed far away. But with its rebirth it was given a change of name which was meant to be permanent. It was to be called No 1 GHQ Reconnaissance Unit. The fact that reconnaissance was but one part of the regiment's function and its major task was to obtain information from those in the best position to know it (under normal circumstances) made no difference: it was to be a reconnaissance unit.

However the War Office and its successor, the Ministry of Defence, have a useful habit of not letting the right hand know what the left hand doeth when it comes to choosing regimental names. Soon afterwards it created the Reconnaissance Corps and Hopkinson was therefore able to propose that the title GHQ Liaison Regiment, alias Phantom, should be re-adopted, to avoid confusion. (Connoisseurs of these matters will note that more recently ((1970) the MOD christened the combined Royal Scots Greys and 3rd Carabiniers, the Royal Scots Dragoon Guards, as if the Royal Scots did not exist. To avoid the inevitable confusion the RSDG are usually called the Scots Dragoon Guards.)

The new GHQ Liaison Regiment initially consisted of a head-quarters and three scout car groups, each containing four officer patrols. The three groups were soon edged up to four and the word 'group' exchanged for 'squadron' which was more suitable to the cavalry panache of the unit. Its strength was rapidly built up to 48 officers and 407 other ranks and from there, more gradually, to 479 plus 92 on reserve. It also had a pigeon loft with 500 pigeons, and a Light Aid Detachment for repairing and recovering vehicles disabled by enemy or other causes. The regiment came under direct command of GHQ Home Forces and was therefore not bothered by enquiries about establishment and authority.

As Hoppy had a genius for 'empire building' the unit did well for both personnel and equipment. The basic unit was a patrol of one officer and six men, equipped with a Daimler scout car, a 15 cwt ($\frac{3}{4}$ ton) truck and three motor cycles. These patrols were designed to be self-supporting for forty-eight hours. Anyone nowadays looking at World War II equipment in a museum will gain a false impression of its capabilities in the hands of most of its users. Three-ton trucks (now the same but called four-ton!) were made to do incredible speeds and cover impossible ground. Most vehicles were fitted with a governor to restrict their speed; such governors were soon removed (illegally) and matronly-looking trucks would hurtle along at 80 or even 90 mph. Wireless sets sometimes operated at freak ranges and guns such as Brens which were designed to be fired from a tripod were frequently fired from the hip!

However, although Hoppy wanted enterprising soldiers he was very careful about those who volunteered. New, unorthodox units are often regarded as a convenient dumping ground for soldiers whose commanding officers give them the highest recommendation for enterprise – without disclosing that it is almost, if not entirely, criminal in nature. They did not get past Hoppy. He recruited largely by getting his trusted officers to recruit their trusted friends.

Much of Hopkinson's success derived from the fact that his training was imaginative and unorthodox. While everyone else was envisaging a possible German landing between Brighton and Bexhill, or at least between Ramsgate and Portsmouth, Hoppy felt that the Germans were not above a sneak attack elsewhere. He therefore sent out patrols to check other possible areas from Wales to the Wash. The prospect of a landing in the area of the Wash is not as fanciful as might be imagined.* Hoppy also appreciated the value of keeping troops busy and in the field.

Phantom now moved closer to the centre of activities. After a short spell at Kneller Hall, near Twickenham, the unit moved to Richmond (Surrey), taking over the Richmond Hill Hotel, and Wick Hall, both of which were in a very run-down state, as their main base. Training took place in Richmond Park, which was then closed to the public, and the officers were billeted in Pembroke Lodge. The Battle Headquarters detachment was in St James's Park, where the pigeon loft was sited. In peace-time it is difficult to take the idea of a pigeon post seriously. In wartime these matters are regarded slightly differently. Pigeons can fly swiftly and directly, usually without danger of interruption, and have been known to travel through areas where the gunfire has been intense enough to wound them though not stop them. The loft was in the care of Lance Corporal Starr, who had enlisted in Belgium, where he was renowned as an expert on pigeons. Starr did not remain long with Phantom. His expertise was employed by Special Operations Executive which attached him to French Resistance. He became Colonel Starr, MC and Croix de Guerre.

Training was rigorous, beginning with early morning PT, and continuing till 6 p.m. There was a midnight curfew. (This was standard practice in most units but these unorthodox formations might have hoped for a little more leeway. Not with Hoppy.) Much of the training time was spent on wireless so that everyone could virtually send and receive at a reasonable speed even in his sleep. And, in practice, an operator might well be almost in his sleep. He will crouch over a morse key, hour after hour, day after day, sometimes getting an hour or two for sleep, sometimes not. Working up to a speed of between twenty and thirty words a minute with absolute accuracy in transmitting and receiving is not a skill which can be learnt without regular, incessant practice. Nor can it be retained without constant practice. There was no nonsense of passing out at twenty-four words per minute and then after a month of idleness being shaky at fifteen wpm. Speed must be maintained and, if possible, increased. Hoppy made his officers become as proficient as their men at morse and motorcycling.

Phantom established a high-speed communication network all over the country using half its personnel while the rest were being trained

* Vide infra.

or re-trained. Hopkinson knew very well that the enemy was not likely to keep office hours, so he trained Phantom to get up in the middle of the night and begin a day's work then, or to miss a night's rest, or to reverse day and night completely.* But the regiment had to be a smart regiment too – not mulishly dedicated to spit and polish at kit inspection but smart enough to take its place with the best. (It is an interesting fact that the best turned out regiments are usually the most effective in battle too. Scruffiness may be all right as a disguise, but when there is no need for disguise the regiment must look good and feel good.) He acquired Guards NCOs to guarantee the drill and turn-out.

Hopkinson was also a good showman. He invited VIPs, such as the Duke of Kent, to visit the unit, and he staged an occasional social event or concert for which he drew on some of his pre-war social contacts. There were also plenty of people in the regiment who had the right connections. One was David Niven, then a major commanding A Squadron. David Niven has appeared so often as a hero in films that members of the general public have begun to feel he was merely a celluloid hero. On the contrary he was very highly respected in the unit for his qualities as a soldier.

One night Niven had been given the task of arranging a concert and the subsequent party. He produced the then famous Debroy Somers band, Leslie Henson, the Crazy Gang and the redoubtable Flanagan and Allen. Time has dimmed the glamour of some of these show-biz personalities but in their day they were the top of the bill in every sense of the word. It was a change from training – but a reward for it too. It was not merely a matter of 'All work and no play, makes Jack a dull boy', but also a subtle way of demonstrating that Phantom was not merely a scraped-together functional unit but was a regiment with a special function which could take its place socially and militarily with the best the army could produce – and without being pompous about it either.

However, Hopkinson knew very well that more than parties and concerts were required if Phantom was to justify its existence, particularly when the immediate danger of invasion had receded by the end of 1940. It may be remembered that in early October German troops had occupied Roumania. With the optimistic ambition of obtaining a little military glory himself, Mussolini had launched the Italian army into Greece at the end of the same month. The Greeks, however, did

---

* This caused other – and higher – formations to be puzzled and often infuriated.

not take kindly to conquest by the Italians, whom they held in low regard, and were soon giving better than they received; the fact that forty-five million Italians were opposing seven million Greeks did not seem to them as important as it had originally seemed to the Italians. The Greeks proceeded to capture Koritza in Albania and went on to overrun a quarter of the country. Mussolini became even more worried when the British launched an offensive in Libya in December 1940, and also crippled the Italian naval base at Taranto with an air attack. These events which were viewed with dismay by Mussolini merely gave a grim resolve to Hitler. He decided there must be no question of a victorious Anglo-Greek army moving in to capture the Roumanian oilfields. He prepared to act.

Hopkinson decided that a move to the Middle East by a squadron of Phantom would be to everyone's advantage. It would give the regiment a function overseas and it would help to answer those critics who, in all probability, would say its continued existence in Britain now that the immediate threat of invasion was over was unnecessary, and that it should be disbanded. Hopkinson decided that a squadron could function very well by reporting directly what was happening on the Greek-Italian front. The War Office agreed. 'A' Squadron, now commanded by Major Miles Reid, Royal Engineers, was chosen for this assignment. At the time it was based on Chilham Castle, Kent.

Miles Reid had had an unusual and exciting career. Originally destined for the Royal Navy, he had spent five years at Osborne and Dartmouth (where he was a contemporary of the future King George VI). Unfortunately Reid was all too prone to seasickness so had left the Navy just before the First World War broke out. He had promptly joined the Royal Engineers, was wounded at Gallipoli, and subsequently gassed on the Somme.

At the end of the First World War he was demobilised and became a business man. At the start of the Second he volunteered, although in his forties. He was sent to liaise with the French on the Howard-Vyse mission. Liaison with the French was not easy as the French still used some military terms which had been unchanged since Napoleon's day and also used Michelin maps on which it was impossible to give grid references. However, the difficulties which occurred before the Germans attacked were as nothing to those which occurred afterwards. Eventually Reid was evacuated and soon after landing in Britain had joined Phantom.

The move was top secret, but as the unit took both Arctic clothing for winter in the Greek mountains, and summer clothing for the Greek summer in the valleys, would-be spies had a difficult time trying to work out its possible destination. 'A' Squadron sailed from Liverpool to Alexandria, whence it proceeded, full of optimism, to GHQ Middle East at Cairo.

Needless to say, when Phantom arrived at Cairo nobody had heard of them and nobody wanted to.* Mild irritation with their presence soon changed to cold fury when it was realised that this upstart squadron wished to pass its gleanings from GHQ ME to GHQ Home Forces. Simply and firmly they were rebuffed.

Greece? That was under surveillance by the RAF. We were not involved in the fighting and there was nothing for Phantom to do there anyway.

Fortunately they found a friend in Major-General Sir Arthur Smith, the Chief of Staff, Middle East. He arranged an interview for Reid with General Wavell. Wavell was a man of imagination. Before the war in a series of lectures at Cambridge he had surprised military conservatives by saying that the modern soldier should be like a 'cat-burglar'. He could see the uses of Phantom but felt they should get themselves acclimatised before getting to work. He therefore sent them off into the desert to be attached to General Sir Richard O'Connor's Western Desert Force Advance Headquarters. They were provided with desert-worthy vehicles but to their chagrin had their transport commandeered and driven to the point of breakdown. Sadly they returned to Alexandria.

But now their luck changed. At the end of December they were flown to Athens. They were re-designated H Squadron instead of A, but it was only a change of letter, and did not mean a change of function.

Although Britain had no wish to become involved in the campaign, which the Greeks appeared to be managing very well without assistance, there was a sizable British military mission in Athens for liaison purposes. Unrealistic though it may seem with hindsight, there was still an Allied belief that the war could be limited, that if Britain did not become involved in Greece the Germans would not do so either, even though their Italian partners were being defeated. Undoubtedly with his forthcoming campaign in Russia in mind Hitler had no wish to dissipate his forces in minor campaigns, but the idea that he would meekly allow a vital strategic area to pass into Allied control and then be a threat to his oil supplies now seems unbelievably naive. But

---

* This was probably because Hoppy had taken too much on himself and failed to inform the War Office adequately.

the Greeks too wished to avoid doing anything to provoke the Germans into invading their territory.

Phantom's objection to their comrades in the military mission was not, however, their naiveté but their red-tape. When the services have little to do the paperwork mounts up. Reid at times began to wonder whether the Mission, with its insistence on peacetime routines, realised there was a war on its doorstep. But to add to his frustration within the mission, there were others outside. The Greeks flatly refused to allow Phantom to observe the activities of their army in Albania. All the regiment could therefore do was to train in the Peloponnese. It established a wireless link with Home Forces in January 1941 and waited. To avoid confusion with the Greek alphabet which in some ways, but not all, is like our own, the P was changed to PHI=Φ. Phantom's training in wireless techniques was rewarded by signals from Greece being received by a No 11 set on Leith Hill.

By March it had been learnt that the Germans had every intention of attacking Greece when it suited them and that the invasion would take place soon. General Maitland-Wilson was appointed to command British forces when that occurred. Phantom was now deployed in the valleys leading into that country – the routes which the Germans must use. It was known that the Germans had some twenty-four divisions in Roumania and that Bulgaria had been forced into an agreement to allow the passage of German troops. Meanwhile Yugoslavia had been coerced into signing a treaty allowing for the passage of German troops through its territory. However the Yugoslavian army upset this plan by staging a coup d'état, and repudiating the treaty. Hitler thereupon decided that Yugoslavia and Greece should be brought to heel forthwith. He had already sent German troops to Tripoli to bolster up the Italians.

On 6th April 1941 thirty-three German divisions invaded Yugoslavia. Six of them were armoured. The Yugoslavs had little to oppose them except courage – they did not possess a single tank or anti-tank gun, and it is hardly surprising that ten days later the campaign was over. Hitler was pleased; he was unaware that this event was also the beginning of another long, exhausting campaign against guerillas and partisans, a campaign which would at times tie up as many as twenty German divisions.

While German troops were pouring into Yugoslavia, others were crossing the Greek frontier and threading their way through the valleys. Phantom, as we saw, had already reconnoitred the possible invasion routes, although in order not to draw attention to themselves

Greece and its neighbours

they had worn civilian clothes. The Greeks had provided transport and a liaison officer!

British involvement in the Greek campaign, as is now well-known, was both a disaster and a mistake. British troops had been taken from the desert where they were badly needed and were plunged into a battle against impossible odds. The rapid collapse of the Yugoslavs, combined with the German success in eastern Greece meant that the Allied forces in Greece were frequently outflanked and generally out-classed. General 'Jumbo' Wilson subsequently said that almost the only reliable information about the state of the battle came to him from Phantom. Unfortunately it was always bad news and the regiment suffered considerably in securing it. The Germans had been astonished to find the British in Greece at all but were also surprised by the stubbornness of some of the British rearguard actions. There was, of course, no hope of saving Greece and the outcome of this Allied gesture of solidarity was that 11,000 troops could not be evacuated but were captured with much valuable equipment.

When it became apparent that evacuation was inevitable Reid established Phantom HQ at Corinth with a wireless link to Athens. However, two days later German airborne units penetrated the area, captured the bridge over the Corinth Canal and cut off the Pelopon-nese from the rest of Greece. As the German parachutists began to land around them, Reid, Sergeant Averill and seven men headed for the nearest high ground. Unfortunately they had only seven rifles and fifty rounds. Even when an Australian carrying a Bren, with seventy rounds, appeared, the outlook could not be anything but hopeless. They were spotted by the parachutists and a brisk exchange of fire took place in which the German captain was killed. An attempt to bring up a box of ammunition merely led to the death of two more members of Phantom. When their ammunition finally ran out the remains of A Squadron headquarters surrendered. In view of the fact that Phantom had killed the German captain, the Germans de-liberated whether to finish them off in revenge : fortunately they de-cided against when Reid pointed out that they had already killed the two members of Phantom carrying the ammunition.

Like the rest of the Allied Forces Phantom had fared badly in Greece. Only nine members succeeded in escaping. Ironically reinforce-ments were already on the way to the unit when it was being obliterated, and these fortuitously arrived in the Middle East just in time for the re-forming of the squadron. The Greek episode was by no means a total loss for Phantom, for they had impressed General Wilson and other senior commanders with their ability to communicate rapidly and accurately from the battle zone. In future Phantom would need all the friends it could get. In the process of formation and establishment its problem had been to prove that it was necessary at all. Its initial forecasts were regarded with scepticism but events had proved that it could do exactly what it said it could. In the future it would encounter a different, less pleasant form of opposition.

Although its ability to send reports direct from the forward areas to GHQ was now appreciated by those in both areas, it was regarded with suspicion and hostility by those commanding intermediate formations. There was an understandable irritation over the fact that headquarters of brigades and divisions were not always given a chance to see the information about their activities which was being supplied to higher formations. There was a further suspicion that the information thus supplied to GHQ was premature, unrelated to the general strategy of the intermediate formations, and likely to be misleading. Direct conversation between the Managing Director and the men on the assembly line tends to infuriate foremen, line managers, and departmental heads. Phantom found that this type of hostility was one of the penalties of success and had to take appropriate measures to counter it.

The experiences of Miles Reid after his capture in Greece appear partly in his book *Last on the List* written in Colditz, and published by Leo Cooper in 1974, and in a book about to be published in 1982. The latter describes Colditz as it was, not as it has since been made to appear in certain books and films.

CHAPTER FOUR

Phantom Reborn

The reinforcements from which the new H Squadron would be created consisted of five officers and fifty-one other ranks. Commanding the draft was Captain Peter Forshall. Second-in-command was Lieutenant Frank Thompson, son of Edward Thompson, an Oxford don. Thompson had a fluent command of Greek and several other European languages and even at Oxford had earned a reputation as a poet and letter writer. His enthusiasm was notable but his soldierly qualities less obvious at this stage. His political opinions were far to the Left. The other officers were Donald Melvin, Edgar Herbert and Graham Bell. All three had joined Phantom two days prior to sailing, and had had no experience of active service. Most of the draft were similarly lacking in experience. Many felt that to be flung into an active theatre without either intensive training or previous operational experience was putting an unfair burden on the newcomers. The fact that they had to create what was virtually a new unit – one which must in no way disappoint the Higher Command's expectations of Phantom efficiency – did not make life any easier. The draft sailed from Gourock on 19th March 1941 in a troopship named *Pasteur*. Like many other troopships it was soon re-christened by those who had to sail in her.

As these events occurred some forty years ago at the time of writing conditions of wartime travel may not always be appreciated by those who did not experience them. After the fall of France all soldiers proceeding on leave or to any destination had to carry all kit, which meant rifle, pack, haversack, steel helmet, gas mask and bulging kit bag with them. Every train corridor was blocked by kit bags – and often with their owners, every luggage rack was full of packs and haversacks. Rifles, steel helmets and respirators had to be carried everywhere, even when a soldier was visiting a cinema (although he was not issued with any ammunition to use on these expeditions). Troopships usually sailed from Liverpool or Glasgow from which ports it was hoped they would be less accessible to German bombers. Their route took them into the North Atlantic where submarines were likely to be less plentiful, almost to Greenland, then down the North American coast before re-crossing the Atlantic to West Africa. Thence they went to the Cape of Good Hope and either or up through the Suez Canal to India. Routing troopships through the Mediterranean past Sicily, Italy and other German or Italian airfields was reckoned too risky. It was not, however, unknown for troopships to be held up in the Clyde fog during the winter months.

Every troopship was crammed with men and kit; five thousand were confined like sardines on former liners which had been built for two or three hundred passengers. But before a man reached the ship he might have spent eighteen hours on the train, sometimes shunted into a siding if an air raid was taking place in a town immediately ahead. Second Lieutenant Bell had eaten a slightly questionable sandwich just before getting on the train. If there was one complaint calculated to turn an uncomfortable journey into a nightmare it was an acute bilious attack. The air raid and pelting rain which met them at Glasgow seemed minor troubles in comparison.

The *Pasteur* was moored out in the river and could only be boarded from ferries, and an interesting climb up a wet rope ladder. The draft embarking on the *Pasteur* included reinforcements for many other units in the Middle East, most of whom had spent the time since basic training waiting in 'transit' camps. Transit camps embodied everything from commandeered holiday camps on bleak seashores to racecourses or disused factories. After a while, boredom or perhaps the arrival of bad news of air raids on their home towns would cause men to go absent without leave (AWOL). Military police usually arrested them on the way or at their homes. 120 members of this draft (though none from Phantom!) were still in handcuffs. In order for the men to stay upright on the pitching ferries, and to ascend the rope ladders, the handcuffs were removed. As soon as the prisoners were on board the handcuffs were put back on – in the rain and the darkness not without difficulty. Then it was discovered that the ship had only four cells for all the offenders.

As the *Pasteur* edged out to sea, it nearly distinguished itself by having a mutiny. Prior to this trip it had been tied up for three months with engine trouble, and some of the stores had been 'overlooked'. These included 300 tons of cabbage which had been stored in the swimming pool. By now the smell of the rotting cabbage pervaded the ship. A mixed fatigue party which was allotted the task of throwing 300 tons of putrid cabbage from the deck into the Atlantic flatly re-

fused. After hasty consultations a new system was adopted. There
would be no general fatigue parties under the direction of a member
of the *Pasteur*'s crew but small groups each under the command of
their regimental officers. Even that was not easy for many of the
officers were seeing their men for the first time on this voyage.

On the voyage they were frequently asked, 'What is Phantom, and
what exactly does it do?' This sort of enquiry could be shrugged off if
it came from outsiders but was rather more difficult to deal with when
it came from newly-joined members of the unit. A limited programme
in morse training was introduced.

At the end of the voyage they were unloaded in the wrong port
and put on the wrong train from it, but eventually reached Mena
camp near Cairo. Their part of Mena was a few acres of sand on to
which, as they arrived, a 3-tonner was dumping tents. They unloaded
stores, pitched their tents, organised the camp and drew their rations.
Nobody seemed interested in them, still less had any information about
their future employment. Forshall's persistent enquiries eventually
elicited the fact that the nine survivors of the Greek campaign were in
a camp in the area; they were brought in.

There was so much bustle and confusion in the area that no one had
much time for small detachments such as this. GHQ Middle East was
still assessing the disaster of Greece and Crete. Had the Higher Command been less preoccupied, H Squadron's fate might well have been
to be dispersed to other regiments as reinforcements. Instead the whole
unit was despatched to a Signals Training School. By the time it had
completed the initial course, its role and establishment had been
decided. It would be used for long-range signals reconnaissance, and
was accordingly brought up to its establishment of eight officers and
eighty other ranks, allotted two 8 cwt wireless trucks (very fast and
mobile), one 15 cwt truck and a new commanding officer. This was
Major Brian Franks, who had come from the Middlesex Yeomanry
with a signals background. However, he became ill and was invalided
home. Subsequently, Franks joined No 8 Commando, and moved from
that to the Special Air Service. He was succeeded by Major Dermott
Daly, Scots Guards and Commandos, whose second-in-command was
Captain George Grant, like Brian Franks from the Middlesex Yeomanry

Before leaving Mena there is one incident to recount which shows
how easily history is made. When the unit was at Mena, Bell was
ordered to build a wall around the latrines, using Italian prisoners of
war in his labour force. It enclosed an area twenty yards long and five

yards deep. Forty years later Bell was back in Egypt on a business trip. Out of sentiment he took a taxi to the long-abandoned camp. He got out and walked towards the wall to see how it had weathered the sandstorms, and perhaps to take a photograph. It was about four hundred yards from the road, but before he reached it he was startled by a challenge and a curt order to 'Come here'. The instruction came from two car loads of armed police who were patrolling the road. 'What are you doing?' they asked. 'Well,' said Bell, 'I was going to look at that old latrine wall I built here during the war.' 'Nonsense,' said the police chief. 'That's not a latrine now, that's a machine-gun post.' He was the police chief in charge of security on the desert road! For a moment Bell thought he was going to be arrested but the police chief, who had recently been on a liaison visit to England, was very friendly. They chatted amiably then Bell was sent on his way without a closer inspection – or a photograph.

Once H Squadron was brought up to strength it began to develop into an effective unit. The nine from Greece were able to contribute suggestions based on personal experience. Captain Gerald Pinckney, who had been evacuated from Greece early in the campaign after an accident, now rejoined the squadron. Further experience came with the seven Commandos who accompanied Major Daly. Lieutenant Carol Mather, from the Welsh Guards, joined H Squadron. Later Mather transferred to the SAS; later still he became MP for Esher, Surrey and still is at the time of writing (1982).

Some restrictions were now placed on the unit's activities. There were three patrols – later increased to five – working with the forward brigade, operating No 9 and No 11 sets. There was a large Marconi set at Kasr el Nil Barracks working to Phantom Regimental HQ in London. However H Squadron was never allowed to send any messages further back than Army HQ. The Army to Cairo link was occasionally used by G Branch for priority traffic if the normal channels were overloaded, but the Cairo-Richmond link was never used operationally at all. (However the Richmond-Cairo link had to be constantly tested in case it should be needed and was popular with all ranks as a means of sending messages home!)

Although the unit now had an operational function training continued and was extended. In September 1941 it had been sent to Syria to gain wider experience in mountainous country. It was considered that the unit learnt more in this ten days period than in the previous three months. As patrols would often have to fend for themselves in the desert, H Squadron attended lectures on navigation and

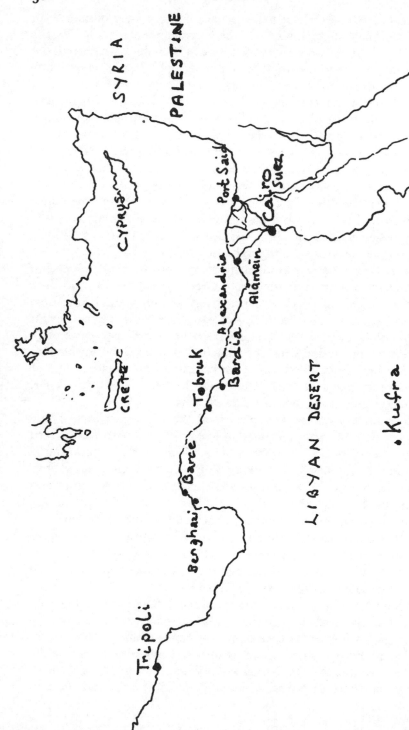

The Western Desert and Eastern Mediterranean

the sun compass by Colonel Ralph Bagnold, founder of the Long Range Desert Group. The LRDG consisted initially of explorers who had spent the pre-war years solving the problems of desert travel, with no official backing. They had perfected navigation, learnt how to conserve fuel and water, could use either sun or stars as guides and had learnt to accomplish miracles with the wireless sets of the time. The LRDG passed on its knowledge to all those in the Eighth Army who wished to make use of it. Phantom owed more to the LRDG than most people.

Forshall, who had done much to stabilize H Squadron in the difficult days at Mena, now left. Thompson was in hospital. H Squadron was now given an operational role in the famous, but subsequently ill-fated 'Crusader' offensive. Crusader aimed to relieve Tobruk and clear the Axis forces out of Libya. The Eighth Army was commanded by Lieutenant General Alan Cunningham, who had distinguished himself in Abyssinia, and consisted in the main of XIII Corps and XXX Corps. The offensive began well but quickly ran into trouble, not least of the difficulties being the inadequacy of the British 2-pdr gun against the German tanks, and the general superiority of the German armour. Rommel, displaying the swift tactical ability for which he was renowned, isolated XIII Corps HQ and drove XXX Corps to take refuge in Tobruk. Auchinleck, the Commander-in-Chief, thereupon flew up from Cairo, replaced Cunningham by Major-General Neil Ritchie, and forbade any withdrawal.

Gradually the situation was stabilized and the Eighth Army was able once more to move forward, clear Cyrenaica and relieve Tobruk. However, in January Rommel received useful reinforcements of which we knew nothing and was able to go on to the offensive again. By the end of the month the Eighth Army was back at its starting point.

Phantom's part in the story was as follows. The squadron was moved from Cairo to Mersa Baggush, some 150 miles west of Alexandria, by mid-September. Eighth Army staff regarded their presence with scepticism, at the best Phantom would be useless, at the worst it could get in the way and be a nuisance. The Eighth Army had been fighting this desert war for a long time and appreciated more than most people the hazards and obstacles of campaigning over vast areas of featureless landscape. Although every scrap of information about enemy movements was vital, it seemed unlikely that a novice formation such as Phantom could contribute much. Nevertheless, a task was found for it.

Crusader was to begin on 18th November 1941 and in the preceding fortnight H Squadron was to assist in a deception scheme designed to create the impression that the offensive – which the Germans knew must begin soon – would come in the south rather than the north. Phantom therefore drove 300 miles across the desert from Mersah Matruh to oasis Giarabub, 200 miles south of the coast and on the Egyptian frontier. With the assistance of a section from the Royal Corps of Signals they managed to produce nine patrols, each of which pushed out into the desert north-west of Giarabub. Bell and his driver, Rifleman Bance, had a lucky escape when their truck went over a mine; neither was wounded but the truck was considerably the worse for the experience.

Undoubtedly H Squadron was doing a useful job but it was a boring one. The patrols had to talk to each other as if they were an Armoured Car Regiment, a form of play-acting which is amusing for an hour or two but remarkably tedious after a few days. A brigade entitled E Force was garrisoning Giarabub and as this was – not surprisingly – the only reasonable sized formation the Luftwaffe could discover in the area they gave it their attention. After one of these raids four Messerschmitt 110s landed ahead of Phantom in the desert. Three then took off again. Two Phantom patrols approached the remaining one cautiously expecting to be raked with machine-gun fire as they came nearer. However, they reached the plane to find only one occupant, the wounded pilot. There was more blood on the fuselage than could be accounted for by the pilot's wounds so they concluded that the rest of the crew members, also wounded, had been taken off by the other aircraft. Doubtless the plane had been hit by anti-aircraft fire from E Force. As far as Phantom was concerned the main interest was in the tribute the episode paid to their camouflage. The German aircraft had flown over the patrols without spotting them.

On the 18th, Eighth Army sent for them again. The next stage of their story was told in an anonymous account which appears in the Phantom papers. At this time H Squadron was the only Phantom unit on operational work. The remainder of the regiment was still in England – we shall see later – but appeared to have virtually forgotten the existence of H Squadron. However, in November 1941, the latter was too preoccupied to consider whether it was a 'forgotten' squadron or not. The essence of the account is:

'We arrived at Army HQ which was now at Maddalena on the wire [Egyptian frontier] on the 19th, and three patrols were sent off at once – Herbie [Edgar Herbert] with No 2 Patrol to 7th support, Carol Mather with No 1 Patrol to XXX Corps HQ, and No 3 Patrol,

Graham Bell, to New Zealand Division. We all got to our formations by midday. No 3 joined 4 NZ Brigade which, in the next few days, fought small actions against the German rearguards along the coast-road to Tobruk. On the XXX Corps front things became very hectic. The Germans had not been bottled up as planned, and a very fierce tank battle ensued which went back and forth along the escarpment of Sidi Rezegh, El Duda and El Hamid for four days; both sides took a fearful beating. Unfortunately our tanks were inferior to the Germans and our losses were considerable. The tank crews were magnificent. Every time they went into action they knew it was a three to one chance against their tank surviving. Herbie was treated as a spy at first by Jock Campbell as he had no notification of the arrival of Phantom and thought the whole thing rather odd. [Brigadier Jock Campbell, VC was one of the outstanding figures of the desert war. In the early days when the standard British anti-tank gun and British tank were found to be inferior to their German counterparts Campbell had devised the "Jock Column" in which a small mixed force with a 25 pdr field gun would make speedy raids on German headquarters, then retire as rapidly as they had come. The Germans found these attacks very disconcerting.]

'No 3 Patrol was very lucky with the Kiwis, were offered every possible assistance, and were able to give some information of the situation to the south. Herbie, blind as a bat without his glasses, and Oxley his driver much the same, spotted what appeared to be some gazelle, so to relieve the monotony of war he chased them in his truck and Moran opened up with a Tommy gun in hopes of adding to the rations. To their surprise three Germans fell off a motor bike and side car and surrendered, so the gazelle turned into the first prisoners of war Phantom took.

'The battle for the relief of Tobruk had not gone according to plan either. The tank battles of Sidi Rezegh left the Germans in command of the battlefield while our forces re-formed. No 1 and 2 Patrols were kept very busy. Rommel made a determined armoured thrust through our positions and went on undeterred, although on a rather uncertain course, and chased XXX Corps HQ and 4 Squadron HQ. Dermot lost his staff car with seven dozen tins of beer. Trooper Prentice was thrown off a truck in the rout and not heard of until some days later.

'Actually Rommel passed to the north of Eighth Army HQ without doing much damage, then returned. In the meantime our forces had regrouped and 4th and 6th New Zealand Divisions made a determined attempt to link up with 70 Division troops in Tobruk. The rear areas were in a hell of a muddle. Our supply columns were frequently waylaid by German forces and we did the same to them. Colonel Dermot Daly captured three German Lancers.

'No 3 Patrol had lost touch with Squadron HQ on the air when they had been chased by Rommel and went back five miles to XIII Corps to see what was up. They went back at night with a liaison officer from New Zealand Division HQ and stopped for a cigarette at what they thought was a quiet spot: suddenly they realised that a few yards off was a party of Germans refuelling a Heinkel Stork Recce plane. They were on a landing ground which the Germans had come back to for a few hours to refuel from hidden petrol! Hunter was about to "have a go" with the Browning mounted on Graham Bell's pick-up truck, when he found it was jammed by a piece of shrapnel from a previous bombing attack. As the 15 cwt truck had part of its radiator missing from a cannon bullet and was being towed, and the wireless truck had also been shot up we decided that discretion was the better part of valour. We therefore left the Germans to their refuelling and supper and pushed on to XIII Corps a mile or so further on. XIII Corps received the news of the German airmen with a marked lack of enthusiasm; they already had a number of German Mark IV tanks a few hundred yards to the west of them and an impassable escarpment on the east.

'On the morning of the 28th, after very heavy fighting the New Zealanders linked up with the outlying troops of Tobruk, and the same night XIII Corps and more New Zealanders moved through this corridor into the town. No 3 Patrol which accompanied them found it a bizarre experience. The infantry of both sides were utterly exhausted, and the column entering Tobruk travelled slowly and cautiously, winding up and down the escarpment, threading its way through endless minefields, feeling utterly naked and exposed in the bright moonlight. It was quiet apart from the rumble of the trucks and the occasional outbreak of cursing when a truck drove into a trench by mistake. It was also a miracle of navigation for the trucks zigzagged through scattered German defence posts for thirty miles losing only one truck. That unfortunate vehicle suddenly found itself facing an anti-tank gun at point blank range!

'Apart from this there was, curiously enough, no incident. Every moment the column expected to be swept with a hail of fire but all that was seen was the occasional light of German cigarettes, and an occasional shout as dozens of dishevelled figures moved about looking for wounded and burying the dead.

'By dawn five hundred trucks had moved through the corridor into Tobruk and No 3 Patrol (Lieutenant Graham Bell) was able to inform Squadron HQ and thus Major-General Godwin-Austin, the XIII Corps Commander, that Tobruk had been relieved. Godwin-Austin promptly sent on a message to Lieutenant General Cunningham, "TOBRUK IS AS RELIEVED AS I AM. THE PRESS MAY NOW BE INFORMED." In the event the news was somewhat premature as the Germans counter-attacked and closed the corridor the same afternoon.

'However, after further heavy fighting the Germans began to withdraw westwards. The Eighth Army prepared to follow but not without caution as everyone knew that Rommel was quite capable of suddenly hooking round and cutting off any unwary columns. But when there was no immediate sign of this happening the pursuit gathered momentum. Four Phantom patrols travelled with the spearheads. One was with one of the Jock columns whose suspicions had now been changed to a warm welcome. Frank Thompson returned from hospital and joined them. Herbie's (Edgar Herbert) patrol reached Benghazi which was now retaken. The Eighth Army reoccupied the positions which they had held a year earlier.

'The situation was deceptively stable. Owing to the very long lines of communication, supply of petrol, ammunition and rations was difficult, and troops in forward areas were reduced to what was felt to be minimal safe levels. The troops began to become bored with inaction. The old adage that war is long periods of boredom interspersed with short periods of intensive activity seemed all too true. There was nothing significant to report. Bell's No 3 Patrol went up to the Guards Brigade HQ and was told, 'You can sleep all day, nothing happens here." At noon on the following day two enemy tank columns suddenly appeared, one on the coast road and one between the Guards Brigade and 1st Support Group. They moved so swiftly that they slipped through the gaps. Desert warfare was in some respects like Rugby 7 a side; there are not enough people to cover the whole field adequately and each side moves tactically to find a gap. The side with the fastest movers tends to win.

'The tanks which slipped past the Guards Brigade were engaged by our 1st Armoured Brigade which was unfortunately no match for the heavier German thrust. H Squadron lost its commanding officer when Colonel Daly's truck was hit by machine-gun fire from a German half-track and set on fire. He was unhurt, but was taken prisoner. XIII Corps found itself outgunned, and almost surrounded, so it headed for the last remaining gap. XIII Corps HQ would probably have been caught if they had not been warned by Phantom patrols that German tanks were heading in their direction. This sudden change of fortune was referred to cynically but philosophically by the troops as the Antelat Stakes in the 2nd Benghazi Handicap.

'With the Germans making deep thrusts into the Eighth Army positions, which had been extended to cover a wide area of desert, there was considerable confusion among the comparatively inexperienced British troops. The only shining exceptions were the Guards Brigade and E Force, which both withdrew in perfect order. Elsewhere hasty attempts to withdraw and re-group led to trucks becoming lost or stuck in salt marches; many men became lost also and were taken prisoner. The Germans, having got command of the coast, were able to push ahead fast while the Eighth Army straggled back through the desert. Benghazi, which had just been reopened and had received thousands of tons of stores, was lost. Msus was abandoned; three months rations and a million cigarettes were burnt to prevent them falling into enemy hands. Corporal McNair had been sent to Msus to draw rations for Squadron HQ. He set off quite unaware of how far the rout had gone and on arrival found Msus in flames. He managed to load up some rations and make his escape just as the Germans came in on the other side. Three days later he arrived in Tmimi having found his way there over 150 miles without a map.

'As everybody in the desert now realised, once one's forward positions were breached there were very few places where one could make a stand. One of them was what was known as the Gazala line, which was a few miles west of Tobruk. Here XIII Corps managed to stabilise the position. Here too Phantom learnt a lesson in security. In those days radio operators did not realise how easy it was to give away vital information, through incautious chatter between aircraft pilots, tank commanders, or infantry patrols. Security was thought to be adequate if Christian names were used. It was the Phantom custom to sign messages with Christian names, but unfortunately the Germans who intercepted those messages assumed that the Christian names were the code name of the formation to which the patrol was attached. This could have been very dangerous if the patrols had been operating in a less mobile rôle.

'Although H Squadron did not know it, they were now at the beginning of a four month lull in the desert battle. Rommel decided to sit on his gains and prepare for the next offensive, whether from our side or his own. For Phantom it was very dull. There was nothing to do except put the equipment into first-class order and ponder the lessons of the past few months.

'There was a slight break in the monotony in March. A convoy had been arranged to take vital supplies from Alexandria to Malta which was under great pressure. As it was well known that the Germans were harassing convoys with aircraft from Martuba airfield, it was decided to mount a Commando-type raid on Martuba and destroy as many German aircraft as possible. Phantom was allowed one patrol on the expedition. But it was only a small-scale enterprise.

'In mid April H Squadron was withdrawn to Mena camp for a refit – all its equipment was much patched and worn. Its performance was reviewed by XIII Corps and the verdict passed that it had well justified its existence. But for the next phase in the desert a slightly different method would be adopted. H Squadron had another assignment. General 'Jumbo' Wilson, who had been impressed by the squadron's performance in the ill-fated Greek venture, had asked for it in his new command – the Ninth Army.

CHAPTER FIVE

Phantom Gathers Experience

While these events were taking place in the desert, the remainder of Phantom was being prepared for future developments. Britain in 1941 made an excellent training ground for a regiment which would have to reach little-known destinations in unknown country. It might be thought that few places would be easier to find than the villages of the United Kingdom; they are all clearly marked on the ordnance maps. The problem which Phantom encountered, and Phantom was by no means alone in this, was the fact that much of the topography had changed since the survey was made; it is virtually impossible to have an absolutely accurate up to date map. Some new roads had been made, others had fallen into disuse, and the great standby of the uncertain map reader, the signpost, had disappeared entirely. For when invasion was thought to be imminent in 1940 a thoughtful government had decided that everything that might help an invader must be removed. That meant all signposts and place names, even the names on railway stations and above shops.

As a training area for map readers Britain was ideal, but the amount of time and petrol lost in futile journeys must have been enormous. The idea was taken so seriously that a lost traveller dare hardly ask where he was for fear that he should be arrested and locked up as a spy or fifth-columnist. To be in British uniform was no help: what better disguise could a German saboteur adopt? Later in the war, when American troops were stationed in Britain, all the place names and signposts were restored. In 1944 when the country was swarming with Allied troops, wearing the unfamiliar uniforms of Free French, Poles, Norwegians, etc., someone is said to have dressed up in a German officer's uniform and walked around in London all day. All he received was salutes.

Those who were not in Britain at the time of the invasion danger may perhaps feel that these reactions were too extreme. They might have thought differently if they had known that an apparently invincible enemy was poised twenty-one miles across the Channel, that our armies had already been crushingly defeated, and that the German air force greatly exceeded our own in numbers.

Phantom's deployment was therefore for the moment designed to give early warnings of invasion; and to identify any which might be diversions designed to draw away defences from the main thrusts. The reconstituted A Squadron – of which, as we saw, the major portion had been lost in Greece and replaced by H – was now stationed at Richmond, and was working with V Corps, which was responsible for the south-eastern coastal area. With it at Richmond was K Squadron which had been formed out of C, which was on standby at Grantham. K was waiting for an overseas posting, which was due any moment. Its commanding officer was Major J. Spicer and its probable destination was the Western Desert. B was in Kent attached to XII Corps, D with the Canadian Army in Sussex. E was in Edinburgh and G in Northern Ireland in case the Germans should develop any activities in that area or to the south. There was another squadron in reserve at Cliveden; this was J.

The regiment had now mysteriously crept up its numbers to nine hundred which was close to what Hoppy had fire requested. But the biggest change was in the autumn of 1941. Hoppy left Phantom to take over command of the Glider Brigade of 1st Airborne Division. He rose to command the division but was killed by a sniper after the landings at Taranto in 1943. He would have wished for no better memorial than to be remembered as the man who had created a unit which did more than many to winning the Second World War.

When Hoppy left Phantom his command was allotted to Lieutenant-Colonel Derrick Hignett (10th Hussars). Hignett certainly put the regiment through its paces. That winter saw a series of exercises designed to familiarize all ranks, even those previously imagining they had a 'chairborne' role, with the experience of travelling under arduous conditions. The one in Wales in winter was generally considered to be the most memorable. As cavalrymen were accustomed to look after their horses and keep them in the best possible condition, so were these modern heirs to the cavalry made to cherish their vehicles. There was no question of having a breakdown and waiting for someone else to recover the wreckage, and if possible repair it. Maintenance became a Phantom speciality and prevention was found to be better than cure. The more serious work was tackled by the Light Aid Detachments. Light Aid Detachments, affectionately known as LADS, had originally been a department of the Royal Army Ordnance Corps with the duty of recovering wrecked vehicles and if possible getting them back on the road. With the creation of the Royal Electrical and Mechanical Engineers the LADS had become a REME province and could tackle every ailment to which a vehicle, wheeled or tracked, was prone. In the desert sobering lessons had been learnt from the German practice of rapidly recovering their own knocked out vehicles, and also some of ours, during lulls in the battle, and bringing them quickly back into use. Sometimes in the desert night recovery teams would fight to recover and salvage vehicles; a useful prize would be a German Mark IV tank or 88 mm gun! By the time Phantom lost the exclusive use of its LAD in 1944 all ranks had profited from its teaching and could do much on their own. The LAD was commanded by Lieutenant R. Owen.

As we saw earlier, Phantom had to begin with whatever vehicles it could acquire, whether ideal for the purpose or not. Usually they were not. Back in England they operated with a Daimler Scout car and a truck to take the overflow equipment. However these were highly vulnerable – even to a rifle bullet. The replacement was a Humber Light Reconnaissance car. This was fast, and had a modicum of protective armour but at just over three tons fully loaded it was too small. It gave way to the White Scout car. Each patrol also had the ubiquitous jeep.

An ambitious plan was envisaged for K Squadron. For a while there was a possibility of this becoming an airborne unit. Airborne units, however, were already well catered for in the role which Phantom could have taken. It was therefore decided that its best employment would be in the Middle East, working alongside H Squadron. At home it was felt that K Squadron, with its officers and seventy-five other ranks, now possessed a sophisticated expertise that would be envied by H Squadron which, it was thought, had had a comparatively routine assignment. Fortunately H Squadron was not aware of this view.

Major W. Hibbert, commanding K Squadron, was despatched to Cairo in August 1942 to request suitable employment for Phantom, particularly K Squadron. An encouraging response came from General Wilson, now commanding Ninth Army defending Palestine, Iraq and Syria. General Wilson, it will be recalled, had been favourably impressed with Phantom in the disastrous Greek campaign. His command, although quiet in 1942, could easily be a vital area in the Germans decided to thrust down through Persia to the Indian Ocean. He asked for at least two Phantom squadrons; another was requested by Lieutenant-General B. L. Montgomery for the Eighth Army which he had recently taken over.

Wilson suggested that a Middle East GHQ Liaison Regiment should be created (in addition to the one with Home Forces). It was to consist of three squadrons, of which one would be H. Hibbert was promoted Lieutenant-Colonel to command it and it would consist of H and K to be joined by B from England. It was given the title of Z regiment but eventually came to nothing. Manpower shortages, caused by the string of disasters we had encountered from Dunkirk to the reverses in the desert, had caused the Higher Commands to veto any increase in establishments. What Phantom had already was all that it was going to get. But just before the plan for 2 GHQ Liaison Regiment received its quietus from the War Office, another squadron, L, had been formed in England. This was sent to train at Penn in Buckinghamshire, where rain seemed to be the only sort of weather. Here it was joined by the nucleus of Z and by G Squadron which had now been brought back from Ireland.

It must have been difficult for many members of Phantom at this time to know who they were and who they belonged to. J became F because there was already a J unit providing a Phantom-type reporting service for the Eighth Army in the desert now that the Eighth Army was under Montgomery's command. Subsequently this J Service would become part of Phantom, but not yet. K and the remnants of F merged. E Squadron, which had been stationed at Edinburgh and was in a very high state of readiness, was alerted for overseas service. By 1943 overseas service probably meant Tunisia.

Having brought the establishment story, which is not an entirely happy one, up to date we can now return to H Squadron, which we left at Mena in April 1942 being refitted for its next assignment. There it received its orders to proceed to Jerusalem and join Ninth Army. In the previous year, on an exercise, No 3 Patrol had visited Arab Legion HQ and talked to Brigadier Glubb. Brigadier Glubb had explained that the key to control of the Syrian area was the allegiance of Bedouin tribes. These were loosely under the surveillance of what was known as French Bedouin control. In all, there were some 250,000 of them, all armed with rifles but also possessing a few machine-guns and a few ancient armoured cars. Under normal circumstances the tribes leave their villages in the fertile valley of the Ante-Lebanon in the autumn and go into the desert where they roam around until the following spring or early summer, then return to their villages as the desert dries up with the summer sun. There were the traditional feuds among them but in general these were very localised and gave no cause for concern to the French.

However, this year had seen a bad winter for rain and the pasture in the desert, poor at the best of times, was worse than usual. This meant that the tribes would all be migrating westward too early and in a disconcerted frame of mind. It would not be too difficult for Axis trouble-makers, particularly Vichy French, to stir up trouble. If the worst came to the worst the Bedouin frustration could be vented in a widespread civil war. If the Germans decided to launch an attack through Turkey towards India, it would be ideal for them to have a Bedouin civil war going on in Syria, for the Syrian desert would then be on the main Allied line of communication. Large numbers would be required to guard our stores against the depredations of marauding Bedouins.

The immediate response to this danger was that H Squadron should have standing patrols in areas where any large scale movements of herds and camel caravans might herald the attack of one tribe on another. The French could then intervene with armoured car patrols and head off the aggressor. Squadron HQ was set up at Homs, a small town in the wheatlands of northern Syria. When the situation appeared reasonably calm the squadron busied itself with mapping wells and tracks near the Turkish frontier. Not least of their tasks was to report on the suitability of surfaces for the movement of vehicles. Squadron HQ moved to Aleppo; 'it was,' the patrols reported, 'an interesting but an idle life. As the patrols moved east so Squadron HQ moved on to Deir-es-Zor on the Euphrates, where it was very hot and with very little shade.'

The next move was to Mosul in the northern Iraq oilfields. 'We camped outside the town with no shade in a temperature of 120° during the day and over 90° all night. The flies were second only to those of Giarabub. It was no fun for the wireless operators sitting cooped up in their trucks bashing away at their keys with flies in their thousands settling on everything. It was a damp heat. Although water was not rationed it all had to be fetched from miles away.'

Major George Grant paid a liaison visit to Tenth Army HQ in Baghdad. Unfortunately for him he chose a day when the electric fans of the Taurus Express had ceased to function. The train had ceased to be an express 'for the duration' * and travelled slowly making frequent stops.

---

* Voluntary enlistments in wartime was described as being 'for the duration (of the war)'. It became a phrase for 'into the unforeseeable future !'

The other troops in the district were 8th and 10th Indian Divisions which were preparing defensive positions against the possibility of the Germans coming from the north. Mosul was hot, dirty and expensive. The only diversions were small, very expensive bottles of beer, and Guinness. There was no ice!

When Rommel launched his attack on the Gazala line in June 1942 it alerted Ninth Army to the fact that an attack might now come through their area as well, thus making a pincer movement towards Cairo, or at least taking advantage of our preoccupation with Rommel's offensive. H Squadron was therefore ordered to move further east into the mountains near the junction of the Persian-Turkish-Iraq frontier at Ruwanduz, about forty miles south of Mount Ararat. Lieutenant Carol Mather left to join the SAS just prior to the move to Ruwanduz. However, they were now joined by Sergeant Averill, last mentioned defending the hilltop against German parachutists in 1941 when most of the original H Squadron was taken prisoner. He had managed to escape from German custody, reach the Greek mountains, live there for nine months, then escape through Turkey. He then reported for duty in Cairo. He was awarded the Distinguished Conduct Meral (DCM). Later he was commissioned but remained with H Squadron.

Patrolling the mountain roads now began to take heavy toll of the already worn vehicles. Springs and steering broke, radiators boiled, tyres burst. It was a miracle they lasted at all in view of their worn condition. The metal was often too hot to touch. Ruwanduz is a small village in a valley at one end of the gorges. The road follows the route the river has carved out through the gorges. On one side there were immense cliffs, perhaps 2,000–3,000 feet high, on the other a rushing foaming river. In winter the river could quickly rise and cover the road. The whole route had been surveyed and peppered with mines and demolition charges in case it should become a battleground. All rations had to cover the 150 miles between Ruwanduz and Mosul. There was little for the patrols to do, for there were few passable routes.

One of their most interesting discoveries was Mersa Zia, an old man from a nearby village who spoke English and who acted as an interpreter to the British Army in Mesopotamia in World War I. 'He got us fruit and, more important, ice. In the winter when the snow comes it gets packed down tight in the crevasses in the mountains, where it stays compressed all the year round. Mersa Zia used to get one of the Kurdish tribesmen to go up with a donkey some 6,000 feet and cut slabs of ice for us. They used to do the whole trip in twelve hours and we would have crushed ice and fruit and condensed milk in the evening.'

But while they were in Kurdistan the fighting in the Western Desert had taken a turn for the worse. Tobruk had fallen. Sadly they reflected that they were 1,800 miles nearer to the fighting at Stalingrad, which was 500 miles as the crow flies, than to their own armies in the Western Desert. Then they heard on the six o'clock news that the Eighth Army was falling back to El Alamein. Hardly had they heard it when a priority message came from Cairo. 'MOVE TO DELTA IMMEDIATELY GIVE EARLIEST TIME OF ARRIVAL.' Their brief interlude as explorers was over.

'We plotted our route over the 1,800 miles to the Nile Delta and sent back a message to the effect that it would take us eleven days. This seemed a fairly sharp estimate for we had to collect up the patrols which were out and check over our transport before undertaking the long trip. But within an hour we received another message. "WHY DELAY. SPARE NOTHING FOR EARLIER ARRIVAL."

'To speed matters up we sent a message to the patrols to meet us at Rutba in three days time. Rutba is half way between Haifa and Baghdad in the Syrian desert. Squadron HQ left at dawn, reached Mosul in a day and pushed on as fast as the inevitable string of breakdown would allow.

'On the Haifa-Baghdad road there was a mass of transport moving west to Egypt in clouds of dust which rolled to the horizon. Most of the squadron had passed through Rutba when a steering arm on one of the trucks broke. Our only hope lay with the British civilian engineers who were working on the road. They had workshops and could easily weld it for us. When asked, the engineer in charge said he was sorry but he was unable to weld our steering arm without permission from his HQ in Haifa and that would take two days. He could not do it without permission because of the company disapproved he would have to foot the bill himself – and that would be impossible. The whole job would have taken five minutes. We pointed out that although it did not matter materially to the war effort if we stayed in Rutba for ever, there was a war on, Rommel was already knocking at the gates of Alexandria and if he had his way might soon be knocking at the gates of Rutba. As a matter of principle, we asked, was it the right attitude to take? He still said "No" and there was nothing left but to tow the offending truck to Jerusalem, which was another three hundred miles.

'Eventually the squadron arrived in Cairo on the evening of the eighth day. After a hurried refit at Mena, where we were refused new trucks and told to do our best with the old ones, we were sent to Burg-el-Arab, between Alexandria and Alamein. There apart from supplying the wireless link for a tank delivery regiment there was nothing to do. It was our worst month of the war. We just sat and waited.'

However a month soon passes. Clearly there was no use for them in the static battle which had now developed at Alamein. But General Wilson had not forgotten Phantom. He himself had recently taken command of the newly formed Paiforce which was the new name for the old Persia and Iraq command. It looked as if this was now going to become a vital theatre, as the German armies were apparently making a success of their drive to the east. To counter this threat a considerable force was being built up in Iraq and Persia; it consisted of four Indian and two British divisions, one Indian Armoured Division and a substantial base contingent. Furthermore, General Anders was in the process of forming the 2nd Polish Corps from Polish prisoners who were now being released from camps in Russia. It consisted of two infantry divisions and some Corps troops. They were being landed at Pahlevi on the Persian shore of the Caspian Sea and being transported by lorry from there to Iraq where they were training.

After a further two weeks at Mena the squadron turned north-east along what seemed to them the most boring of all roads – that across the Sinai desert to Jerusalem. Thence to Rutba and Baghdad where the temperature was 120°F, and humid as well. But as they travelled on towards their ultimate destination of Khurrumabad both temperature and scenery changed dramatically for the better.

They described it thus : 'From the flat and arid desert you suddenly come up against the first wall of mountains of Persia; the road crosses by the tortuous route of the Paitak Pass with a summit of about 6,000 feet and drops down the other side on to a plateau. There is a vastness in Persia that we had not seen before. Huge mountain ranges were separated by great valleys and plateaus. Ultimately, climbing higher and higher by stages you reach the high plateau of Central Persia which continues to the Indian frontier on the extreme east, and the Elburg mountains up to the north.'

At Khurrumabad they set up camp near Tenth Army HQ. Melvin now left them to join his old regiment, the 5th Camerons, which had recently arrived in Egypt. They were joined by Lieutenants Ian Reid, from the Black Watch, John Pearson-Gregory from the Grenadier Guards and J. Adam from the Royal Corps of Signals.

Although it was the custom in World War II to laugh at some of the administrative bungles made by the Army its successes received less attention – and they were many. Here in Persia the situation was an administrator's nightmare. Persia is extremely hot in summer but in winter this area could experience 40° of frost. Communications were totally inadequate; there were only two roads of any use from Iraq to north Persia, one running through Khaniquin–Kermanshah–Hamadan–Teheran, the other through the Persian Gulf through Ahwaz–Kurrumabad–Sultanabad–Qum–Teheran. There was only one railway. The freight capacity of the railway was 1,200 tons a day, but only twenty tons of that was available to the British as the priority was aid for Russia. Vast quantities of supplies for Russia were also being brought up by road by the UKCC (United Kingdom Commercial Corporation) who were responsible for the transporting of the stores.

In spite of these handicaps Paiforce was pressing ahead urgently with its plans. Large defensive positions were being built in all the big mountain passes, with dug-in gun positions and food and ammunition dumps. These preparations had the aim of protecting Abadan and the head of the Persian Gulf. Although it was far distant from this area a primary objective was to keep it out of effective German bombing range. Practically all the high octane aero spirit for the Royal Air Force in the Middle East and India was produced there.

Abadan was, of course, within bombing range already, but as the distance was too great for the bombers to have fighter escorts they would have to fly unescorted, and the only way they would risk that would be at night. As the valleys between the mountains in Persia were very wide and flat, it was possible for Paiforce to construct numerous landing grounds. The Russians flatly refused to co-operate in any joint defence policy for Persia for they said that Stalingrad would never fall and therefore any plans made for the defence of Persia were quite unnecessary. Provided the Germans did not break through the Russian defences by mid-November, the immediate danger would then be over for snow on the mountain routes would make them scarcely usable. The Russian zone of occupation of North Persia was north of the 35° grid line, and anyone who went across it or even near it was immediately arrested.

Not least of the problems was lack of maps and the Royal Engineers were conducting a survey of the country as fast as possible in order to produce new and up-to-date ones. The only maps in existence had been made some time in the nineteenth century and were extremely inaccurate. Phantom was employed on reconnaissance trips in north

Persia up to the borders of the Russian zone. Sometimes they were accompanied by senior officers of the Xth Corps planning staff who wished to see for themselves which were the most suitable sites for battles, or ambushes.

In October the squadron moved further east to Hamadan in the centre of the carpet industry. Then, as it became apparent that the Germans were going to get no further at Stalingrad, all but two divisions of Paiforce were moved out of the country for the winter. H Squadron returned to Baghdad, and stayed there for nearly three months. As it was now winter, conditions were considerably pleasanter than on their last visit. Reid now went to India to be an ADC to General Wavell, the Commander-in-Chief, and Lieutenant Norman Radcliffe, of the Manchester Regiment, came in his place.

The threat to Persia and the oilfields seemed to have receded. General Wilson returned to GHQ Middle East in Cairo. H Squadron was now instructed to return for the last time over the roads they had learnt to know so well. After a few weeks in Cairo they were sent to Sidi Bishr Camp at Alexandria. It was now the spring of 1943. Much had happened since they were last in the desert. In the previous November further Allied landings had taken place in French North Africa. In January the Eighth Army had entered Tripoli. Early in May the North African campaign ended with a crushing defeat for the Axis powers. 250,415 German and Italian troops became prisoners of war. The next stage for the Allies would be Sicily.

CHAPTER SIX

Europe Again

Before venturing on the next stage in the Mediterranean we must look at the remainder of the regiment and its employment.

By mid-1942, the war had been continuing for nearly three years. It had produced some spectacular disasters for the Allies: Norway, France, Greece, Crete, Singapore, Tobruk, had all been the scene of defeats which had looked inauspicious for a successful outcome. The brighter spots had been few but had included the Battle of Britain, Wavell's campaigns against the Italians in East Africa, and Auchinleck's successful holding action against Rommel at 1st Alamein. America was now fully committed but so far had merely sustained a humiliating defeat at Pearl Harbour. The Russians were still falling back in the face of the German onslaught. Sebastopol and Rostov had fallen; the Panzers were pushing toward the Caucasus, and not till August would they receive a check at Stalingrad.

Morale among the Allies badly needed a boost. Now that the Germans were heavily entangled in Russia it seemed that there was an excellent opportunity to stage a large-scale raid on the French coast. This would have the advantage of raising morale, giving some battle experience to the large numbers of troops who were now available in Britain, show our American allies that we were doing our best, and act as a minor Second Front to take some of the pressure off the Russians. In those days there were numerous cries to 'open the Second Front now' and even to-day there are still a few railway bridges where the slogan may be read as clearly as when it was painted on in 1942. The fact that there was already a second front in existence in the Middle East appeared to have escaped the notice of the amateur strategists.

It therefore seemed to Churchill and his advisers that a substantial raid on a portion of the French coast would do no harm and might provide useful lessons for the greater invasion which would come later – which it certainly did. So, under the code-name of 'Operation

Jubilee', an extensive 'reconnaissance in force' was planned for the Dieppe area. There had been other tentative plans, such as projected raids on Guernsey and Boulogne, but they had been cancelled.

Dieppe was a substantial operation. It involved two Canadian infantry brigades; one Canadian tank brigade; No 3 Commando; No 4 Commando (both British Army); 'A' Commando, Royal Marines; a detachment from No 10 Inter-Allied Commando; a detachment from the United States Rangers; and J Squadron of Phantom.

There was a strong naval contingent, including eight destroyers, and there was considerable air support. The landing party totalled close on 6,000.

In the event the raid was an almost total disaster. The Allies had 3,670 casualties, and lost a destroyer, 29 tanks, numerous landing craft, and 106 aircraft. The Germans lost 591 men and 48 aircraft. Hitler and Mussolini were pleased, the Allies humiliated and the Russians totally unimpressed by the Allied sacrifice. However it is worth mentioning that there were valuable lessons learned from Dieppe: one was that beaches must not be too steep to take tanks and the second that a port would not be taken without great losses, if at all, by frontal assault. Cherbourg, it will be recalled, was later taken from the landward side.

J Squadron was commanded by Major the Hon J. J. Astor (Life Guards) and incuded Captain B. Hutton-Williams, Captain J. Fane, MC, and SSM Harrison (5th D.G.).

Phantom had three patrols in the landing. Captain A. Sedgwick's patrol was with No 4 Commando (which was the only major unit to capture its objective), Captain Fane's was with the main Canadian attacks, and Lieutenant M. Hillern's was with No 3 Commando. No 3 Commando encountered a German coastal convoy on the way over, and lost many craft. Captain Fane's patrol fared equally badly; their landing craft was hit by enemy gunfire and was unable to land at all.

The heaviest casualties occurred to Hillern's patrol which, after being attacked by German E boats, struggled to the land, where it found itself surrounded by remnants of other units. Many boats had blown up or been set on fire when the Germans attacked. This was thought to have been largely due to the fact that spare petrol was carried in tanks slung round the sides of the ships. Immediately after landing at 6.45 a.m., Hillern's patrol tried to make wireless contact with the other units, but had little success. The units it was trying to contact were under heavy fire and were fighting for survival. Before Hillern's patrol could establish regular contact the order came to withdraw. Although they used smoke to cover their retreat, they were swept with periodic machine-gun fire for the Germans had now located the main British positions and estimated their possible lines of withdrawal.

In Hillern's patrol one man was killed and two others wounded. It was obvious that the raid had now turned into a rout. Hillern destroyed the code-books and the radio then led the patrol back to the beach. There was not a boat in sight. As German fire was still periodically sweeping across the sands, the patrol established itself in a cave. Hillern, seeing a boat drifting a mile out, began to swim out for it. He had not gone very far when a machine-gun opened up on him from the cliff above. He called out once, then disappeared.

The patrol stayed in the cave firing at whatever targets presented themselves. By 3 p.m. their ammunition was exhausted. That was the end of Hillern's patrol. The two others had managed to get away in the general withdrawal.*

Dieppe might have been considered a useful experience but Phantom had had enough of this sort of useful experience at the time of Dunkirk. It was clear that the unit could be used in a number of rôles but it was pointless to put them into static situations where communication was already adequate. Thus far the best rôles had been the identification of forward positions for cooperation with RAF and Artillery, specific tasks of reconnaissance, liaison with other nationalities, and the rapid transmission of material from battle headquarters to General Headquarters.

However, later in 1942 there took place an operation in which Phantom *was* properly used. This was 'Operation Torch', the landing of a joint Anglo-American force in French North Africa. Command was given to an unknown American officer, Lieutenant-General Dwight D. Eisenhower, who had never previously commanded in the field. In the even this was an inspired choice because he had a better understanding of military decisions than most people at the time suspected and also had the vital quality of being able to produce a harmonious relationship among the Allies. But in late 1942, as well as the misgivings about the appointment of this untried commander, there were considerable fears about the wisdom of removing such a large force of Allied troops from the United Kingdom, thus leaving it dangerously weak. However, the landings were made on 8th November

* A report by one of the survivors appears on p. 152–5.

1942 and the invasion forces pressed on to Medjez-el-Bab, thirty miles south-west of Tunis. The Germans reacted swiftly and poured in reinforcements. Heavy rain and supply problems then resulted in a stalemate. Although the Germans were now in danger of being caught between two converging forces they had plenty of fight left in them. But in March Montgomery won the Mareth battle and on 7th May Tunis and Bizerta fell.

E Squadron of Phantom, commanded by Major M. S. B. Vernon, covered the landings of First Army. First Army, in fact, was rather a high sounding title for a unit which was not much more than divisional strength. It was bombed on arrival, and then bogged down by incessant rain. Three patrols went out: one to 36th Infantry Brigade, one to 78 Division, and one to 36th Reconnaissance Regiment which was also part of 78 Division. In spite of the atmospheric conditions contact was maintained, although, as we saw above, there was less movement than had been expected. A patrol commanded by Lieutenant Stileman was sent to work with the Free French, and proved its value when the French came under heavy German attack in December 1942. Another patrol was attached to 1st US Armoured Division.

One of the benefits of Anglo-American co-operation was the introduction of the jeep. These handy little vehicles seemed to have the versatility of motor cycles but to be less vulnerable and more stable and comfortable in bad weather. Working with American and French forces did, however, make special demands. The obvious exxample was the phonetic alphabet but there were plenty of other instances where co-ordination had to be made. Often confusion occurred because both British and Americans were using the same words – with different meaning. A British speaker on an American telephone might be asked during a pause if he was 'through'. The British caller, knowing that his opposite number had gone to collect the required information and would return shortly, would gratefully murmur 'Yes'. He would then be disconnected, 'through' having a different meaning to the two people.

The value of Phantom was made clear when First Army requested that a second Phantom squadron should be sent out. The allotted squadron was K which was under the command of Major J. A. Warre, MC, whom we first encountered in the early days in Belgium. In the meantime E Squadron was deploying six patrols. Stileman's and Adam's were with V Corps, Mackinlay's was with 26th Armoured Brigade, Macintosh-Reid's was with 78 Division, Fraser's with 1st

Guards Brigade, and Macdonald's with Marshal Juin's French forces. Squadron headquarters was near Lavendure.

In February Phantom was fully stretched for that was the month in which Rommel decided to hit the newly arrived Americans at the Kasserine Pass. But by the end of the month the situation had stabilized once more. In this month K Squadron arrived in the theatre.

The squadrons agreed to pool, and exchange, patrols if the need arose. E Squadron was ordered to cover General Patton's attack on Gafsa. K placed its squadron HQ with Patton also, and both operated to rear links at Army HQ at Aain Beida. When Patton launched his attack on Gafsa, Warre lent two patrols to E Squadron to cover V and IX Corps, and sent his No 2 Patrol to 34 US Infantry Division for the attack on Fondouk No 3 (Demetriadi) to 9th US Infantry Division for the El Guettar area, No 5 to 1st US Infantry Division (attacking with the 9th), and No 6 (Dawson) to 1st US Armoured Division. K Squadron's work was apparently much appreciated; for the moment everything seemed to be going right and E Squadron was also working very well with the French advance to Sedjenaine.

'Battle honours' were won when Demetriadi's patrol joined in the fighting, knocking out two anti-tank guns and taking forty-one Italian prisoners.

In April both squadrons were at 1st Army HQ near Souk-el-Arbra. Phantom personnel were present at the historic meeting of 1st and 8th Armies. E's task was to cover 9th Division and the French 19th Corps. K's brief was to cover 2nd and 5th US Divisions when 18th Army Group had been formed for the final assault on Tunis.

In May E Squadron had patrols with 4th Indian, 6th and 7th Armoured, 4th British Infantry, and the French forces. No 3 and 6 patrols arrived in Bizerta with the leading units on 7th May. By the 13th it was all over and the squadrons rendezvoused at Carthage. One patrol from each squadron took part in the Victory Parade which was held in Tunis on 20th May.

The North African campaign had been a success for Phantom in that it had been able to prove its value in modern warfare as a personal intelligence service at the disposal of the C-in-C. It also demonstrated that its earlier successes were 'no flash in the pan' and that the new and expanded regiment would have continuous, fresh and increasing uses. So that none of their experiences since Torch was wasted, the regiment instituted a comprehensive system of reports from unit commanders. These would then be related to the training taking place in the United Kingdom, to see if any amendments needed to be made to the latter. Although the experience of H Squadron further east in the desert had been noted, the situation was different in that H Squadron had had to learn its lessons on the campaign; the other squadrons had had previous training.

It was appreciated that many of the lessons learnt in one theatre might have little relevance in another but there are certain immutable truths about all campaigns. It was noted that officers tended to take too much kit; this cluttered up transport. Jeeps, it was decided, should if possible replace existing motor-cycles. A roomier, better-designed reconnaissance vehicle was an urgent necessity. Lastly, although Phantom had made many friends who were prepared to testify to its uses there were still plenty of staff officers who remained to be convinced. The fact that patrol commanders were usually lieutenants meant that their standing in headquarters was minimal. Subalterns were not usually allowed access to operations rooms and the fact that Phantom need to be there created awkward and embarrassing situations. Subsequently when the achievements of Phantom had been thoroughly assessed the decision was taken to raise the rank of patrol commanders to captain. Even so there would still be occasions when an officer arriving at the formation to which he had been assigned would be greeted with the words: 'Phantom – who the hell is phantom and what is it supposed to do?'

But there was the other side of the coin. The GCGS Home Forces visited North Africa and reported on his return :

> The two Phantom squadrons under 18 Army Group have done excellent work. Their information was accurate, and owing to their exxcellent communications, up-to-date. On battle days about 75% of the information coming in was from Phantom.

The code-name for the invasion of Sicily was 'Operation Husky'. The decision to invade the island had been made at the Casablanca Conference of mid-January. At the same conference Churchill and Roosevelt agreed that the cross-Channel invasion of French could not take place till mid-1944. They also agreed that the doctrine of 'unconditional surrender' should be applied to Germany. The last decision was subsequently criticized because it was felt that after the successes in the Mediterranean and the realisation that the German attack on Russia had failed to achieve its object the German High Command might be prepared to capitulate. But 'unconditional surrender' served to make them fight every inch of the way on the retreat.

Before the Sicily invasion was launched the Allies had an easy
victory over the island of Pantellaria. Here a three-week bombardment by the RAF led to the surrender of 11,000 Italians. But Sicily,
where there were twelve Axis divisions, two of which were German,
was altogether a tougher nut to crack.

Like every other unit Phantom eagerly awaited information about
how its component parts were to be employed in the Sicily landings.
E and K squadrons felt that their recent experience could be put to
good use. It could have been put to even better use had there not
been an unnecessary delay in launching the invasion. If this had taken
place almost immediately after the conclusion of the African campaign,
the Allies would have found the island very lightly defended.

General Eisenhower was to be the Supreme Commander. Under
him were Admiral Sir Andrew Cunningham, General Alexander, and
Air Marshal Tedder.

The land forces consisted of the US 7th Army (two and a half divisions) commanded by General Patton, and the British Eighth Army,
of four and a half divisions, commanded by General Montgomery.

The original plan had been to make two widely separated landings,
in the north-west and south-east of the island, but Montgomery had
objected to this plan which was described as 'a violation of the principle of concentration of force'. The final plan had the British army
going in on the south-east and the American army going in on the
south coast.

There was a deception plan in operation at the time designed to give
Hitler the impression that the Allies were not planning to invade Sicily
at all but instead were going to descend on the Greek mainland. Hitler
was already inclined towards this view so we helped to confirm his
suspicions by the curious and macabre operation known as 'The Man
Who Never Was'. In this the body of a man dressed in the uniform of
an officer in the Royal Marines was floated ashore in Spain, carrying a
secret letter from Admiral Mountbatten (then Naval C-in-C Mediterranean) to Admiral Cunningham, stating this very point.

Meanwhile back at home Phantom had a new commanding officer
as Lieutenant-Colonel McIntosh had replaced Lieutenant-Colonel
Hignett. Pearson-Gregory had returned to the Grenadier Guards and
had been replaced by Lieutenant Freemantle-Bates. Major Grant,
commanding H Squadron, was then somewhat surprised to learn that
an assault detachment of six officers and eighteen other ranks was
coming to the Middle East 'for a special job'. Soon afterwards he received a note from GHQ MEF that the squadron was to be fully

trained and equipped for operations by 1st August 1943. The instruction continued:

A total of ten men including officers and other ranks will have an elementary knowledge of Turkish. This will allow for at least two Turkish speakers per patrol.

Patrols will be trained to operate in a mobile role, making full use of their transport over bad rocky roads or hilly terrain. You will ensure that your transport is capable of this work.

Vehicles will carry sufficient petrol for a 200 mile round trip and rations for ten days.

Patrols must be capable of operating in both summer and winter conditions.

The unit will also be trained to supply road reports and going information in a form universally read and understood.

Patrols must be capable of maintaining wireless communication with squadron HQ at any distance between ten and five hundred miles. The Anchor Detachment at Squadron HQ must be capable of working up to one thousand miles.

Everything in this instruction was simple enough and could be implemented immediately, except for the Turkish speakers . . . A teacher was acquired from the Berlitz School of Languages in Alexandria, but unfortunately she did not speak a word of English. French had to be used as an intermediate language.

For good measure it was decided also to run a Greek class. Two of the squadron, Captain Thompson and Lieutenant Averill, already knew the language well.

All these pleasant diversions came to an abrupt halt when forty of H Squadron were suddenly despatched to join Captain Sedgwick's assault detachment. This detachment was already under the command of Major Grant of H Squadron and Grant was wondering how he could possibly carry out all the tasks likely to fall to the squadron without an increase in numbers. In fact the deficiency was made up by three officers and six other ranks from Major Vernon's squadron. In spite of the need to assist in the Sicily invasion, it was still considered by the Higher Command that H Squadron could play a full part in 'Operation Accolade', which involved an expedition to Leros and probably other islands not far removed from Turkey.

However, for the moment all attention was to be given to the Sicily landing. There was much visiting of various headquarters from

GHQ to Brigade for special briefings. One form of training was to work on a wireless network for which one unit was 1,500 miles distant. The hope that from now on almost everything could be and would be carried in a jeep was rudely dispelled by the introduction of standard infantry training. This was made harder by the need to carry loads heavier than anything an infantryman normally has to carry. A fully loaded infantryman usually carried 72 lbs but this weight could easily be increased by extra ammunition, grenades etc. The main burden for Phantom was the wireless. They were now using the 48-set. Even if a man was not carrying the set he might have to carry the batteries. 48-sets worked well over distances averaging forty miles but on occasion could manage much more. Once 250 miles was achieved.

Training exercises for invasion had disclosed the fact that for Phantom to be fully efficient it was essential that the patrols must be in the craft of the commander of the landing formation. They also needed transport themselves if they were to continue working for more than short periods and operators on headquarters ships must be Phantom squadron operators or those under direct control of its commander. XIII Corps, for whom they were working, ensured that the first of these needs was met; unfortunately the others were left in abeyance. XIII Corps had informed its division that Phantom information was invaluable. Nevertheless the fact that the patrols were left without their own transport on landing and sometimes had to proceed to a different formation from the one they had arrived with made life somewhat difficult. In the event bad weather, among other causes, upset the timing of the landings.

In spite of heroic efforts, Grant never managed to establish adequate co-ordination with the other squadrons, E and K, who were operating from Tunis. In an attempt to achieve it he sent Christopher Mayhew (later a British Labour MP. He resigned from the post of Minister of Defence (RN) in protest against the reduction of naval strength). Every effort had been made to ensure that operators at both ends of a line were Phantom personnel who knew all the problems of this somewhat specialized form of activity, but this was not always possible, with unfortunate results.

Sedgwick had a surprising encounter for the following reason. Sicily was the scene of the first Allied Airborne operation of any size, and it was far from a success. It took off from Kairouan in Tunisia in 400 transport aircraft and 137 gliders. Conditions were difficult owing to the high wind and the fact that the pilots had had too little training. Many of the parachutes landed far from their objectives and some of

Right: 'HOPPY'
Lieutenant Colonel
(later Major
General) G. F.
Hopkinson, founder
of Phantom. A
dedicated soldier but
with an enormous
sense of humour.

Below: A break on an exercise. Phantom at ease.

Valenciennes, 10 May 1940. Leaving.

First rendez-vous, Mielen-sur-Aeist, St Trond – 1430 hours.

First rendez-vous, Mielen-sur-Aeist - 1435 hours.

HQ in an orchard at Neerlanden. *Left to right:* P. Purves, Driver Higgins, T. Newton-Dunn, Lt. Col. G. F. Hopkinson, Lord Charles Banbury.

Tervneren, 12 May 1940. After thirty hours riding. *Left to right:* Geoffrey Sunley, Christopher Cadogan, Peter Purves.

Conclusion of a power dive by a
Junkers 87, Neerlanden, 1940.

Armentieres, 1940.

Above: Casualties, 1940.

Below: Dunkirk 1940

Survivors from Dunkirk on board the *Marquis*. *Left to right:* L/Cpl Tiffin, L/Cpl Middlemiss, Lt Purves, Capt Gabriel, Lt Jackson, L/Cpl Fisher, Capt J. S. Collins. Driver Housden, Lt Sunley, Lt Cadogan, L/Cpl Swann, L/Cpl McGee, L/Cpl Anderson.

Left: Christopher Cadogan and Stella Zilliacus at their wedding, July 1940. *Right:* L/Sgt Tinsley, 'F' Squadron – 'one of the best W/T operators.

'F' Squadron exercise, Suffolk 1941 – 'Tea break'.

Phantom 'B' Squadron at Cliveden. *Left to right:* R. Raw, G. F. N. Reddaway, Lord Banbury, J. A. Warre, MC, W. F. Thompson, Hon M. L. Astor.

Right: 'K' Squadron and 'E' Squadron, North Africa 1943. *Back row:* Hugh Randall, Percy Pennant, Hugh Coming. *Middle row:* Springett Demetriadi, Mark Mainwaring, Johnny Macdonald, Edward Oliver. *Front row:* Tam Williams, Tony Warre, Hugh Fraser, Norman Reddaway.

Left: D. Brook-Hart, A. Mackinlay, A. Crawley-Boevey.

Above: Archbishop Francesco Petronelli wearing the Silver Medal of Military Merit conferred by King Victor Emmanuel at Trani. The Archbishop had shown consistent bravery during the German occupation. Lieutenant Denys Brook-Hart, leader of first British patrol to enter Trani, is on the right.

Left: Taken at Torgau on 26 April 1945 at the first meeting between the United States and Russian armies. The British soldier lighting the cigarette is Driver G. McNulty (Phantom). The soldier facing the camera is Russian.

the gliders came down into the sea. On one of the latter was Major-General Hopkinson, the co-founder of Phantom. He was hauled out of the sea and pulled over the rails of the Headquarter ship by Sedgwick. The conversation ran as follows :

Hopkinson, with water dripping from him : 'Hello, Alistair. What are you doing here?'

Sedgwick began to tell him but Hoppy had too much on his mind to listen. 'Well, goodbye,' he said, 'best of luck. I must get the navy to lend me a boat and get ashore.'

When the landings were completed certain facts came to light. The 22-set had not proved as reliable as had been expected; in fact the 48-sets had done better. As the Allies pushed inland the leading formations were constantly changing. In order to keep up at the front, and thus up with the news, Phantom had constantly had to change from one HQ to another. This had been remarkably difficult before they acquired their own transport.

Lieutenant Freemantle-Bates and Corporal Watts were both wounded. Watt had some miraculous escapes subsequently but owed his survival largely to his own persistence. The hospital boat on which he was meant to have been evacuated was torpedoed. He was not, however, on it, as he had decided he was not sufficiently badly wounded to be unable to report back for duty. Others thought otherwise but as soon as he got back to Egypt he walked out of hospital and reported to the squadron again.

The Tunisian detachment which consisted of three patrols commanded by Captain J. Fane, MC, had no complaints. All their patrol commanders were Scots and they were working with Scottish battalions.

Regrettably Sedgwick had had a different experience. He felt that the squadron had been hampered in a number of ways. In fact most of these stemmed from the manner in which it had been drafted into the battle. Whereas the other units had some official recognition, Sedgwick's establishment was so unorthodox and unexpected that there were clashes with those other units who felt they were already covering his tasks adequately and resented his presence. The Army was now becoming very conservatively minded about specialised units, which it was very much inclined to dismiss scornfully as 'private armies'.

It was perhaps inevitable from the nature of the task that embittered clashes should occasionally occur. Originally the Phantom problem had been to find acceptance with the Higher Command, then there had been the dissatisfaction when intermediate formations felt they were being by-passed, and now there was resentment from other signal links. The fact that Phantom was graded with such a high degree of secrecy did little to help matters. Units which move around in a cloud of top secrecy are intensely irritating to more orthodox formations. In the early days Phantom had been massively tactful and diplomatic in its relationship with other units. In parts of the Sicily landings this requirement seems to have been overlooked. It is, of course, difficult to be restrained and courteous in the forefront of a battle when one appears to be surrounded by people less competent than oneself. But if one is the sort of unit that Phantom was, that is as much a part of your military skill as all the others.

One of the units used in the Sicily landings was the J Service which would soon become a part of Phantom. J Service was so similar to Phantom that it seemed extraordinary that it could have grown up alongside and almost in rivalry. J Service was introduced in 1941 at Tobruk when, if there was to be an effective break-out, everyone must know what everyone else was doing. It was particularly important to know of the activities of armoured units as these were likely to change rapidly. The original J Service was the creation of Major Mainwaring. J was essentially a listening service. Signals operators would simply listen to everything on the air from forward units. By this means headquarters could quickly be aware of sudden changes in our own dispositions and, as the service monitored enemy broadcasts too, of the approach of German or Italian forces. This method differed from Phantom in that Phantom obtained official information from forward headquarters; J would receive 'chatter' from tank commanders and other radio networks about events as they were happening. Phantom provided a slightly later, more balanced, picture. J Service listened to broadcasts which were made in clear and could pass them on quickly, whereas Phantom material was often delayed by coding.

J was then further developed by Major Mainwaring and had eighteen receivers and three transmitters. It also used a Fullerphone, when direct telephone lines were laid. The Fullerphone was a product of World War I (the invention of a Captain Fuller) which had the advantage of being secret until more sophisticated devices were introduced. Telephone lines were, in fact, laid and used for frequently than might perhaps be imagined in desert warfare. When, however, the war became mobile everything depended on radio.

J proved particularly useful at the Alamein battle of 23rd October

1942 for it was able to provide absolutely up to the minute information about the movements of enemy troops. To do this it needed to be particularly mobile itself, otherwise the opposing formations could move quickly back out of range.

The value of J service was quickly recognised, particularly over the following :

1. It identified bombing targets by reporting lines along which enemy formations were withdrawing. It also gave the results of the bombing.
2. It supplied information of the movements and numbers of enemy armour.
3. It gave indication of the spirits of forward troops.
4. It supplied the first news of enemy withdrawals.
5. It gave information which enabled our own headquarters to deduce changes in the enemy's tactical planning.

Like Phantom, J suffered from considerable handicaps. It had no fixed establishment or organization, and equipment had to be borrowed or begged. In the early stages J worked solely for the benefit of Army HQ and Corps could only make use of it when J was near them or when they could put a set on the J circuit. XXX Corps was the first to recognise the need and to make provision for it.

However in January 1943 J received its establishment at last. It was to have one Royal Signals officer and forty-nine other ranks. The Staff officers working to it would be part of Army HQ. It would still have a slightly Cinderella-like existence but at least it now had a standing. In general the Army tended to be sceptical of units that did not seem to belong to anyone in particular. Even units like the LRDG and SAS which had given ample proof of their value were constantly having to wage a battle for survival. The most mysterious units of all were the SLUs. These were the Special Liaison Units whose task was to pass top-secret information from Ultra intercepts to those entitled to receive it. SLUs did not merely have to be secret; they had to be secret without appearing to be secret.

J continued to demonstrate its worth as the campaign across North Africa continued. It was considered to have been particularly valuable when Rommel made his counter attack in March 1943 and again in the attack on the Mareth line.

When First and Eighth Army joined forces, a detachment from the Eighth Army J joined First Army J at First Army HQ at Souk El Arba and received information from both armies. At the end of the battle First Army J was recalled to 18th Army Group; it was disbanded on 1st June 1943. Eighth Army J then returned to Eighth Army HQ to prepare for the invasion of Sicily.

However this was not quite the end of First Army J, for two of the officers were then attached to 7th US Army to organise a J service. Eighth Army J was still fully in existence, and one part of it landed on the southern beaches with the main Sicily landing, the other, five days later, at Augusta. However, as with Phantom there was not much for such a specialised unit to do in Sicily. There was little rapid movement, there was an existing telephone system, and there was little scope for intercepts. However a few J officers who stationed themselves with brigades produced useful information. It would have been clear to anyone who had time to take an impartial look that there were too many people involved in a communications task which was not very onerous.

However as the campaign gathered momentum, and more landings were made, J became increasingly useful. It had its problems too, for when the leading troops advanced through hilly country it was not always possible to keep in touch with forward units. The range of radio speech transmission in those days was strictly limited. In the past 'keeping up' had been dealt with by 'leapfrogging'. J units had divided into halves and one had gone forward as far as possible, then passed information back to the other half. Then the rear party would leapfrog forward.

At this point we must leave J for the moment and take a look at what is happening in Phantom.

After the Sicily landings H squadron felt somewhat ill-used. It had been asked to provide a platform and personnel for Sedgwick's assault party and had done so with misgiving about the ability of this mixed unit to perform a Phantom task. The fact that Phantom Assault Group had been praised by GHQ did not really convince the remainder of H squadron. H squadron was now split into three parts; one at Alexandria, one in Malta and one on the SS *Rajula*. When it had been reassembled it went on a training expedition to Syria. In November 1943 it was given a new establishment. It was now to have fourteen officers and 115 other ranks. This would give it six patrols and two J sections. K squadron was disbanded and helped to make up H's numbers. Major J. A. Warre, MC, returned to the Lancers. He had been with Phantom since the beginning and made an enormous contribution to the successful establishment of the regiment. The Turkish idea was abandoned – those who had learnt Turkish would now have to find a different use for it or forget it. A planned expedition to Rhodes was also abandoned.

The Sicilian campaign only lasted thirty-nine days and ended on 16th August. However, although the Axis lost some 150,000, mainly in prisoners of war, they managed to evacuate 100,000 of whom 40,000 were German. They also managed to remove many vehicles, tanks and guns.

Nevertheless prospects looked very good for the Allies. The invasion of Sicily had triggered off a revolution inside Italy by which Mussolini had been deposed and imprisoned in a remote hotel. King Victor Emmanuel put the government in the charge of Marshal Badoglio and the latter, though pretending to be working with the Germans as actively as ever, was in fact secretly negotiating with the Allies. On 3rd September an armistice between Italy and the Allies was signed at Syracuse. However, the Germans had been expecting something of this sort and they promptly seized Rome. Victor Emmanuel and Badoglio were nearly captured. Regrettably, the Allies had waited six weeks. Had they moved into Italy as soon as Mussolini had been deposed, the long, gruelling Italian campaign could have been shortened. But there were considerable reservation among the American leaders about whether we should commit ourselves to the Italian mainland when we already had the Pacific campaign on our hands and the D Day landings in France were scheduled for less than a year ahead. It was only when the Italian army showed its willingness to capitulate in Sicily that the Allies could agree that a move to the mainland in the near future was eminently desirable.

Accordingly, on 3rd September Montgomery had taken the Eighth Army across the narrow Straits of Messina and landed it at Reggio, and on 8th September the American Fifth Army had disembarked at Salerno. The Fifth Army contained a British force which landed just south of Salerno. Unfortunately for the Allies, the delays mentioned above had enabled Field Marshal Kesselring to take decisive steps to retain the German hold on Italy. Nevertheless Naples fell on 1st October, and Kesselring withdrew to the Volturno. The Americans then forced him back to the Gangliano. By December the Allies appeared to be making steady though not particularly rapid progress. At the end of December the needs of Overlord – the projected invasion of France the following summer – meant that Eisenhower, Montgomery, Tedder and Bradley all departed to take up new appointments in England. General Wilson – Phantom's old friend – took over Eisenhower's job as Theatre Commander, and Lieutenant-General

Sir Oliver Leese took over the Eighth Army. General Alexander commanded 15th Army Group which consisted of the Eighth Army and the US Fifth Army. The latter, which was commanded by General Mark Clark, contained five American, five British and two French divisions with a Polish division in reserve. The Allied armies totalled nineteen divisions, while Kesselring had eighteen; however some of Kesselring's forces had to be stationed in northern Italy, in case of insurrection there.

At this stage the war settled into a stalemate. The Germans clung resolutely to their Gangliano position and were not dislodged till the end of the following May. By that time the monastery at Cassino, which overlooked the battlefield, had been bombed to rubble. An attempt to break the deadlock at Gangliano, by making a landing further north at Anzio on 22nd January, had proved a dismal failure. The Germans had no difficulty about containing the landing with its 50,000 British and American troops. The break-out from Anzio did not take place till the Gangliano had been forced four months later, and therefore ranks as one of the less glorious episodes of the war. Churchill referred to our invasion force as 'a stranded whale'.

In January, H squadron was overjoyed to receive instructions to sail for Italy. However, the move was postponed and the sailing did not take place till March. They then landed at Taranto.

But while H squadron was pondering on past lessons, training and trying to get itself reorganised, E squadron was having a much more interesting time. E squadron was commanded by Major the Hon Hugh Fraser, whose original regiment had been the Lovat Scouts, commanded by his brother the legendary Lord Lovat. Later he would join the SAS and much later still would become a Conservative MP and Secretary of State for Air.

E Squadron, delighted that four months in limbo were over, embarked on the HMS *Aurora* at Bizerta on 11th September, but to its surprise was only allowed to take four jeeps. Considerable resource was displayed to take other equipment which experience had shown to be essential; some of it was put on a cruiser and two other jeeps were conveyed on a tank landing craft. The latter arrangement was the product of diplomatic work by Captain Norman Reddaway, whom we last spoke of swimming away from the transport *Aboukir* after it had been torpedoed off Dunkirk.

The arrival of Phantom in Italy was described by Denys Brook-Hart in a report written in the following month (October 1943). It ran as follows:

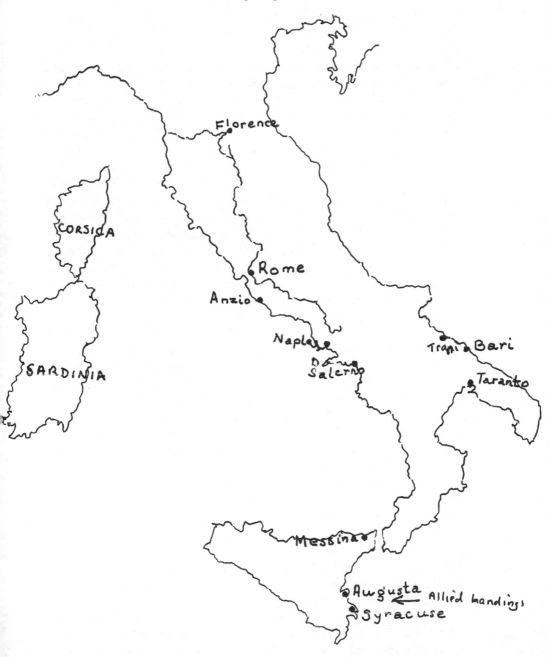

Sicily and Italy

'The cruiser *Aurora* left with two other cruisers at last light and steamed flat out across the Mediterranean, passing on the way the major portion of the Italian Fleet which had surrendered to British Naval Forces. In the evening of 12th September we arrived off Taranto Harbour and offloaded into a mine-sweeper – the only type of vessel able to get through the obstructions and mine fields. Most of the squadron was assembled on the quayside in the dark without becoming split up in the general confusion. Within five minutes of landing, we were told that a German armoured division was advancing on the town and that our chances of holding on to the city were extremely small as the airborne personnel had no armament apart from their small arms and half-a-dozen six pounder anti-tank guns. However, we commandeered several large Italian lorries and moved off in the dark through the outskirts of the town, which was in ruins through Allied bombing. After travelling for some time, about one hour, and having seen no sign of life, either from our own forces or the native population, we discovered we were several miles in front of what should have been the front line. The squadron withdrew a mile and leagured for the night in an olive grove by the roadside.

'Such equipment as we had been able to take with us was offloaded in heaps under the olive trees, and the following day the squadron commander joined us with our orders. It was reliably reported that the Italians had just started fighting the Germans in Yugoslavia, and that the entire Allied occupation of Italy would be only a matter of hours. As it was difficult to obtain reliable information of enemy movement on the east coast of Italy, we were assigned to the job of patrolling this area behind the enemy lines, and to keep contact with the withdrawing enemy forces from the rear.

'With feverish activity we sorted out from the heaps of equipment on the ground, such wireless apparatus as we could fit into jeeps to start a communication system.

'In the midst of this we were given the news that Lieutenant-General Hopkinson, the first commander of Phantom, had been shot through the head by a sniper whilst watching the progress of one of his company's attacks. General Hopkinson died just as we completed our arrangements for patrolling.

'By good fortune I discovered that most of my equipment was intact, and I was therefore the first patrol to be fitted for field operations. On the 14th I left Taranto in company with Peter Stileman and an enlarged patrol to go through to Bari on the east coast. We drove via Massafra and Monopoli by a circuitous route and arrived in

Bari early in the afternoon. This drive passed without incident, except for an incredible number of punctures which the Italian population mended very rapidly. The Italians were, without exception, very friendly and helpful. The road blocks through which we passed were manned by the Fascist Blackshirt troops, but we overcame the difficulty of explanations by driving straight through them at about 60 mph before they had time to make up their minds which side they were on.

'On arrival in Bari we found the town in a ferment of excitement and confusion, and decided it would be hopeless to try and establish a headquarters there. The Italian XIX Corps was in occupation, and had not yet made up its mind as to which side it was on. Accordingly, we set up a small headquarters in the inevitable olive grove outside the town, and established communication with our control station set. At this time an Italian destroyer manned by a German crew steamed close inland and proceeded north along the coast taking a good look at us. They passed on, apparently not believing what they saw, and took no action.

'I then patrolled eight miles north of Bari and contracted a major road block manned by Bersaglieri. I understand from their commander that they were willing to defend the town with their one gun, provided that the eight shells available were supplemented by the British. On returning to the town we contacted the General commanding the Italian XIX Corps and told him that he could consider the town under British occupation. Whilst he was unwilling to take any definite action against the Germans in the area, we assured him (untruthfully) that a large column of British tanks was on its way up at that moment, and he became a great deal more co-operative and willing to come over to our side. I then contacted the Colonel of the Bersagieri, and arranged to have a number of his motor cycle troops under my command.

'On the 15th I went out in the jeep to Bisceglie, and there contacted an outpost of seven Germans in a house off the main road; whilst keeping observation on this party, they slipped out of the back entrance and got away in a private car to the north.

'On the 16th another portion of the squadron came up, under the squadron commander, and we established a joint headquarters just outside a village to the west of Bari. In actual fact, at this time we had expanded to about fifty men with vehicles and equipment within half a mile of the main German forces occupying the village. This did not appear to stop us driving freely on all the road systems, or on the main road which would have been used by the enemy had he decided to enter Bari. On this day I was assigned the task of patrolling out as

far as possible in order to get information on the main enemy dispositions. My patrol was supplemented by two civilian cars, in which we
had a Tommy gun party, and two Italian motor cyclists who filled
their kitbags with grenades and a good deal of high level talk about
their bloodthirsty aims.

'By midday we reached a point two miles north of Trani where the
road stretched in a straight line into the town. As there was little cover
on the road we decided to pull off into the garden of an Italian villa
and tried to get observation of the town from the roof. In the garden
we found a new packet of German cigarettes lying outside the villa
door, indicating that an enemy patrol had passed through shortly
beforehand.

'From the roof we could see a great crowd of people in the streets
of the town and what appeared to be a manned road-block on the
outskirts. After a short conference we decided to put a patrol into the
town and endeavour to make physical contact with the enemy. We
proceeded into the outskirts and were immediately stopped by Italian
civilians who gave very confused reports of enemy in all parts of the
town. However, it seemed apparent that there was a party of Germans
in a school building not far away. Accordingly, I dismounted from the
jeep with six men and made an approach to the building. On arrival
we found that the building had been recently abandoned by the enemy
and was still smouldering from fires they had started in some of the
rooms.

'Owing to the confusion in the town and the impossibility of free
movement amongst the thousands of civilians we decided to get out to
the north. We took the main road through the outskirts and drew
alongside a large cemetery. At this point I was just giving orders to
take the jeeps under cover in the cemetery when two lorryloads of
Germans appeared from behind us through the outskirts of the town.
They stopped about 200 yards away, got out and went into a wine
factory. It was obvious that they did not realise who we were or what
we were doing on the road. Fortunately we had got two jeeps into the
cemetery and the patrol was dispersed behind cover on each side of the
road. Within a few minutes we had almost decided to open fire with
our one Bren gun on the German vehicle.

'At this point we saw another lorry full of enemy coming from the
north down the main road. As we were then trapped, there was no
alternative but to put an ambush into operation immediately. The
enemy from the north must have seen our motor cycles in the road as
they slowed down to about five miles an hour. At this point we threw

the first grenade into the road as the nose of the lorry came past the cemetery wall. This had the effect off shattering the windscreen and wounding the driver. We then opened up with our Tommyguns and Bren guns into the midst of the enemy at point blank range. The enemy to the south then opened fire on their own vehicles. At this point an Italian priest appeared from behind the cemetery and guided us up some steps and through a back way down to the sea-shore where, with our two remaining vehicles, we were able to with-draw to the south of the town.

'On the 18th two patrols with a battalion of Bersaglieri attacked and occupied the crossroads at Mellito.

'On the 19th, with the same force, my patrol moved out twenty miles to the west of Bari and occupied Santaremo in the wake of the retreating German parachute battalion. Unfortunately all road bridges were mined and blown up as we arrived and it was therefore impossible to advance further.

'On the following day the Eighth Army contacted us with their advance forces and we moved with their reconnaissance detachments through Andrea to Carato.'

A slightly different experience of the Italian campaign was that of Anthony Crawley-Boevey :

'After the North African campaign Phantom's role appeared to be in doubt, but obviously we must have made a great impression as the high command used us for the assault on Pantellaria and Lampedusa and finally Sicily. General Hopkinson also insisted he wanted Phantom to accompany his division on the mainland of Italy at Taranto. We duly embarked on HMS *Aurora* at Bizerta, two days before the official armistice with Italy, as part of 2nd Airborne Division.

'On our way into Taranto we witnessed the most magnificent sight of the whole Italian Navy steaming out of the port in order to sur-render at Malta. Our four cruisers steaming full speed ahead in the opposite direction fired a broadside in salute to the surrendering enemy. I was sitting with my brother officers on the upper deck, in-cluding Tam Williams, the famous actor. Tam suddenly dived under the tarpaulin we were sitting on and we all laughed at him and convinced him that they were only blank charges that were being fired. Once the firing started a very red faced and portly airborne brigadier raced up on deck and shouted at everybody to get down and asked what the devil was happening. Tam Williams then explained to us that it wasn't the shooting that sent him under the tarpaulin, but the brigadier who was his first father-in-law and whom he did not want to see very much!

'On arrival in Taranto our first cruiser went up on a magnetic mine with heavy loss of life and therefore we were a bit apprehensive when it was our turn to move into the harbour and tie up to the jetty. We were all right and disembarked, but we were told the sad news that General Hoppy had been severely wounded. Two days later I had the honour to be selected to attend his funeral in the military cemetery. It was a very moving moment. We were very proud to show the white P on the black background which was his very own military insignia on our uniform.

'Once again Phantom together with Popski's Private Army and the SAS were organised into an ad-hoc armoured car Regiment. We commandeered a number of civilian trucks and Italian Breda machine guns from the Italian Army and with the few jeeps we had, set out for Bari.

'We entered Bari without opposition and established this place as our base. We had our officers mess in the main hotel and all the Italians mobbed Tam Williams in the bar, as he was appearing in the local cinema which was showing *Wuthering Heights*. They could not understand that a film star could be fighting for his country. He did a wonderful public relations job for us and Spumante wine appeared from everywhere, which the Germans never enjoyed, to celebrate the arrival of a real live film star.

'We enjoyed Bari which had seen very little of the war. We went out on patrol every day and had the odd skirmish with the Germans who had not yet arrived in force. The Italian army was everywhere, but were not impressed with the British Army and their commandeered vehicles. I was sent up the coast to Barletta to try and contact the Bersaglieri Brigade of the Italian Army who was supposed to be in some strength in this town. I arrived there in my jeep and with an Italian army officer who acted as interpreter. I had about twenty soldiers following behind in a mixed assortment of impressed vehicles each carrying a Breda machine-gun on the roof of the truck. I went straight to the local barracks and asked to see the General. I was taken along a number of beautiful marble-lined corridors and passed very handsome Bersaglieri guards with their black feather helmets blowing in the wind. They presented arms to me as I passed and I have never felt before or since so important.

'My interpreter led the way, as he too was a Bersagliero, and we at long last reached the General's office. We waited outside a high mahogany double door and the two guards outside knocked on the door. I did not know what to expect. After what seemed a considerable time (probably two minutes) the door opened and the most extraordinary figure appeared. He was very tall, almost bald, dressed in pyjamas and sporting an eye-glass. He smoked incessant cigarettes in a very long cigarette holder. He introduced himself as General "something or other" commanding the Bersagliero Corps. He spoke perfect English and ordered my interpreter to stay outside. I went into his very impressive office. He knew we had landed at Taranto, but wanted to know where the Eighth Army was in the toe of Italy. He hoped he would meet General Montgomery within the next few days! I pointed out that General Montgomery was a long way away and that I had no information about the progress of the Eighth Army. He said he did not think he would hold Barletta very long against the Germans and wanted me to produce some tanks. He knew nothing about the whereabout of the Germans but was obviously very scared about his isolated position. I told him that the British Army would look after him and after two glasses of Marsala wine I beat a retreat as graciously as possible. I often wonder if he realised that I was only a lieutenant without any authority! Anyhow my report went back to 2nd Airborne Division HQ in Taranto and I often wondered what happened to this General and if he ever met Monty.

'My last appearance with Phantom ended with the capture of Termoli. Myself and four soldiers mounted in a jeep with portable wireless and batteries were sent to join the Special Services Brigade, who were embarking on their LCA's at Manfredonia, a little port south of our objective Termoli. I reported to Brian Franks, the Brigade Major who had been a Phantom officer himself but gone on to higher things in the Army. Brian could not have been kinder and made sure that I and my troop got everything we wanted. We left Manfredonia in the evening and I had no idea what I was in for as I had never had any training in amphibious warfare. It shows just how flexible any Phantom officer had to be.

'We sailed up the coastline all that night and were not allowed to smoke or even speak except in a whisper. The Commandos were very impressive chaps and the naval officers so calm and matter of fact. In the early hours of the morning we transferred to the final assault craft and landed on the beach. I didn't even get my feet wet. It all seemed too easy as we ran up the beach. However by the time we reached the sand dunes and our first objective I was cursing the heavy battery I was carrying. Our jeep with my driver whose name was

Driver Balls RASC, the most delightful cockney you could ever wish to meet, was in the follow up flight and we would not see him for some time, so we had to leg it into the town. As a cavalry officer I was not used to this sort of treatment.

'The first excitement was when we reached the railway line which was just off the beach. Here we found a train waiting with steam up. The Brigadier commanding the SS Brigade jumped on the footplate of the engine and stuck his revolver into the driver's guts and told him to let out all the steam. The Italian driver was a very frightened man and acted immediately. There was an awful blow of steam and the engine went dead. This train was just due to evacuate the German garrison, we gathered.

'We pushed on towards the town and suddenly all hell was let loose. The Commandos woke up the sleeping Germans and the battle began. It was quite a battle and we saw several dead in the streets, but by breakfast the vital bridges over the River Biferna were captured and I had the honour to report this fact to Army HQ. Thank goodness the wireless set got through right from the start as the only aerial I had was a long bit of wire that we had to throw up to the top of a tree.

'Eventually we met up with our jeep and how delighted I was to see Driver Balls and his cheerful face. I then had my more reliable and conventional vehicle set which made life easier. We had a quiet day and we heard reports that the Brigade coming up from the south were on their way, but meeting some resistance. We wondered what the Germans would do when they found that the SS Brigade held the vital bridges over the Biferno river which they would have to cross if they hoped to get away to the north.

'The next morning we made contact with the land forces and I suddenly had a message to return to Squadron. I could not believe it as I still felt I had a job to do especially as the Germans were starting to react and the Brigadier was getting worried about his position. However I was told to get back as soon as possible and was assured that the road to the south was open. We got into the jeep and set off to the south to the map reference we were given for Squadron HQ. Our last sight of Termoli was of burning buildings and we could see the Germans were giving it stick. As things turned out, it was a good idea that we were departing. Hugh Fraser, our Squadron Leader, perhaps did not want to lose a troop, we thought. We at last found Squadron HQ some thirty miles south of Termoli and instead of being welcomed as conquering heroes as I hoped, we were regaled by a very grim Hugh who told us that we had been disbanded. I could not believe it, but I gather he got a message that morning from General Montgomery's Chief of Staff to say that the C-in-C would not allow private armies in his army. "You will disband immediately." Hence my hurried departure from Termoli.

'I had no alternative but to return to my own regiment, the 7th Queen's Own Hussars after that, as there was no future obviously for Phantom in Italy. I got back to my regiment via the Phantom Squadron in Baalbeck in Syria whom I stayed with for a month.'

By the 20th this interesting task was over. They were first ordered back to Taranto, then sent to do some recces for the Canadians and for XIII Corps. For these duties their patrol contained one truck, one jeep and one motor cycle. The Canadians were described as being extremely amiable and cheerful to work with but at the same time difficult because they were unwilling to part with any information unless it had been confirmed from top level. General Dempsey approved strongly of the work E Squadron was doing but could not retain its services for the War Office had ordered that it must now be disbanded. Many of the E squadron were transferred to J squadron, the remainder sailed for England on 25th December 1943.

One day when nothing much was happening Fraser and Stileman wondered if they could slip through the German lines and pay a visit to Rome. To do this they acquired an Italian railway timetable. From this they suddenly realised that it would be possible to use the railway telephone system for passing messages. This discovery came in very useful later in the war when they were helping to rescue survivors from Arnhem, for they used the Dutch railway telephone when other lines were not available.

Meanwhile a somewhat complicated organsation was functioning for the advancing armies. Not least of Phantom's problems was the terrain. Mountainous country not only made movement difficult; it also interfered with wireless communication. When forward units moved quickly they soon became out of range of HQ sets; when they moved slowly the signals area became congested. J Service was functioning well and supplying a lot of information; it had established a useful link with SIAM (Signals Information and Monitoring) which was its American equivalent. But as soon as movement stopped the enemy used land lines in preference to wireless. Tapping those telephone lines was not in Phantom's province. This situation occurred several times in Italy, notably at Cassino. In Italy, in 1944, therefore, Phantom was found to have a limited use. It had carried out all its tasks adequately but in the circumstances, with increasingly heavy demands on manpower, it was inevitable that the activities of specialist units such as Phantom would be examined critically. The conclusion reached was that the regiment had considerable value but neither the J Service nor the normal Phantom activities were vital in a slow-moving campaign such as Italy. Whether the conclusion was true or erroneous would be seen later. However there was one criticism which required immediate action. At the beginning of October 1944 J Service was declared to be insecure and was ordered to use cipher in conjunction with the one time pad.

The one time pad requires a little explanation. So far the officer in charge of J Service had been using his discretion over which messages should be sent in clear (as having no security implication) and which should be sent in a special J code. Now this more complicated system would be required.

The one time pad was an essential part of an unbreakable code. Contrary to popular view, every code cannot be broken if a certain lengthy procedure is followed; even computers have not changed this. As the name implies, both sender and receiver had a pad from which sheets could be torn off. Each page contained special enciphering information of a random type. Each enciphered letter belonged to a different system from the others. When the message had been enciphered the page was torn off and destroyed. It could not be used twice nor was it likely to fall into anyone else's hands. The sender likewise used his page to decipher the code and then destroyed it.

Of course nothing is completely infallible. An enemy might manage to steal and copy the one time pad, or a computer might work through several million combinations quickly enough to arrive at the solution in time. But both possibilities were considered to be highly unlikely.

However, in view of Phantom's expertise it was now decided that even if there was no urgent requirement for the regiment's services it would be a mistake to disband the unit; if the battle became mobile again recreating a new Phantom would take too long to organise.

By this stage in the war it had become apparent what could and what could not be done by Phantom's component parts. J was at its most useful when listening in to armoured formations and interpreting their actions – providing it knew all the code names. Phantom, on the other hand, could collect information from areas where wireless silence was in force, and then pass it back along special channels.

While Phantom was thus sorting out its internal problems, the war was relentlessly ploughing forward. As we saw earlier, the preparations for the invasion of France were proceeding rapidly during the first five months of 1944. It was not thought that Italy could ever be more than a secondary theatre as far as winning the war was concerned. However, as a secondary theatre it was extremely useful in trying down a number of first-class German divisions which the Germans could have used elsewhere. The Italian terrain did, however, enable the Germans to use their troops to excellent advantage in delaying the Allies. Rome was not taken till 4th June 1944, two days before D Day. (The capture of Rome by General Mark Clark was heavily criticized for by turning aside to take the city he had enabled the main body of the Germans to retreat up the peninsula.)

Elsewhere progress to eventual victory was slow, difficult, and costly in manpower. In the Far East the Americans under MacArthur were clawing their way back across the Pacific island by island, and British forces in Burma were slowly wresting the initiative from the Japanese; on 7th June 1944 (the day after D Day) the Japanese were retreating from Imphal and Kohima. On the Russian front the Germans were now being pushed back, but the battle there was by no means won. Huge quantities of supplies were being sent to the Russians from Allied sources; they included millions of barrels of oil. At sea the battle between submarine, destroyer, merchantman and aircraft continued unrelaxed. And in Britain, civilians who had thought that the worst of the bombing was now over suddenly had to come to terms with the fact that it was not. First the Germans launched what was known as the 'Little Blitz' in early 1944 and then, seven days *after* the invasion of Normandy, the first V1 flying bomb fell on London.

As preparations for the invasion of France continued, it was obviously necessary, in the interests of security, that plans must be kept as secret as possible. This necessary secrecy usually meant that those involved in the plans were unaware of what was in store for them until the very last moment. Inevitably when there is an absence of genuine information there is a superfluity of speculation and rumour to fill the gaps. In early 1944 Phantom, like everyone else, was wondering what the future held for it. It was known that it would be used in the battle but precisely how and when was not revealed. The second-in-command of Phantom in Britain, Major John Morgan, who had been with the unit from its earliest stages, had been sent to Italy (Siena) to obtain a report on Phantom's experiences in Africa and Italy. He then delivered his findings to 21st Army Group. 21st Army Group was the name given to the combination of the British Second Army and the American First Army which would be under the command of General Montgomery for the invasion.

However, Morgans visit accomplished considerably more than a normal fact-finding mission. It led to discussions, the result of which was that Phantom and the J Service were now formally amalgamated as 2 GHQ Liaison Regiment. With that we can leave them for the moment and look at the situation back in England.

Here, as with other units earmarked for the invasion, military life had consisted of exercises, training, and ponderings on what was intended for the big day. Phantom 1 (1 GHQ Liaison Regiment) was now under the command of Lieutenant-Colonel A. A. McIntosh; Lieutenant-Colonel Hignett had been forced by sickness to relinquish his post the previous year. Phantom had six squadrons in Britain : they were A, B, C, D, L and F. On the assumption that there would be five corps involved in the landing (an assumption which proved correct) it was contemplated that each of the first five would be allocated to a corps. F Squadron would be left as a spare for future, and possibly different, employment. Although the regiment had now been in existence for five years, it was still experiencing difficulties inherent in a secret unit.

Many people in the Army had never heard of Phantom; unfortunately they included a few who should have done and who were responsible for its supplies. This became apparent when the regiment took part in an exercise in early 1944. The basis of the exercise was that Second British Army was to represent an invasion force and First Canadian Army the defenders. It was, of course, precisely the sort of situation which the Italian-based squadron had found to be the most frustrating, for the area was too congested to give Phantom scope for its proper employment. Nevertheless it enjoyed some successes and derived great benefit from the experience of being fully stretched.

Not least of its problems was the fact that the regiment was now using a different and more powerful wireless, the 22, which was replacing the 11. Unfortunately the first 22-sets had a tendency to break down without warning; the failures were attributed to careless assembly. However a bonus of the exercise was the regiment's popularity with the Canadians; they liked Phantom so much they wished to create a similar unit of their own.

The exercise, code-named 'Spartan', had used for squadrons, A, B, C, and D. 'A' Squadron had up till this point been commanded by Major David Niven (Rifle Brigade) but now he had been taken off to be a Lieutenant-Colonel in General Eisenhower's Headquarters. His place was taken by Major J. E. Dulley (Northamptons). The other squadrons were commanded by Major D. L. Russell (Roughriders),

Major P. D. Pattrick (Royal Artillery) and Major J. M. Hannay (Queen's Own Cameron Highlanders).

But there were other clouds on the horizon. There was the fear that the regiment might disappear altogether in one of General Montgomery's sweeping moves; this fear was not allayed by the knowledge that his Chief of Staff, General De Guingand, was still unconvinced of the regiment's usefulness (and he had known it in North Africa). The clouds passed away and later, when the regiment was engaged in the European battle, De Guingand was generous in his tributes.

John Morgan, who was with the regiment at its beginnings and eventually commanded it, says that Phantom always seemed to have an influential friend when it was in danger of being dispersed. After Dunkirk it was Alan Brooke who had been favourably impressed by the regiment in France. Now in 1944 it was the Canadians who, after their Middle East and Italian experience of working with Phantom, simply and categorically demanded it: Phantom and no substitute. In 1944 John Morgan was sent to act as liaison officer at the American Headquarters in Bryanston Square. He found them generally very polite but distant: there were also a few Anglophobes who clearly resented his presence. He tried for some time to find common ground and eventually decided to make himself an expert on baseball. This established lasting friendships but also made him a baseball addict himself. He has subsequently visited America many times, is an acknowledged expert on the game and is the only Englishman who has ever been allowed to give the commentary on a broadcast of a top-level game. His house is full of baseball trophies!

A question still unresolved was who or what should be Phantom's parent body. So far it had depended heavily on the Royal Signals which had supplied a steady stream of very competent operators. But the function of Signals is conveying information, not acquiring it, and although Signals often finds itself maintaining links in highly dangerous and isolated places this is not its primary function. Furthermore, although many Phantom officers came from cavalry regiments, it was not a cavalry or reconnaissance unit. Nor, in spite of J Service, was it an Intelligence unit. Ultimately, in spite of the unresolved doubts as to its true parentage, it became a part of the Royal Armoured Corps.

From its early days Phantom had favoured what might be described as a 'country gentleman' attitude to soldiering. Vehicles and squadrons had borne the names of famous horses or even trains. In the new organisation a slightly more serious note was introduced and the names of birds were given to patrols. Thus such words as 'Fulmar', 'Kite', 'Gull' and 'Gannet' came into everyday use.

F was having a more active, though highly secret role. It was commanded by Major the Hon J. J. Astor and had been attached to the SAS Brigade which was commanded by Brigadier R. W. McLeod (later General Sir Roderick McLeod).* The SAS rôle was very different from Phantom's, for their aim was to destroy enemy installations, from aircraft to railway engines, well behind the enemy lines. The brigade consisted of 1 & 2 SAS regiments, 3 & 4 French Parachute Battalions, and a Belgian Independent Parachute Squadron. 2 SAS was now commanded by Major Brian Franks who appeared in this narrative as a squadron commander in Phantom.

F Squadron's tasks were many and various. Two squadrons went to 1 SAS and two more to 2 SAS. One of the latter was commanded by Captain John Hislop, a man with an international reputation in horse-racing. The French and Belgian regiments had their own signals who worked to F Squadron HQ. All were Phantom-trained. The patrols carried Jedburgh sets which did not require batteries and could be carried by two men. There were also some midget receivers for picking up the code messages which the BBC transmitted to agents in the field. Reports of Phantom patrols working with the SAS appear later in the book.

L Squadron's assignment was scarcely less arduous than F's. It had been sent to Scotland to work with 52nd Lowland Division. 'Work' involved learning the art of mountain warfare over the central highland region. 52nd Division was a territorial unit but was the only official mountain division in the Army. It was commanded by Major-General Neil Ritchie who had been first appointed to, then removed from, command of the Eighth Army in Africa. L Squadron approached its assignment with a sense of foreboding, for they knew Ritchie's history and they suspected that he might feel that part of his undoing was the quality of information which had been supplied to him – partly by Phantom. However, it was not in Ritchie's nature to bear malice to anyone, so L Squadron was accepted without prejudice.

Scotland's mountain region offered ample opportunity for learning what happens to wireless transmissions in rugged country – an experience which others had known in the uncomfortable conditions of Norway and Italy. Weather makes no difference to the scheduled programme; if the ground was covered with snow the wireless was carried

---

* See *Special Air Service* by Philip Warner, Kimber, 1971.

on sleighs or pack ponies. Needless to say when this arduous training was completed the mountain campaigns were over and their only prospects were northern France, Holland or Germany.

As June 1944 approached, Phantom received its orders and trod carefully to ensure that none of the reputation for efficiency which had been won by hard work would now be lost by carelessness. Major Pattrick established an excellent relationship with the Canadian Divisional Commander who saw that Phantom communications were neither over-used nor misused.

Eventually Phantom's task was set out on paper in the form which the army has found useful, even though at first sight it seems a little pompous and long-winded.

Object 1. To produce at Army/RAF HQ, the most up to date picture of the battle possible and to keep the picture maintained.

The need for this picture arises because :

a. The fighter bomber squadrons of the RAF are controlled from Army/RAF HQ. The intervention of these squadrons is one of the most effective weapons in the hands of the army commander. Their correct and opportune employment is dependent on up to the minute information as to the progress of forward troops.

b. The commitment of reserves at the decisive moment is a question of timing and effective calculations and can only be made on the basis of up to the minute information as to the present state of the battle.

c. The forward planning of administrative facilities is a major pre-occupation of the Staff at Army, and again, calculations can only be made on the same basis.

2. To produce at Corps HQ an identical and simultaneous picture of information available at Army.

Method 1. With every division in the line there is a Phantom patrol. The patrol can obtain the information from any source in the divisional area. The means whereby the information is obtained is at the discretion of the patrol officer as he alone knows the conditions in his own area and can decide which, of several alternatives, is likely to be the most profitable. When obtained, the information is transmitted from Squadron HQ at Army HQ by wireless. High grade cipher is used. Each message quotes the source and time of any item of information, giving the rank and appointment of the Staff Officer supplying it.

2. With Armoured Divisions a J patrol usually supplements the information obtainable from the Phantom patrol.
3. With every Corps there is a Corps patrol whose function is to listen in on Phantom and J patrol rear links and pass on the information thus obtained to Corps staff.
4. With Army HQ is the HQ of the Army Squadron whose function is :
    a. To act as control to the outstations.
    b. To pass information to army staff.
    c. To administer its own squadron.

Each squadron had an establishment of 23 officers and 187 other ranks, organised as follows :

1. Headquarters (consisting of Signals, I section, and Administration . Total 1·1 officers and 83 other ranks.
2. Nine patrols (7 each of 1 officer and 6 other ranks and 2 each of 1 officer and 10 other ranks. Total 9 officers and 62 other ranks.
3. J detachment (3 officers and 42 other ranks).

Incoming information to be dealt with as follows :

1. One copy of all direct to AIR (i.e. the section of the staff dealing in Air Support for the Army).
2. J messages to be marked on the unconfirmed map together with all other unconfirmed information. The map to be kept in the Army ops room.
3. Making of this map to be a Phantom responsibility.
4. One copy of all Phantom messages quoting source of information to be passed to the marker of the confirmed map.
5. Any message on which action might be taken to go direct to the department concerned.

CHAPTER SEVEN

D Day and After

D Day, in which Phantom was to play a small but vital part, was an enterprise of such magnitude that it can only be described very briefly or in great length and detail. There is only scope for the former method here, although we include some personal stories later.

The Allied plan was to assault with 37 divisions of 15,000 men each. They would be landed on five beaches in an assault area fifty miles wide, between the Orne and the Vire estuary. Of the assault beaches the Americans had two: Utah and Omaha, and the British (which included the Canadians) had three: Gold, Juno, and Sword. The left flank of the British would be protected by a drop by 6th Airborne which would land east of Caen, and the right flank of the Americans would similarly be protected by the US 82nd and 101st Airborne divisions which would drop in the area around Carentan.

The initial assault was to be carried out by the British 3rd Division on Sword, the British 50th Division on Gold, the Canadian 3rd Division on Juno, the US 1st Division on Omaha and the US 4th Division on Utah.

Each beach was subdivided into smaller areas but these do not concern us here.

As is now well known, the period of waiting and attendant uncertainty in the weeks before D Day was a strain on all concerned. Squadron commanders were expected to keep their units cheerful and interested. As movement was heavily restricted and mail censored, this was not by any means an easy assignment. It was some consolation to know that the situation was the same for everyone.

A spy hoping to unravel the mysteries of Phantom would not have been helped by the fact that there was no special cap badge. The only unifying factor was the 'P' on the black background. Otherwise members of Phantom still wore the insignia of their previous regiments and cap badges had a misleading diversity. However when the Army adopted the black beret Phantom too wore black berets. It would be possible therefore to see a man with a parachute badge and a black (not red) beret. Hills records that it was not always even as simple as that. One of the early recruits was a trooper of the Royal Tank Regiment. He decided to change his badge to that of the 12th Lancers. Warre noted this and, knowing that the man had never served in the 12th Lancers, ordered him to take it off. Unabashed the man substituted the badge of the 11th Hussars, which he liked the look of too. This prospered until Hignett, of the 11th Hussars, arrived to command the regiment. Surprisingly he could not recall the man in his regiment either. But there are plenty of regiments in the British Army with attractive badges and after this enforced change the man's luck held.

On 'the day' there was no Phantom patrol with 6th Airborne. The task of 6th Airborne was to prevent the Germans demolishing two bridges near Bénouville as these were essential to the second part of General Montgomery's breakout plan. This meant capturing the bridges and holding them, not an easy task in an area where the enemy was concentrated. Strong winds made the task of locating dropping zones extremely difficult in the dark. The mission was successful but the subsequent realisation that Phantom would have been useful if available was not overlooked in later planning.

Rear HQs were at Dover and Selsey. Phantom had one patrol with 50th Division, one with 3rd Canadian and one with 3rd British. The patrol with 50 Division was attached to 231 Brigade whose task was to capture the vital port of Arromanches. They were to go in with the 2nd Devons, veterans of many bloody battles.

The journey had not been pleasant. The water was still rough, the transports were crowded and unstable, and the future problematic. But once ashore there was no time for personal thoughts. Captain Brook-Hart, who was with 5 Patrol reported a roughish crossing but a successful landing near Ouistreham. Thence the patrol moved to Hermanville, then inland to Colleville. They had a 22-set and two R107 receivers, and worked to Dover. They were listening for information from 6th Airborne, but the division was not using wireless except in emergencies, and No 3 Reconnaissance regiment from which they obtained nineteen messages. Soon the patrol was able to report on the problems 231 Brigade were encountering near Arromanches and that 69 Brigade was edging towards Creuilly. Messages for bombing Port-en-Bessin and concentrations of enemy troops near St Leger were sent to 2nd Army HQ through Phantom from HQ 50 Division. On the average, messages from the front were taking little over an hour to reach the Commander-in-Chief at Dover. This time included collection, verification, encoding, transmission, decoding and submission. When one considers that each of these took place in a different area the time is gratifyingly short.

The patrol with the Canadians (Balfour-Paul's) was late in landing owing to the inevitable congestion, shellfire, mines, and the like, but managed to pick up some information and transmit it from the LCT (Landing Craft Tank) on which they were pitching and rolling. A little later messages were picked up from 6th Airborne reporting success in securing objectives.

By evening it was clear that in spite of all the problems of extricating information from such a confusing situation Phantom had done all and more than could have been expected. The patrols had been able to come up quickly with information about a rapidly shifting scene. There would never be another day like this and Phantom had acquitted itself well. So much for Gold, Juno and Sword.

On Utah and Omaha events had been even more complex. The airborne assault by 82nd and 101st US Divisions had been disastrous. Their dropping zone was badly flooded and numbers of parachutists, weighed down with equipment, were drowned. Nevertheless those troops who did manage to reach their objectives were able to prevent the Germans concentrating on the beach landing areas. The Utah landing was a theoretical disaster but a practical success. Owing to the loss of their radar boat 4th US Division were unable to locate their proper landing point and therefore came ashore one mile south of their intended destination. Their commander, Brigadier Theodore Roosevelt, then took them straight inland instead of trying to move to the destination originally planned; it was a wise and successful decision.

At Omaha the scene was considerably less happy. The area was much more heavily defended than the attackers suspected. Two Phantom patrols were assigned to report on the American position. They were those of Captain W. S. Macintosh-Reid, and of Captain Maurice Macmillan.* Their task was not lightened by the fact that some Americans mistook the 'P' for some German regimental badge. However, Phantom was not involved in the initial assault. Both squadrons embarked on 8th June. Macintosh-Reid arrived the day he embarked, Macmillan was delayed till the 12th. Once they were on the scene it was clear that there was an urgent need for the sort of service Phantom provided, and the Americans responded promptly by detailing an officer and twenty-five enlisted men for Phantom training. However,

* Son of the future Prime Minister.

it was impossible to train these as a separate unit in the available time, so gradually they were absorbed into Phantom by attachment. This was not the end of the American wish to have its own Phantom for a plan to form a Phantom unit was, in addition, sent to Washington for approval, which it obtained. Of those selected most were then attached to Phantom for training, but the war came to an end before this fully independent American Phantom Regiment was established.

Meanwhile Macintosh-Reid was now with US VII Corps, en route to capture Cherbourg; Macmillan was with US V Corps at Issigny. L Squadron, which we left in Scotland busy training for mountain warfare, now found itself suddenly posted to Normandy with the task of providing a Phantom service down to Corps level on the American sector.

Phantom had an immediate appeal to the Americans because it clearly fulfilled an essential need and did so by making the best use of modern technology. Furthermore it was apparently unflappable. However crowded the system, however hard-worked the operators, Phantom managed to convey an atmosphere of efficient calm. It was by no means what their members felt on numerous occasions.

L Squadron, as we saw above, came into the battle as US VII Corps was moving towards Cherbourg. US VIII Corps was moving west across the Carentan peninsula, US XIX Corps was closing in on Carentan. From L one patrol under Lieutenant M. F. Cleghorn (Royal Fusiliers) went to XIX Corps and one, under Lieutenant A. F. L. Borman (RA) to VII Corps. On 22nd June VII Corps moved towards Cherbourg. Expenditure of ammunition was heavy and as a result shortages began to be worrying. Macintosh-Reid sent off the corps' urgent request for further supplies, particularly of 105 mm, and was able to report as step by step the Americans recaptured this vital port.

As the war went on, the importance of Cherbourg increased, for the Germans clung tenaciously to their hold on other major ports. Unfortunately the BBC announced the capture of Cherbourg two days before it actually occurred. This was not the only occasion when rumour was passed as fact. Phantom was sometimes accused of being behind with the news of great events. Its reply was terse – 'We report events when they occur, not when people hope they will occur.'

But, of course, it was not roses all the way. Some Americans were still suspicious of the British presence in their HQs; some went further and were pronounced Anglophobes. Many formations felt that to have the Phantom station in the middle of their area was equivalent to telling the Germans their exact position. Even when Phantom was moved to what was deemed a safe distance, the comings and goings were criticized as giving away hints to potentially unfriendly eyes. But, overall, results told. Even General Patton, not noted for his cordiality to things British, gave Phantom a nod of approval.

British and American forces linked up at Escures, near Port-en-Bessin, on the afternoon of 8th June. Phantom was proving very useful in helping to map out bomb lines and ensure that our own bombs and shells did not fall on our own advanced units. A Squadron was now with 51st Highland Division, south of Creuilly; B was also in this area.

However, as the German realised that the main attack was now in the west of Normandy and not in the Calais area as they had expected they were rushing up reinforcements to contain the invasion forces. Much of their armour was concentrated against the British flank. Fourteen German divisions, including armoured, were confronting seven British. On the other flank nine German divisions, including two armoured, were confronting fifteen American divisions under Bradley (with four of Patton's in reserve). Caen fell on 9th July and on 26th General Patton's Third Army began to overrun Brittany. On 7th August the Germans made a counter-attack in the direction of Avranches but it was held at Mortain by Bradley while Patton, veering north, launched a thrust at Argentan. The Canadian First Army now pushed forward to Falaise. The result of this was that the German 5th Panzer and 7th Armies were trapped in the Falaise pocket where they were pounded mercilessly by Allied aircraft and artillery. At the end of the battle the Germans had lost 10,000 killed, and a further 50,000 taken prisoner. Without accurate information from Phantom, telling British American and Canadians exactly where the other's units were, undoubtedly they would have fired on each other as the gap was being closed.

On 15th August three American and seven French divisions were landed near Cannes, in what was known as Operation Anvil. This had the effect of causing the Germans to abandon the south of France, but did not materially affect the rest of the fighting. The critical battles were taking place in the north. Paris was liberated on 26th August. Patton pushed forward to Lorraine; Montgomery confounded his critics, who thought him unadventurous and slow, by pressing on rapidly to Brussels and Antwerp.

It was all too clear that in a war of rapid movement, of sudden stops and changes, it was vital for the Higher Command to know exactly where the advanced units were, what sort of opposition they

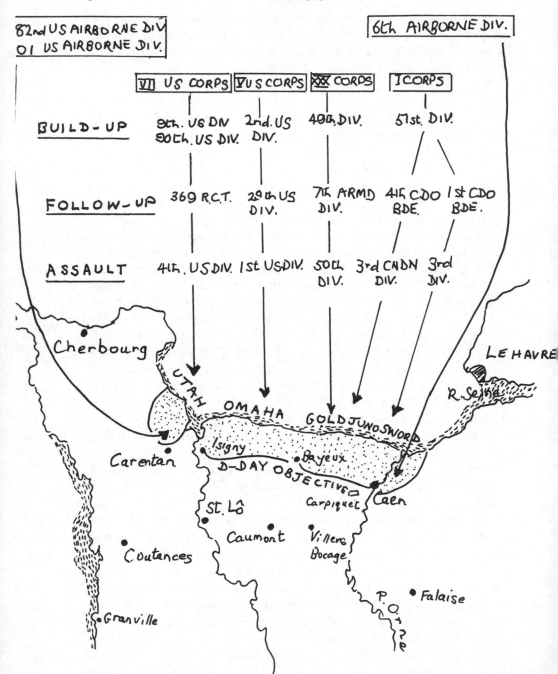

(Phantom patrols were attached to the forward units).

The D-Day Landings, 6th June 1944

were encountering, and how far the situation was fluid. This gave Phantom every justification for its existence. Particularly was this so around Caen where strategic points changed hands several times. The breakout from the Caen area was known as 'Goodwood'. Here A Squadron, with B in reserve, was heavily committed.

Phantom was in fact even more popular with forward troops than it was with the Higher Command for, as is sadly well known, air forces are all too liable to bomb their own troops under the impression they are assisting them. This happened in Normandy to an American regiment which was almost wiped out by its own air-support. Phantom began producing its air maps from reconnaissance. J Sections were overwhelmed with information; there was so much going on and so much to hear that it was almost impossible to interpret it. But at least it managed to report on positions and therefore prevent a successful thrust from being the target of our own gunners. Phantom soon realised that the fluidity of the battle would have to be matched by its own flexibility. A Phantom patrol therefore went where it was asked to go, not where, by the original Order of Battle, it should have been.

But mistakes were sometimes made. On 14th August as First Canadian Army went into attack it was bombed by our own Lancasters. The Phantom patrol (Captain Michael Astor's) with 2nd Canadian Armoured Brigade got off fairly lightly with three men wounded. But the Canadians had their consolation too. They took part in the recapture of Le Havre, Dieppe and Ostend; their pleasure in doing so was matched by that of 51st Highland Division who re-took St Valéry where their earlier comrades had been trapped in 1940.

In fairness to the air forces it should not be forgotten that they were often fired on by our own gunners.

We can now take up the story of F Squadron again. As we saw, it was as highly trained as the SAS units to which it was attached. By an interesting coincidence, when some of that training had taken place in Scotland, F Squadron's headquarters were at Auchinlecks, in the Strathclyde region. Field Marshal Sir Claude Auchinleck, who as Commander-in-Chief Middle East had given David Stirling permission to form the first SAS unit, was a direct descendant of the Auchinlecks who had lived in the area since the twelfth century.

The F Squadron patrols were spread very widely. Some went to Brittany, one to the Ardennes. Captain Hugh Fraser was with the latter. He had the unpleasant task of reporting the Waffen SS atrocities in the area. F Squadron maintained close links with the Maquis but the Maquis often proved alarmingly independent; F Squadron and the SAS worked on the basis of the finely calculated risk. The Maquis, on the other hand, often seemed to ignore or not to see a risk and to trust in luck or another deity. F Squadron knew very well that if any-one was captured their fate would lie with the Gestapo, not with some prisoner-of-war camp commandant.

The work was immensely satisfying but equally gruelling. The Ger-mans were seeking them actively, food was short, supplies, including ammunition, wireless, etc, had to be carried by hand often over very difficult country. Jeeps occasionally arrived by parachute, but occasion-ally a jeep found itself confronting a German armoured vehicle and that was another jeep gone. The cost in casualties of this particular operation in which a total of ninety-two men were involved (mainly, of course, SAS) was high, for thirty-one were killed, twenty-eight after capture, by the Gestapo. 'Special Forces' often incur the envy and dislike of their comrades in less glamorous activities but when units like F Squadron become operational there is no glamour, a little too much activity, and often a very unpleasant sequel.

Back with the main thrust the Canadians had very sensibly laid down what they felt was their requirement from Phantom. It ran as follows. For:

1. *Operations*: General information on progress down to battalion level. Intentions – change of plans.
2. *Intelligence*: Identification and re-identification. Gossip on the enemy.
3. *Air*: Line of forward troops, or estimated line, by any and every means.
4. *Royal Engineers*: Constant information on state of bridges.
5. *RAF Intelligence:* Information on enemy air.
6. *Staff Duties*: Information on own troops down to battalion.
7. *Adjutant and Quartermaster*: Road surface and traffic news.

Inevitably, as Phantom built up its system and sent out its tentacles, its offices became shopping centres for information. It found itself very short staffed for such an onerous assignment. L Squadron established a detachment at Montgomery's own headquarters. This was apart from the main headquarters and numbered about thirty in all. To have the Commander-in-Chief living apart in what was felt to be a small, vulnerable entourage was a constant worry to the security staff. How-ever, as that was the way Monty wanted it, that was the way it was.

Although Phantom's rôle might have seemed to an outsider to be free and unhampered, it involved a lot of hard, detailed, regular work. The service proved itself useful in a number of different ways. There was, as always, the original one of mapping the 'bomb line' so that our own aircraft did not bomb our own troops. It also passed the latest information about the state of a battle at top speed to GHQ. But there were other developments which were almost as useful. As a division went into the attack, with Phantom reporting on every point gained or lost, other Phantom units were functioning in divisions on the flanks of the attacking division. The flanking units were therefore kept fully informed of the progress or otherwise of the assault division, and could therefore work out their own policies in relation to results.

Eventually this led to what was known as the 'Golden Arrow' Service. 'Golden Arrow' provided a complete report on the activity along the entire front for Corps conferences each morning. So important did this report become that before long Corps conferences began with the reading out of the Phantom situation reports. On one occasion, in a Corps which remains nameless, the Phantom officer responsible for producing the report overslept. He woke up five minutes before the Corps conference was due to start. Knowing he had no chance of producing an up-to-date situation map in five minutes, he decided to report that there had been a technical hitch and the required information could not be available for about half an hour. He fully expected the Corps conference would continue without him, using the information they already possessed. To his amazement the Corps commander postponed the conference for thirty minutes. Fortunately for the Phantom officer, he was not asked to explain what sort of technical hitch had occasioned the delay.

On a normal day three copies of the latest sitreps were delivered to the Chief of Staff, the G2 and the G3. Once the service was established with them it worked even better with American and Canadian units than it did with British. In the American sector some of the patrols were of mixed British and American personnel; they worked in complete harmony. Relations with the Canadians were also very friendly. The latter, with the utmost amiability, referred to Phantom as 'Those bloody Limeys'.

A typical message, from August 1944, was this (sent on 28th August):

Phantom Msg No 550   281835   Third US Army   VIII US Corps
Source G3 VIII Corps 1830 hours. Div advance held up by strong enemy position on high ground area Q-9903. 2 Div making

two fold attack, one on above mentioned high ground. Two: on high ground T-0001. When successful G.3. believes further advance possible.

On that occasion the optimistic forecast was correct. On other occasions the message was more sombre: (Sept 11th 1944)

Phantom Msg No 1013   111829   Ninth US Army
   Source Msg G3 VIII Corps. Brest fortress wall is surrounded by anti-tank ditch 15–20 metres wide and varies to 15 metres in depth. The wall is made of earth and rock and varies in width from seven to 20 mettres and from eight to 15 metres in height. Enemy positions are located on top of and along the wall. Breaches in the wall for roads and blocked and heavily defended.

Brest, of course, was not the only walled town which provided unexpectedly tough resistance to modern weapons. The idea that ancient walls would promptly collapse into rubble when attacked by modern artillery had proved an illusion early in the war. Boulogne had surprised the Germans in 1940; subsequently other crumbling fortifications from France to Burma had proved equally obstinate and unyielding.
   One of Phantom's most useful feats at this time was to match two messages, both in the British sector. One said that an infantry unit was moving forward to attack a German position, the other said that the RAF were going to bomb that same position. The RAF were actually in the air and on their way when Phantom was able to get a message to the infantry and delay their attack.
   Of course, all messages were not of action. There had been a fascinating series of reports right back in 1940 when Phantom had been instructed to report on the possibilities of a German landing in the Wash area. Phantom was already in the district, reporting on weather. When an invasion is in prospect few things are more important than accurate weather reports in coastal areas. The question was: Was the Wash a possible invasion area? Ever since Erskine Childers' book *The Riddle of the Sands* had been published in 1903, there had been a lingering fear that this area might be used for a diversionary landing even if not a main one. The task of finding out the feasibility of such an action in 1940 had fallen to Phantom. The problem to be solved was whether the Germans, and Dutch skippers who might happen to sympathize with them, knew all the tricks of the tides and shallows in the Wash. It may be remembered that less than a year

before the *Royal Oak* had been torpedoed in the allegedly secure anchorage of Scapa Flow, and Scapa Flow had frequently been visited by trawlers, German and Dutch, between the wars. The findings of Phantom as far as the Wash was concerned was that a landing was just feasible but unlikely.

Another series of messages would bring a smile to the face of a veteran soldier. At the start of World War II the standard headgear with battledress was that was then called a forage cap or 'Cap : Field Service'. (The Army had yet another name for it which is hardly suitable here.) A forage cap was like a small flat tea cosy. In theory the side flaps could be pulled down to keep the ears warm. Forage caps were probably better than the old cheesecutter but they were still hopelessly impractical. It was instructive to watch a squad of recruits drilling. Every few minutes a cap would slide from its owner's head on to the ground. The drill sergeant would often pick them up and at the next halt redistribute them. Off duty soldiers would either tuck the forage cap into their pockets or under their shoulder straps, neither of which helped the appearance of the cap or the owner. They were not waterproof and they were not warm. They looked their best when worn by girl friends. Phantom wished to change to a beret like that worn by the Royal Tank Regiment, which later became the standard form of headgear. There ensued a series of messages about the relative cost of purchasing FS caps and berets and the subsequent cost of dry cleaning each. Few FS caps can ever have seen a dry cleaner; they soon became greasy but were then scrubbed clean. But Phantom realised that if you are dealing with the bureaucratic mind you must think like a bureaucrat in order to make your point. They won the argument.

In 1944 a typical squadron day had a schedule like this :

1. Collate information about all local Allied positions (which would have been obtained the night before).
2. Obtain copies of all the operation orders and code names for the day. (Code names were a headache, for they were usually only issued at the last minute and might be changed with very little notice.)
3. Obtain casualty statements.
4. Give a continuous picture of the operational situation, basing it on situation reports.
5. Report any minor changes in plans.
6. Report all possible information about the enemy, especially what

might be learnt about the condition and use of roads, bridges, railways etc.

7. Report results of operations.

This sounds straightforward enough, and often it was. There were exceptions however such as when the squadron took up temporary headquarters in a nunnery at Overpelt in Belgium in 1944. There the presence of starlings in the chimney caused constant showers of soot, and the nuns who remained in the nunnery showed an all too keen interest in the operational map.

By 1944 the standard pattern of a squadron was as follows:

1. A Captain or Lieutenant
2. A Corporal or Lance Corporal
3. Nine other ranks, of whom half were spetcialists – operators, encoders etc.

The equipment was:

1. White scout car and trailer
1. 107 Receiver
1. 22 Set (later Canadian 9 Set and, latest of all, a 52 Set)
1. Issue petrol cooker (which proved useless and was replaced by privately owned primus stoves)

The Autumn of 1944 saw Phantom back in the areas where their military existence had begun in 1940 but the situation now was a far cry from that in those distant days. The Guards Armoured Division retook Brussels. Brussels is one of those lucky towns which in spite of being captured and recaptured in two world wars has seen very little actual fighting within its boundaries. 11th Armoured Division entered Antwerp soon after. The main bridge had been saved from German demolition by the prompt and courageous action of a Belgian. However, there had been no chance of preventing the Germans blowing the bridges over the Albert Canal. 30 Corps was now advancing towards the Dutch frontier. The Canadians captured Blankenberg. The Americans were pushing ahead though Patton was repulsed at Metz and checked at Lunéville. The German army had now recovered from the recent onslaughts and had stabilized its line. The Germans' stubborn defence of the Channel ports and the fact that they were still holding the approaches to Antwerp was creating many problems for the Allies.

Montgomery, who was now showing initiative and speed of which neither his friends nor his enemies would have thought him capable, was anxious to thrust forward into Germany. Unfortunately, for the reasons mentioned above, there were insufficient supplies to maintain both Montgomery and Patton, and the latter, in spite of setbacks, was doing remarkably well further south. This dilemma led to the Market Garden operation which was a disaster for the British 1st Airborne Division, and a setback for the entire Allied cause.

Since D Day, when 6th British Airborne and 82nd and 101st American Airborne Division had dropped to protect the flanks of the invaders, there had been little need for airborne units. This was because the ground troops were attaining their objectives without needing airborne drops ahead of them. However, the need to outflank the Siegfried Line and to establish an army over the Rhine led to the sanctioning of a decidedly risky operation. It was to take place in daylight, close to numerous Luftwaffe bases, and it could only be successful if the corridor behind the landing force could be kept open. To add to the problem there was a shortage of transport aircraft.

Phantom's part in this projected operation was to provide a streamlined airborne squadron. The regiment was by no means unused to airborne operations for aircraft had been used on exercises and a number of people had been trained as glider pilots. Each of the three divisions taking part, which were the British 6th Airborne, 101st American, and 82nd American, would have a Phantom patrol with them. As a back-up 52nd Lowland Division was to be landed by Dakotas as soon as a suitable airfield (preferably Dielst) had been captured. This too would be linked by Phantom. Phantom also had a unit at 1st British Airborne HQ. This aerial assault force would land along a line running from Eindhoven–Nijmegen–Arnhem, and capture the road bridges over the Maas, the Waal and the Neder Rijn. The Guards Armoured Division and 30 Corps would force their way through as the airborne units secured their objectives.

In the event eight important bridges were captured but the ninth, the vital one at Arnhem, was not. This was due to the fact that 9th Panzer Division was unexpectedly close to Arnhem, and so too were the German generals Model and Student. The operation has been fought and refought in films and books so there is no need to devote more space to the broader aspects here. To those taking part events seemed to have an inevitability. The Allied airfleet, collectively entitled 1st Allied Airborne, had been standing by for various similar operations for the previous month. When Market Garden was postponed for

24 hours, this seemed like yet another damp squib. The supposition proved sadly wrong.

Phantom HQ Squadron was commanded by Captain J. P. Astbury (Royal Signals) and Captain R. J. T. Hills (Life Guards). Eventually, on Sunday 17th September, at 11.30 a.m., after a few more days, they were airborne in their gliders. At 2 p.m. Phantom arrived. As happens with gliders, there were accidents on landing, but none was fatal. Glider 13 broke its tow rope and came down near a German aerodrome. Its occupants were soon captured. Unfortunately they included Astbury, but fortunately they fought long enough to give them time to destroy all secret material.

101st gained its objectives without encountering much trouble but its fellow countrymen in 82nd took longer. But the operation was far from complete. The Germans were fighting back vigorously, with all the advantage which close-by airfields gave them. By 21st September Nijmegen had been taken, but Arnhem was full of German troops. The occupation of Nijmegen was distinctly uncomfortable, for the German aircraft now attacked the town like angry wasps. Bad weather hampered our own air effort which had to travel from much further away. Desperate attempts were made to push through to relieve the remnants of the much battered 1st Airborne Division. But they were of no avail. On the 25th an orderly withdrawal was begun and two thousand men were ferried back across the Rhine that night without the Germans apparently realising what was happening. Phantom, of course, were the last to go.

Captain D. Brook-Hart was awarded an immediate Military Cross for his part during the operation. But overall it had been a disastrous week for the Allied cause. Had the operation succeeded – and it could have done if the British had been a little less cautious and the Americans had concentrated their effort instead of adopting broad advance tactics – the war could have been ended in 1944 and thousands of Allied lives saved.

CHAPTER EIGHT

A Deceptive Calm

Although the Western Allies were unaware of it, the Germans in the north had been almost totally exhausted, both in manpower and supplies, by the Arnhem battles. But to their surprise and dismay those forces received less than a fair share of the meagre resources available for reinforcement. On Hitler's direct orders, most of the new tanks, Mark IVs and Vs (the big Panthers), were sent to the south where it was hoped to give Patton a surprise. Patton was not easily surprised. When the Germans mounted an offensive at Lunéville on 18th September they were immediately thrown back. By 23rd September two German tank brigades had been cut to ribbons. Another German offensive three days later was equally unsuccessful. These events created in the minds of the Allies the idea that the Germans were now contained and would gradually be pushed backward. It was to prove a costly delusion.

However the principal weakness of the Allies at this moment was not complacency but indecision. There was no clear understanding of what strategic objective should be pursued next. By approving the policy of advancing on a broad front Eisenhower had failed to cross the Rhine, failed to take the Antwerp estuary and thus make the port usable, and failed also to make sufficient headway in the Saar-Frankfurt area. Yet all the time he was aware that each of his divisions was trying to cover a ten mile front, and this was, of course, totally at variance with the accepted military maxim of concentration of force. It should have surprised no one that the capture of Aachen took a month, whereas it should have taken a few days.

Supplies were coming in from Cherbourg and from Mulberry Harbour at Arromanches but they were slow in arriving. Many in fact were 'lost' and did not arrive at all. Dieppe and Ostend had been taken by the Canadians but these were very small ports and the vital need was to open up Antwerp, Dunkirk, Calais, Boulogne and Le Havre. Each of these contained a last-ditch German division which

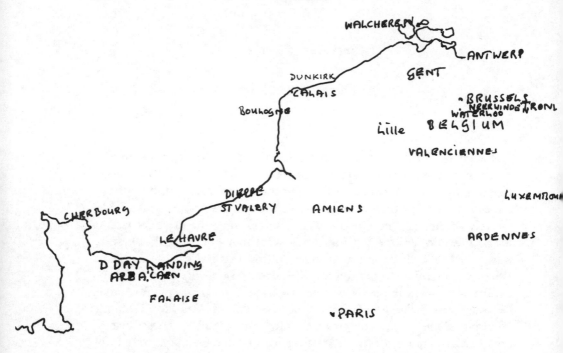

WALCHEREN

ANTWERP

DUNKIRK

GENT

CALAIS

BOULOGNE

BRUSSELS
NEERWINDE TROND
WATERLOO

Lille

BELGIUM

VALENCIENNES

LUXEMBOU

CHERBOURG

DIEPPE

ST VALERY

AMIENS

ARDENNES

LE HAVRE

D DAY LANDING
AREA. CAEN

FALAISE

PARIS

RENNES

LE MANS

FOUGERAY
'DUNHILL' AREA'
(F. Squadron)

ORLEANS

'LOYTON'
AREA

TOURS

DIJON
'HOUNDSWORTH
AREA. F. Squ.

France and Belgium

(Sketch map shows 1940, Valenciennes—Trond—Dunkirk; 1944, Normandy—Waterloo, and areas 'Dunhill', 'Loyton' and 'Houndsworth' where 'F' Squadron operated with the SAS)

had been ordered to destroy the harbour and fight to the last man if necessary.

In the event the task of regaining them proved less exacting than had been expected. Two British divisions captured Le Havre in less than two days; at Boulogne and Calais the Canadians took a little longer but as they were only able to deploy two brigades for the task their achievement was remarkable. Unfortunately all the ports had been well mined and damaged by their German occupants and it took a further month to get the docks into some sort of working order. Even then the unloading facilities were totally inadequate, as the Germans had destroyed all the large cranes.

One of the first to re-enter Calais was Rifleman Turrell who had seen the town in 1940 when, with other members of Phantom, he had been engaged in a rearguard action before being evacuated. Another notable figure (in every sense of the word) in Calais was the tallest man in the German Army. He was 7 feet $3\frac{1}{2}$ inches tall and was captured by the French Canadians.

Antwerp was clearly going to be a difficult task, for the port, although in our hands, is fifty miles inland. The Germans still clung tenaciously to Merxem on the northern side of the town, as that enabled them to shell the docks. But before any ship could ever reach Antwerp it had to run the gauntlet of Welcheren Island at the mouth of the estuary. Here the Germans had a powerful array of guns, and these were matched by others nearby on the mainland.

Fortunately for the Allies Walcheren was reclaimed land. It was therefore decided that RAF Lancasters should bomb the dykes and flood the island, which they did successfully. However the Germans were still able to occupy some coastal strips. Only after desperate fighting by Canadians and several British regiments was control of the island achieved. Clearing the channel took a further three weeks.

The Phantom officer who had the pleasure of sending off the message stating that the Canadians had reached the North Sea was Peregrine Worsthorne, later to become known to millions from journalism and television, especially from his column of political comment in the *Sunday Telegraph*. He had been commissioned into the Oxford and Bucks Light Infantry in 1942; in 1944 he applied to join Phantom, with whom he served for the remainder of the war.

This period of the campaign consisted of hard slogging in the most unpleasant weather conditions anyone could have expected. Even normally trouble-free transport found the mud and prevailing conditions too much. A vehicle may be highly mobile but when its wheels sink out of sight in the mud there is little the occupants can do about it. It happens often. Nevertheless patience and perseverance appeared to be winning the struggle. North of Maastricht the British and American columns linked up. Strasbourg was taken by a French armoured unit on 23rd November. Phantom was first to report the capture. At first the report was not believed but when it was confirmed Phantom gained considerable kudos from having reported such a vital piece of information so speedily.

But successes were still slow in coming. A tactical problem was set by the Schmidt dams. If the Allies attacked successfully their leading units could all be swept away into the Roer or Maas, if the Germans opened the dams. It was therefore decided that the dams should be destroyed by air attack and the Allied forces advance after the floods had gone down. However, the air forces were unable to destroy the dams and eventually, in December, it was decided to risk everything in a straightforward ground attack. It succeeded, but by then the Allies were about to face a totally unexpected and unnerving problem in the Ardennes.

The fact that the Ardennes offensive has been the subject of spectacular films and exciting fiction has somewhat obscured the basic causes. Although the offensive took the Allies by surprise, it should not have done. Since the previous July Hitler had been amassing a reserve of 250,000 men and 1,100 tanks for the counter-stroke which would be commanded by his most able general, von Rundstedt. That Allied intelligence remained so completely unaware of this huge concentration is one of the mysteries of the war. But even without the knowledge of this dangerous massing of German force, there were many reasons for expecting trouble in the Ardennes region. It was here that in 1940 the Germans, realising French weakness in the area, had broken through. There was little about the Ardennes which the Germans did not already know. Before the 1940 breakthrough they had studied the area very carefully; in the campaign itself they had learnt other facts from experience. Yet in 1944 the Allied High Command was so confident of victory that it had allowed an 85 mile front to be covered by a mere five divisions, a thinner spread than anywhere else. Furthermore, of those five divisions three had scarcely recovered from heavy fighting in the Aachen area. The American First Army, which had been allotted the dubious pleasure of holding this sector, was short of all supplies, including guns and ammunition.

Phantom Regimental Headquarters at this time was at Waterloo

(Belgium) in the Waterloo Golf Club Clubhouse. Belgium was rapidly returning to normal – or so its people felt. Golf was again being played on the Waterloo links. From here Phantom linked to the patrols deployed in the forward areas and back to the 21st Army Group Headquarters in Brussels. Phantom HQ was so overcrowded that it might be more fitting to say that its occupants were crammed together.

For security reasons and also to give the transmitters the best conditions for sending and receiving, this part of Phantom was sited about a mile from the ops room. Choosing the best site for the transmitters was by no means an easy task; it required that technical knowledge should be combined with an 'eye for ground'. Fortunately at Phantom HQ, these qualities were displayed by Major Lord Cullen who had come to Phantom from the Royal Signals and was now senior signals officer. He disclaims the technical knowledge; nevertheless equipment never seemed to break down when under his command. He acquired the Waterloo Golf Club House for Regimental Headquarters; it was not merely comfortable but was excellently sited for transmission and reception. After the war he became Amateur Tennis Champion in his mid thirties and again five years later. At the time of writing he is a Lord in Waiting (Government Whip) in the House of Lords.

Organisation was flexible. There were direct links to Canadian, 2nd British Army and 12th US Army. It was pleasant and encouraging to know that the Phantom service was appreciated and fully utilized. The feeling of satisfaction was, however, somewhat diminished as the volume of traffic grew. This meant that resources were strained to the limit. Some relief was obtained by bringing over extra personnel from England and by borrowing Americans on the spot but even with these the regiment was fully stretched. Part of the problem was the number of 'special requests'. These came from unit commanders with a special interest in certain localities. A partial solution was found by making a regular broadcast of sitreps to thirty-five out-stations. The service did not entirely remove the demand for special information but it certainly cut it down. Conditions in the area varied considerably. As mentioned above, the weather that winter was appalling. This did not affect the Phantom units at Waterloo or 21st Army Group too badly but was felt by those at Montgomery's headquarters, where they were in tents and caravans. The only means of heating was the ubiquitous oil stove. The stoves of that vintage were considerably less efficient than their modern counterparts. They polluted the atmosphere, smoked when affected by draughts, and occasionally caught fire. More than one fire was caused by someone putting a chinagraph talc near the stove and forgetting it. Talc is readily inflammable when it heats up, and once it begins to burn goes ahead merrily. Curiously enough, it is often the irritants rather than the hazards of war that stay in the memory. Many of those in north-west Europe in 1944–45 remember the cold and damp discomfort more clearly than bombs and bullets. Some people's most lasting wartime recollection would be of a smelly smoking stove which covered everything with smuts and oily slime. That, and never being really warm, day or night.

There was of course a widespread belief that the war was now reaching its final stages and that until the weather allowed for a spring offensive there was little to do. The main objectives had been achieved. Immediately after the Normandy landings a new threat had appeared, the V bomb. Now, however, the V bomb sites had mostly been over-run and Britain was in no further danger from them. It was merely a matter of crossing the Rhine and sweeping through Germany. . . .

The Germans, however, thought otherwise. They had a good idea of the tangles in the Allied supply lines and they knew how thinly some sections of the Allied line were held. And they knew, or thought they knew, that if a tremendous thrust was put in through the Ardennes it could break through, split the British and American forces, turn north and recapture Antwerp.

On the 16th the moment of truth arrived. Stileman, with V US Corps, sent his first message at 9030 hrs :

Enemy artillery fire activity along the whole corps front this morning. 106 Division report counter-attack by one company area 0393 and further small counter-attacks area 0390. 99 Division : Command post 3rd Bn 394 Regt area P.9799 receiving small arms fire. Unknown strength counter-attack made slight penetration against 1st Bn 393 Regt but no details yet. 3rd Bn 395 Regt repelled attack. Enemy patrol activity continuing.

These moves were in fact slightly to the north of where the big thrust was being launched. The deployment of the American forces was V Corps around Eupen, VIII Corps around Malmédy and VII to the east of Aachen. These corps were collectively Lieutenant-General Courtney H. Hodges' First US Army. Antwerp lay a mere 100 miles away to the north-west. North of First Army was US Ninth Army (Simpson) consisting of two corps only, and to the south Patton's Third US Army consisting of III, XII and XX Corps. Unfortunately, owing to shortage of Phantom personnel, there was no Phantom patrol with VIII Corps.

V Corps then received the full weight of SS General Sepp Dietrich's VII SS Panzer Army. The Americans were pushed back but fought tenaciously. The German aim was Liège but they never reached it; they were brought to a halt on 19th December. V Panzer fell on US VIII Corps, which, as we saw, was very thin on the ground. The Germans reached the outskirts of Houffalize and Bastogne. In the south the German VIII Army had limited success in trying to push round the southern flank of Third Army but it was soon brought to a halt.

The Germans had surprised the Allies in every way. They had attacked unexpectedly, in appalling conditions, they had infiltrated Allied positions creating confusion and disaster, and they had produced more tanks and aircraft than anyone had expected. But they had some surprises themselves; they did not break through in the north as they had hoped and once VI Panzer was checked that was virtually the end of the hope of recapturing Antwerp. The Americans, although taken by surprise, rallied quickly and put up an admirable defence. Although V Panzer hammered away at Bastogne it failed to penetrate. Brigadier-General Anthony McAuliffe was invited to surrender on 22nd December when the town was completely surrounded and had been bypassed. His reply was the single word 'Nuts', which subsequently became his nickname.

But the Germans had not stopped. A thrust was still going forward to Dinant and Namur. The Panzers had now driven fifty miles into the Allied line. But Second British Army stopped the Dinard thrust, First US Army counter-attacked VI Panzer and drove it back, and Patton's Third US Army pushed through to Bastogne. Here a major battle was still taking place. Von Manteuffel, commanding V Panzer Army, was determined to crush Bastogne and then use his entire strength in a drive forward, in the direction of Namur. On 30th December his army and Patton's fought it out in the snow. By 8th January the Germans could do no more and began to withdraw. The Allies had lost 77,000 men but the Germans had lost 70,000 and had had another 50,00 taken prisoner. Not least of the contributions to Allied victory was the performance of the Allied air forces, even after receiving tremendous blows from the Luftwaffe.

For Phantom it was almost like Belgium in the early days. They were constantly on the move and almost every piece of information they reported had an ominous ring.

One Phantom member suddenly plunged into the battle was Captain the Hon Michael Astor. On 18th December he was told to report to US XVIII Airborne Corps which, with US V and VII, made up the remains of First Army. As the Americans were now particularly alert to German spies operating behind our lines in British and American uniforms, his welcome was at first somewhat restrained. Eventually when he located the corps HQ it was in a farmhouse. Here he met the redoubtable Matthew B. Ridgway, later to be commander of Allied forces in Korea. Ridgway radiated confidence, which was not misplaced, in the ability of the Americans to fight off the German attack. Astor's task was to transmit daily information to Montgomery, who had now been sent by Eisenhower to command US Ninth and First Armies. This appointment was no reflection on the Americans but recognised an administrative need as Bradley was too far away, in Luxembourg, to take the responsibility. A few eyebrows were raised and a few thoughts voiced about how the Americans would take the appointment. There was no need to worry : it worked perfectly. And Montgomery subsequently wrote : 'The battle was won primarily by the staunch fighting qualities of the American soldier.'

CHAPTER NINE

The Final Stages

After the Ardennes offensive had been checked, the Allied forward drive was continued. In spite of the conditions, for snow and frost had been followed by thaws and floods, the line crept forward. Houffalize was retaken on 16th January. On the same day the British XXX Corps began to straighten the line along the Roer, a proceeding which took ten days of gruelling fighting. During the month one patrol of Phantom, operating between British XXX Corps and VIII US Corps, passed 1080 messages.

During February the Allied advance continued and by the beginning of March the whole of the west bank of the Rhine was in Allied hands. In Phantom, B Squadron with the Canadians was now carrying the main burden. 'A' Squadron with 2nd Army was having a quieter time. But the fact that there was less to report did not mean that there was less going on. To those not immediately concerned it may have seemed that it was all over bar the cheering. To those on the spot battling against a determined and fanatical enemy fighting on the frontiers of the Fatherland it seemed somewhat different. The fact that the Germans had 60,000 battle casualties and lost another 293,000 taken prisoner during early spring gives the true picture.

Luck, initiative, and a German oversight gave the Allies a tremendous advantage at this moment. On 7th March an American sergeant led a platoon of the US 9th Armoured Division over the intact bridge at Remagen. As they began to cross, the Germans, who had not realised the Americans were so close, belatedly began to fire on them. Not a man was hit. Soon other American units followed the first and a bridgehead was established.

The Germans then threw everything they had at the bridge, using shells, V2 rockets and dive bombers, but the structure lasted miraculously for ten days. By then the Americans had built other bridges close by.

The magic message announcing the first crossing of the bridge had been sent just after 5.30 on the evening of 7th March.* It ran:

Source Maj. G3 III US Corps at 1735 hrs 9th Armoured Division. Unconfirmed report that Combat Command B infantry elements are across Rhine river at F 6520 (Remagen) with railway bridge intact.

The Americans lost no time. At 9 a.m. Phantom was able to send another dramatic message:

Source Major G3 III US Corps at 2030 hrs. Three infantry companies over Rhine. Railway bridge at Remagen has been de-mined, is in good order and convertible.

'Convertible' meant being made suitable for road traffic which was at first done by putting down wooden planking.

Even so, the operation was still in a very delicate state. Bradley sent five US divisions across the river and hoped fervently that the bridge would not be destroyed before another could be built. If the worst came to the worst the American divisions would be cut off and would probably be eliminated by the huge German forces which were now converging on them. But the bridgehead was held and was extended to an area twenty-five miles wide and ten deep.

Hitler was, of course, enraged. He had four officers court-martialled and shot; however, the officer responsible for failing to demolish the bridge had already been taken prisoner by the Americans. Another victim of Hitler's fury was von Rundstedt, who was dismissed and replaced by Kesselring.

Useful though the Remagen crossing was, it had no effect on the general Allied plan. The northern crossings of the Rhine, in an amphibious operation, were timed for 23rd March. However Patton, learning that the section of the river south of Mainz was virtually unguarded, went over at Oppenheim on the night of 22nd March. The main crossing, preceded by aerial and artillery bombardment, involved Second British Army, 1st Commando Brigade and Ninth US Army. Not least of the problems was the speed of the Rhine current. If a DUKW did not achieve its landing spot it was likely to be swept further and further down the river. The late William McElwee, then

* It had been preceded by a telephone call from Captain Hutton-Williams to G1 (ops) 21 Army Group (TAC).

commanding a company in the 2nd Argyll and Sutherland Highlanders used to say that one of his fellow officers, seeing a DUKW
being swept downstream with the driver doing little to prevent it,
shouted at the man, 'Get your bloody whip out!' Although no horseman, the surprised driver accelerated vigorously and achieved the
needed landing.

The next day the British 6th Airborne and the US 17th Airborne
crossed the river. In less than a month the whole of the Ruhr was
enveloped and 400,000 German soldiers had been taken prisoner;
Model, the German commander, shot himself on 21st April. Events
were now occurring at headlong speed. Patton had reached Frankfurt
on 29th March. On 12th April the Ninth US Army reached the Elbe,
where they were only sixty miles from Berlin.

With all this proceeding, Phantom was more stretched than ever.
One interesting effect of the long period of co-operation with Canadian
and American units was that Phantom seemed to have crossed
national boundaries; in the field at least it had become an almost
international force. The patrol with 17th US Airborne were by this
time wearing American uniforms and even rank badges. It saved much
trouble and unnecessary explanation. This patrol had a lucky escape
when landing. Their Waco glider, one of a flight of five, was hit by a
mortar immediately after it touched down but they were already
clear. The patrol was commanded by Captain R. A. Bryce.

Captain Brook-Hart was with British 6th Airborne. He landed at
11 a.m. Two hours later he was able to report:

Source Commander 6th Airborne Division, at 1300. Hamminkeln
captured. 5 Para Brigade report all their objectives captured and
casualties light. 3 Para Bde attack going OK.

But it was no walkover. Here and there the Allies came across pockets
of German resistance where the Germans were fully determined to
fight to the finish, and did so. The 'usual channels' of communication
would have been ill-suited to such a fast-moving situation.

Massive problems began to appear as the large numbers of surrendering Germans were supplemented by liberated Allied prisoners of
war. Many of the latter were sick and the Germans for some time
before had ceased to be able to supply the camps with rations.

Geoffrey Brain, who had come into Phantom in 1940 from the
Wiltshire Regiment, had landed in France soon after D Day. From
then on he had had little rest, having been in Caen, the Falaise battles

and across France into Belgium, Holland and Germany. For most of the time he was with the 1st Polish Armoured Division. He recalls that some time before the invasion, on an exercise in England, a transport plane had crashed and caught fire. The nearest Poles grabbed axes and hacked their way into the burning plane, rescuing several trapped men at great risk to themselves. Falaise produced some very uncomfortable moments but to his surprise he survived shelling and bombing unscathed and moved forward over the old battlefields and into Belgium. When Ghent was liberated the Cathedral bells played English hymn tunes! For a time he was at Breda, then hastily sent to the Ardennes, where he was attached to the American First Army. That was a winter to remember. Later he crossed the Rhine with 3rd Canadian Division, but was soon back with the Poles. Polish discipline was strict. He recalls the case of a Polish sergeant who had entered a German farmhouse, shot the farmer and raped the wife. He was tried and sentenced to death for having disgraced the name of Poland. His defence was that that was what had happened to his own family when the Germans had entered Poland in 1939. The answer was: 'Barbarians may behave like that: we do not.' The man was executed.

Near Wilhelmshaven they overran a concentration camp which was almost exclusively for Poles. One of the Poles met his sister – a living skeleton. Bodies lay in heaps. There were lampshades made of human skin, some still bearing tattoo marks on them.

Wilhelmshaven was bitterly defended but suddenly resistance crumbled and they were in the town. The Germans had scuttled some ships in the harbour and the naval personnel were still defiant. However, the Polish commander said to them: 'Do what you like to the harbour. It was once a snipe shooting marsh and that is what it is going to become again.'

Dennis Russell had joined Phantom from the Roughriders (County of London Yeomanry) and stayed with them through the war. He stressed the fact that when, in the early days, Phantom was struggling for recognition, confidence was built up by their being present on every important exercise. Phantom was seen, recognised and soon trusted. Endless practice brought the regiment to such a high level of efficiency that it could function anywhere, on the move, in any form of country, in any weather, day or night. The skills acquired by the relentless practice proved invaluable later.

His squadron was the one stationed at Dover to provide the bogus signals traffic for the deception plan prior to D Day. The aim was to deceive the Germans into believing that the Allied landing would be made in the Pas de Calais. A huge volume of detectable signals traffic was sent to an imaginary army allegedly based in the Thames estuary and East Anglia. The deception plan was so successful that even when the real landings took place further west the Germans for some time believed that was only a feint to obscure the direction of the main attack.

At the end of hostilities Russell was sent to Denmark which, it was feared, the Russians might try to occupy. The whole Scandinavian area was highly sensitive with over a quarter of a million German soldiers in the area, numerous Russian prisoners, and some fears about Russian military intentions.

Those whose path took them into the concentration camps are unlikely ever to forget the experience. All through the war men had known that this was a crusade against a tyranny with something immensely evil inside it. Even then no one was quite prepared for the horrors of the extermination camps; Ohrdorf, Belsen, Buchenwald, Auschwitz, to name but a few. And while almost unbelievable horrors were being disclosed, and the needs of liberated prisoners reached crisis point, the fighting still continued. Bremen was invited to surrender but refused. The messages ran: 'Telephone communication established with general commanding Bremen by undamaged line to Achim and surrender of the city demanded.'

After the rejection of the surrender message two divisions attacked the city. The next message ran:

Source GOC 52nd Div 1130 hrs 25th April. Attack going well so far. Main difficulty rubble but expecting to meet strong opposition shortly.

Eventually the Russian army and the American army joined up – or rather met – at Torgau. The Russian unit was 58th Russian Guards Division; the American unit was 69th Division of US V Corps. This historic meeting was reported by Captain B. E. Hutton-Williams. The actual meeting place was the command post of US 273 Regiment at Trebsen, which lies some seventeen miles east of Leipzig.

The Americans knew only too well that if the Press knew of the impending meeting it would not be possible to prevent the most extreme statements from being passed out as fact. A complete black-out was imposed of all outgoing news. This unfortunately was extended to

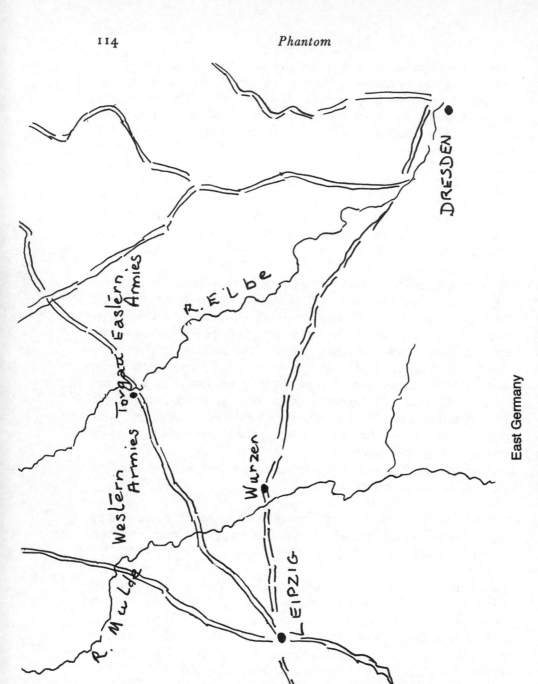

East Germany

(The Western Armies met the Russians at Torgau)

Phantom. Hutton-Williams managed to get out a message reporting : 'I confirm personal contact made,' but unfortunately this was turned down by the censors and never sent.

But the privilege of being an eye-witness to the historic moment when the Russian and Western armies met 'somewhere in Germany' in April 1945 then fell to Captain Brent Hutton-Williams, whose account follows :

'In April 1945, when, where and how a meeting between the Red Army and a Western Allied Army would take place was a matter of overwhelming interest and importance. The link-up was expected to signal the end of the war in Europe, but there was a liaison problem. No inter-allied communication arrangements existed between the forward elements of the converging armies. If they fired on each other by mistake this might cause a highly embarrassing incident or even lead to armed conflict between allies.

'The Allied Occupation Zones in Germany had been agreed at the Yalta Summit Conference of February 1945 when Stalin extracted concessions from Churchill and Roosevelt in return for Soviet entry into the war with Japan.

'In February 1945 the Western Allies were held by the German Army west of the Rhine. It was not until 7th March, following a swift break through that the First US Army secured intact the railway bridge over the Rhine at Remagen and established a bridgehead on the east side. The Ruhr was encircled and the speed of the Western Allies advance from the west into Germany was far faster than that of the Russians from the east. As a result by April 1945 the Western Allies, particularly the Americans, were occupying areas in Germany which according to the Yalta Agreement were to be occupied by the Russians.

'No one, it seemed, amongst the forward elements of the Americans knew for certain the Red Army's intentions or had any idea what it looked like on the ground. Tac/R (Tactical Reconnaissance by air) was not much use if you were not certain what you were looking for.

'The danger of a clash between the Eastern and Western Allies in central Germany was appreciated by the Supreme Allied Commander in the west, General Eisenhower, and caused him to order the First US Army not to advance beyond a readily identifiable physical feature on the ground, namely the river Mulde, and not to patrol more than 10 kilometres east of it. In fact, the First US Army, having encountered negligible German resistance during the first fortnight of April, might well have had its spearheads on the river Elbe by about the middle of the month.

'There was no talk of the Yalta Agreements amongst the soldiers at the time. The good old military dictum "Here I am and here I stay until ordered to withdraw" prevailed and this point of view somehow reached the Germans who logically believed that the Western Allies would maintain their positions and stop any further advance westwards by the Russians.

'On the morning of 23rd April 1945 I was ordered to report any contact which might be made in this area between the forward elements of the American and Russian armies. The First US Army consisted of 3 Army Corps, each of three divisions and covered about 100 miles of front. It seemed to me, as we set off on the long journey east to my first port of call, US 76th Division HQ at Burgstadt, that a lot of good guesswork and a lot of luck were needed if the mission was to be accomplished successfully.

'On 24th April there were no indications of any possible contact with the Red Army on 76th Division front, but there were rumours of Russian activity further north, and I decided to investigate. At 6th US Armoured Division HQ there was nothing to report, but at 2nd US Infantry Division HQ, there was a lot of conflicting rumour and unconfirmed information. As it seemed that Red Army contact was imminent on 2nd Division front, I decided to spend the night at 2nd Division HQ at Bad Lausick

'April 25th dawned overcast and hazy. Since visibility was so poor Tac/R would not be effective. Neither on the formations on the flanks, 69th Division to the north nor 6th Armoured Division to the south had anything to report, nor had the 23rd Infantry Regiment which had patrols operating east of the river Mulde.

'Whilst I was still at 2nd Division HQ there was a rumour that contact had been made by 273rd Regiment of the 69th Division. This was confirmed on the telephone by the G2 (Intelligence officer) at 69th Division HQ at Grimma. I took off for 273rd Regiment command post at Trebsen, a small town on the river Mulde some twenty miles east of Leipzig.

'On arrival at 1900 hours I found a much harassed Regimental Commander, more intent on fighting off the onslaughts of the Press than on his strictly military duty. It was only on my pledge that I had nothing to do with the Press that I was allowed into the Operations room. The information available consisted of one message received during the afternoon from a patrol of 273rd Regiment, "Mission accomplished, am making arrangements", whereupon radio contact had been lost. There was no further news.

'After a brief telephone conversation with a battalion or company HQ, the OC 273rd Regiment stated that confirmation of a Red Army contact might be forthcoming shortly. Seconds later a telephone message from US V Corps (69th Division's senior formation) was received in the operations room, saying that a news black-out had been imposed on all Red Army contact information. An excited US Lieutenant burst in accompanied by two Russian officers and a general mêlée of back-slapping and hand-shaking followed. I gathered from the young American officer that contact had been made with the 58th Russian (Guards) Division and that the Russians did not intend to cross the river Elbe. I had to get out of the emotionally charged operations room to get my W/T message sent. Outside there was tumult. All and sundry, with or without excuse, were trying to enter the room I had just left. The OC 273rd Regiment had to clear the operations room and post sentries.

'My wireless set was still at US 2nd Division HQ. My driver had to carry written messages reporting the contact about twelve miles to the operator at Bad Lausick in the dark, over bad roads, across a forward area, without knowing the password. He returned later to pick me up.

'Just before 2200 hours I managed to get back into the operations room. It was then I heard that an official meeting at divisional level would take place at Torgau on the Elbe on the following day. When we reached 69th Division HQ early on 26th April I found that the Divisional Commander's column had already left for Torgau. My good friend the First US Army liaison officer was however waiting for us. He had a map tracing the 69th Division's route.

'We set out to cross the forty miles of no-man's-land which separated the Eastern and Western Allies on our own. We went flat out, two jeeps in front and the unwieldy scout car bringing up the rear. We had to go back on our tracks only once. Surprisingly it was a German soldier who showed us a way round a blown bridge which barred our way.

'We also passed small groups of German soldiers marching west, in good order, to surrender to the Americans rather than to the Russians and civilian refugees with household chattels piled high on small carts or in perambulators.

'On the outskirts of Torgau all was quiet. I stopped the patrol. Almost immediately a heavy machine gun opened up. Pretty rapidly we put a building between the patrol and the direction of this surprise attack. I then went into the town slowly, with the scout car following, ready to dive for cover in case of need. We entered a square. Russian troops were dancing and drinking, as at a country fair. On the far bank of the river Elbe I could see the formal Allied delegations about to meet. There was no chance of getting vehicles across as all the bridges had been blown. I went over myself in a racing skiff propelled by a Russian boatman who was primarily concerned with finding and evacuating to the east bank Russian so-called "slave-labour". These women had been doled out as servants to German housewives by the Nazi authorities after the German invasion of the Ukraine. The Russians, it seemed, were worried in case they had become indoctrinated. We had a stout strong Ukrainian aboard, seated in the stern and the skiff had just about two inches of freeboard.

'I experienced some difficulty in getting into the official meeting hall, it was so heavily guarded by American MPs and Russian sentries. The latter had probably never seen a British uniform before in their lives. When I did get in, the party was in full swing, trestle tables littered with empty glasses, bottles of vodka, chunks of fat ham, raw onions and black bread. Tough-looking Red Army officers, many wearing medals, were already full of high spirits. The Americans were subdued and correct by comparison. Behind the top table at which the Generals and their senior officers were seated, the Union Jack was displayed equally with the Stars and Stripes and the Red Flag.

General Reinhardt, commanding the 69th US Infantry Division, proposed the toast of Marshal Stalin, which was duly drunk. General Rusakov commanding the 58th Red Army (Guards) Division replied with a toast to Stalin, Churchill and Roosevelt. The Russian officers seemed unaware on 26th April 1945 that President Roosevelt had died on the 12th and been succeeded by President Truman. The fraternising continued with the American officers surprisingly singing "Roll out the Barrel" and calling for a Russian song in return.

'With another perilous trip across the Elbe over and W/T reports of the meeting between the Allied Divisional Commanders sent from the west bank, another Phantom mission was completed, and so to all intents and purposes was the war in the West.'

Although the war was effectively over, however, the fighting was not. The final stages would not be reached for yet another week even though Hitler committed suicide on 30th April. 6th Airborne reached the Baltic and on 3rd May they too made contact with the Russians.

The Italian war was over and von Rundstedt had been captured. As the Allied armies moved forward across Germany they had often been surprised to find there was more food there than they had seen since Normandy; the Nazis had had no inhibitions about plundering conquered territories so that their own nationals could be adequately fed.

The official cease-fire was ordered for 5th May and the formal surrender ceremony for the 8th.

Although Phantom was under the impression it had now sent its last message in Europe this was soon found to be a fallacy. But before continuing any further we must link up with those members of Phantom whom we left in Italy in mid-1944 when we diverged to the story of the D Day landings and the campaign in north-west Europe. As mentioned above, following the liaison visit of Major John Morgan in December 1944, who had recommended that the Phantom Liaison Squadron and the J Service should be amalgamated, the official merger was approved and Phantom and J now became 2 GHQ Liaison Regiment, Central Mediterranean. The commander of the new regiment was Lieutenant-Colonel R. B. Y. Mills, MC, RTR. Phantom Regimental Headquarters was at San Domenico, close to 15th Army Group Headquarters which was in Florence itself. No 1 'J' Squadron was with Eighth Army, and No 2 with I Canadian Corps. Both Phantom and 'J' had patrols at Corps HQ in Eighth Army. Phantom also worked to IV Corps and Fifth Army Headquarters; J worked to divisional headquarters. This arrangement was more economical and probably more efficient as it meant a saving on the number of people used in corps patrols. The saving thus made was used to supply a patrol to II US Corps which had previously not been covered. Reorganisation made the regiment busier than ever, for both Phantom and J had to be operated while the changes were taking place. Corps patrols now had two officers on the establishment for they had to pass information back to 15th Army Group, to give information from their divisional patrols to their own headquarters, and to intercept on any interesting Phantom net. The American Corps was not affected but a special teletype machine was established at Allied Forces HQ and 15th Army Group, and was used to transmit any messages of special operational importance.

There were other changes and moves at this time. Captain Shaw's detachment at HQ Eighth Army amalgamated with HQ No 1 J Squadron and the combination was then known as B Detachment. The new formation was commanded by Major Power. Captain Drysdale became Adjutant and Major Allen, who had been in charge on

No 2 J Squadron at HQ I Canadian Corps, took over A detachment at HQ Fifth Army.

Meanwhile Captain McBain's patrol in Greece had been sending valuable reports to AFHQ via Captain Pike's patrol (installed in the Royal Palace at Caserta). By the middle of February however the situation in Greece no longer warranted a patrol there, so McBain was ordered to Crete, leaving his patrol to work with 18 L of C (Line of Communication) Signals. Captain Pike's patrol went to B Detachment and Captain Shaw took a patrol to HQ 10 Corps.

As the units settled down in their new places it seemed that this was an efficient arrangement which could continue happily for some time. Alas for hopes, the War Office ordered that the four patrols working with I Canadian Corps should move with them to Europe. Replacements were requested but refused. This meant that Phantom could be very tightly stretched in the future. It was a situation they had experienced before !

For their next part in the final battles of Italy the 92nd US Division was ordered to put in an attack to take Genoa. However their moves were meant first to confuse the Germans as to where the next blow would fall. A patrol was requested for the division, so one was made up from RHQ and Captain Bluett commanded it. For a week it was very busy but when the division's objectives had been reached it was able to return to HQ for further assignments.

Events were now moving rapidly. Captain Gimpel's patrol accompanied 10th US Mountain Division when it crossed the Po on 25th April, Captain Shaw's patrol from 10th Corps HQ now joined 88th US Division which was moving quickly towards the Brenner Pass. 1st US Armoured Division was probing ahead fast. Captain Graham Bell sent a somewhat unorthodox message saying : 'I doubt if even God knows where the forward elements are' and received a reply from RHQ : 'Situation well in hand. God sending angels on reconnaissance.' The 'angels' in fact were aircraft which had been detached for the purpose.

Over a hundred operational messages were reaching RHQ daily, the wireless groups had to be changed frequently, the duty officers were required nearly all day in the regimental operations room, and for ten days it took two duty officers to write the morning summary. That summary had to be in the War Room at 0630. However those who had had to work all night were apparently much consoled by seeing Florence at her best in the early morning sunlight.

When it was learnt that the Germans were ready to surrender, a mission was despatched to HQ German Army Group C. It was accompanied by Graham Bell's patrol after they had driven through the night to meet it at Villafranca, near Verona. Bell's patrol sent messages from Colonel Brissach at Bolzano, and to General Mark Clark in Florence. Bell stayed in Bolzano for a week then returned to RHQ with a barrel of beer and fifty bottles of champagne. The latter came in particularly handy as Major Brown, the Signals Officer, was being married a few days later.

The commander of the German forces in Italy surrendered on 2nd May but that was by no means the end of Phantom's duties. There were roving bands of Germans unaware of the situation, or aware of it and unwilling to surrender. There was a German Corps Commander who said that having taken the oath of allegiance to Hitler himself he could not surrender his command till Hitler ordered it or died. (Hitler was in fact already dead.) Tens of thousands of prisoners were moving to the various grouping areas. The boundaries between Russian and British troops in Austria had to be settled and all movements reported. Finally, firm action was being taken to force Marshal Tito of Yugoslavia to present his claims to Trieste at a peace conference and not to try to annex it by force of arms.

Finally 2 GHQ Liaison Regiment concentrated at Varese from where they were transported home.

CHAPTER TEN

End of Message

While the war in Europe was drawing to its close the eyes of Phantom were turning east. Major J. A. T. Morgan flew out to India on 20th May to examine the needs of and for a 3 GHQ Liaison Regiment. This was formed immediately after his return to Richmond on 8th June. The initial employment was to cover Fourteenth Army, which consisted of two corps and nine divisions. The regiment would need to be more flexible than ever, for units in South-East Asia Command were as likely as not to be waterborne or airborne.* But while the regiment was still being formed Japan surrendered and 3 GHQ Liaison Regiment, which had by now established headquarters at Bunde in Germany, wondered about its future. It was believed that the move to Bunde was the result of a War Office decision to continue Phantom after the war as a part of the regular army.

But in the general rundown Phantom was reduced to an Independent Phantom Squadron, Royal Corps of Signals. It was given an establishment of six patrols and a headquarters. All but the patrol officers were to be signals personnel. Then, as the cynics and realists expected, it was disbanded.

Meanwhile the remainder of the other regiments were still finding work. Four patrols were sent into Denmark to serve the Supreme Headquarters Allied Expeditionary Force Mission. F Squadron went with 1st Airborne Division to Norway. Another detachment went to Berlin on 4th June to work with British Headquarters. But gradually Phantom was fading away.

On May 1st 1947 Phantom was reborn as a regiment in the Territorial Army. It became part of the Royal Corps of Signals and was entitled 'Army Phantom Signals Regiment (Princess Louise's Kensing-

---

* K. V. Rose recalls that they were visited by someone from the War Office who taught them how to commit suicide if captured – not the best way of building morale.

ton Regiment)'. Permission was granted to wear Kensington badges and to carry the Kensington's colours.

Some of Phantom's former members groaned inwardly at seeing Phantom finally passing under Signals control; they had misgivings that the Signals would stifle some of Phantom's initiative. There were others who took a broader view. During World War II when regiments were classed as either 'Fighting Arms' or Services, the Signals had been very definitely among the 'fighting arms'. Although there were cosy niches in rear formations much of Signals work was, and had always been, highly dangerous, the more so for the fact it was exposed, or otherwise easily located by the enemy. The most dangerous job in World War II was said to be that of Brigade Signals Officer (in World War I it had been Forward Observation Officer of the Artillery). Signals were of course everywhere. Although Phantom officers had come from many different regiments, the other ranks came mainly from Royal Signals which had a valuable supply of intelligent, capable, well-educated soldiers. No regiment could hope for a better mixture, as was proved on many occasions. However there was no doubt that among senior Signals officers there were those who resented a wartime creation like Phantom usurping the regiment's task, displaying skill and imagination, and doing a job which Signals would like to have done themselves.

The Kensingtons had a long and honourable history. Although the regiment officially dated from 1859, there had been a Corps of the Kensington Volunteer Association as early as 1798. This had been disbanded in 1802 but was re-embodied (under a slightly different name) in 1803. The latter was disbanded in 1814.

In 1859 the 4th Middlesex Volunteer Rifle Corps was founded by Lord Truro but in 1885 this took up headquarters in Kensington High Street: it took on the sub-title of The West London Rifles and wore a grey uniform with red facings and a black belt. It gained a battle honour in South Africa in 1900 and in 1908 was adopted by the Royal Borough of Kensington and became 'The Kensington Rifles'. In 1908, as a result of the Haldane Reforms, the Kensingtons were joined to the 2nd Middlesex to form the 13th County of London Regiment. However, in 1909 Princess Louise, Duchess of Argyll, who resided at Kensington Palace, gave her name to the new regiment and constantly supported 'her Kensingtons'.

So great was the rush of volunteers in 1914 that a second battalion was formed, the 2/13th. The 1/13th was in action in France soon after the outbreak of war. It took part in most of the major battles:

Neuve Chapelle, Aubers Ridge, Somme, Ginchy, Arras, Vimy, Cambrai and Ypres. It served with distinction but suffered many casualties.

The 2/13th came into action a little later but served first in France and then in the Middle East. It landed at Salonika then had various tasks before being engaged in the Palestine campaign. During the latter it acquitted itself magnificently but not without heavy casualties.

Between the wars the Territorial Army had a lean time. In 1937 the TA was reorganised and Princess Louise's became part of the Middlesex Regiment. Although with headquarters at 190 Hammersmith Road it was outside the Royal Borough, the regiment was granted permission to retain the name, badges and connections. It now became a machine-gun regiment.

The 1st Battalion was in continuous action in the campaign in France in 1940 and the survivors were eventually evacuated at Le Havre on 12th June. In 1943 it first saw action in Sicily but then continued throughout the long Italian campaign. Among its battle honours were Cassino and Sangro. When the war came to an end the battalion had reached Austria. From then until September 1946 it was engaged in rounding up Germans themselves, and assisting in relief work. From April 1946 it was in Greece, near Patras.

The 2nd Battalion, after various home duties, was sent to Iceland. It returned in September 1942, trained further in the British Isles, and then was back in action at Caen in June 1944. From then onwards action was continuous. For five months it battled around Nijmegen. When the latter town was liberated a street was named after the regiment. The 2nd Battalion was disbanded in 1946.

Army Phantom Signals gave the Kensingtons a new role and much new equipment to master. Ex-members of Phantom and Royal Signals joined. In 1951 the Royal Borough of Kensington re-adopted the 'Princess Louise's'. It provided liaison and communication for the Coronation procession of Her Majesty Queen Elizabeth II. In 1954 the regiment went to Germany for an Army Exercise instead of attending a normal home training camp. In 1959, when it celebrated its official centenary, the regiment was obtaining all the volunteers it needed. The post-war commanding officers have been:

Lieutenant-Colonel R. Wasey, MBE, TD, 1947–51
Lieutenant-Colonel D. C. Cocks, 1951–54
Lieutenant-Colonel R. Hammond, TD, 1954–57
Lieutenant-Colonel B. R. Wood, OBE, TD, DL, 1957–63

Colonel Wood, who continued to command the regiment till the end, wrote the following:

'When Princess Louise's Kensington Regiment was given the role of Phantom on re-formation of the TA in 1947, and as such had to become part of the Royal Corps of Signals because wireless sets were used, it was fortunate enough to secure the services of General Sir H. Colville Wemyss, KCB, KBE, DSO, MC, as Honorary Colonel. He had held several of the highest offices in the British Army and finished his career as Military Secretary in 1946. He was the first and to date the last Royal Signals officer to reach the rank of full General. Our subsequent history was to prove the inestimable benefit of having one of the Royal Signals' most distinguished sons as Honorary Colonel of Royal Signals' newest unit.

'The Battle Royal exercise in Germany in 1954 was quite a challenge. It was the biggest Army Exercise held since the war. As we arrived in Germany we had to take over "mothball equipment", vehicles, wireless vehicles, wireless sets not used for years and get them in order within twenty-four hours of proceeding on a 10-day exercise. We operated Forward and Listening Patrols and had a presence in the Joint Operations Centre at Army HQ. We understood we did very well on the exercise and the long hours and hard work for the TA did not discourage recruits or members continuing service.

'In 1959 it was learnt that Phantom was considered rather a luxury in view of the advance in communications etc over the last few years and the role was to be discontinued and the Regiment converted to a Trunk Signal Regiment in 1960. This was particularly horrifying for me and most of the officers, none of whom were true Signals. We had converted from Infantry, RAC, machine gunners, gunners etc and easily coped with the staff duties side of Phantom and using R/T and indeed morse but Trunk Signals was beyond most. However, all went on courses and I continued to command the Regiment as a Trunk Signal Regiment until 1962 with most of the original officers and senior NCOs. After that I became a Group Commander of three TA Regiments in a UKLF role.

'In conclusion whilst I appreciate that Phantom had outgrown its usefulness in combat conditions I still think that in this nuclear age if the worst comes to the worst there will still be room for chaps who can tell someone somewhere what is happening either on R/T or by morse or in the Phantom Code and this particularly of course in the UK. I have tried to put this over in the last few years but with little success!'

Part Two

CHAPTER ELEVEN

Personal Viewpoints

A strange aspect of war is that those who are shaping events are seldom in a position to know what is happening outside their immediate area and can only guess at the overall picture. In fact what actually happened in certain battles may never be accurately known until years later, and perhaps never at all. Sometimes those who have essential information are killed, sometimes valuable papers are destroyed; sometimes for reasons of 'security' files are 'weeded' and the truth obliterated for ever. Official documents are published and are, generally, accepted although doubts are sometimes expressed by their readers. Regimental histories tend to be partisan but often contain interesting information which may not have been published elsewhere; they have a very limited circulation. Undoubtedly the most interesting accounts of war come from personal memories. They may not contain an entirely accurate account of an operation but, provided they have been written before memory fades or imagination makes additions, they provide a fair and interesting version.

Phantom was unusual in that it had an exceptionally high proportion of intelligent and well-educated officers and other ranks. Initially the Phantom requirement was for mobile and personable young men who could obtain information for intelligence purposes. The idea was not new: Napoleon had employed young cavalrymen for the same purpose. But after 1943 when there was more than a sufficiency of units to engage in reconnaissance the rôle of Phantom changed from being a discoverer to being a collector. From then onwards the requirements of a Phantom liaison officer were very demanding. He had to be a high-quality news reporter, capable of obtaining facts but equally capable of passing them on without subtraction, addition, or comments. One of the rarest skills in the world is the ability to pass on information without adding your own view and thus distorting the original.

One of the earliest members of Phantom was Christopher Cadogan.

Diaries, like cameras, were forbidden on active service but he kept one. Before the war, Cadogan had begun a promising career at Eton and Oxford, and had been called to the Bar at Middle Temple. He was an excellent skier, enjoyed life, was a practising Christian and had been adopted as Liberal Candidate for Bury St Edmunds in 1939. He was engaged to Stella Zilliacus, the exceptionally attractive daughter of a well-known Socialist MP; they had met at Oxford. Eventually Stella, who spoke fluent French and had had some nursing experience, was able to visit him once in France by becoming a First Aid Nursing Auxiliary and arranging to work for a few days in the French hospital at Valenciennes.

That was mid-April. Just over three weeks later, on 10th May, the 'Phoney War' came abruptly to an end and the Blitzkrieg began :

Christopher's Diary

Friday, 10th May, 1940 : At about 5 a.m. loud anti-aircraft fire along the Franco-Belgian front and the continual drone of German re-connaissance planes woke us up. The machines were low and plainly visible, the AA fire inaccurate. Going back to bed for the third time I suspected nothing, being by now inoculated by a series of scares and flaps.

At 6.30 a DR arrived bringing me (as orderly officer) an urgent message saying that the French and ourselves were now on Alert No 3. This hieroglyph meant nothing to me so I took it next door to Tommy Newton-Dunn (GSO3) who immediately told me to wake everyone, then proceed to barracks to see that the men were up. He went off to the Colonel. I should have liked to see Hoppy just then. 'I consider myself privileged and lucky to be able to fight in two wars against the Germans' he had said to the Hospital Commandant : the approaching possibility of fighting the Germans always brought a lively smile to his face.

At 8 a.m. I discovered from the BBC on our barracks wireless that Holland had been invaded by Hitler to protect it, and we would soon be called in to protect Belgium. The men were no trouble, my job consisting of issuing passes to batmen etc. whom the French quite rightly refused to let out of barracks. Soon after, Bertie Woolcock deciphered a message from HQ, BAFF [British Air Forces in France] which indicated that this was the Real Thing.

The next hour or so we spent in hurried but orderly packing. I think the outward show of calm and discipline was more than mere appearance and deeper than a pose, because everyone was glad that *Der Tag* had at last arrived, that this meant the end of a period of waiting, of boredom and niggling anxieties and petty disputes.

Certainly as we cruised up the road to Mons, I had an almost shocking feeling of relief and exhilaration. I knew I oughtn't to like war – and fundamentally I didn't – but I had been one of thousands urging the government to stand up to Hitler; to meet aggression with force and not meek concessions. For years the struggle had been in vain; a terribly thwarted enterprise, an effort blocked and impeded by the deadweight of complacent inertia. And now, though the same old treacherous gang of ineffectives was still in office, we had been compelled to call a halt to Hitler.

We crossed the frontier at Blanc-Misseron at about 10 a.m. – the first British troops to do so – led by John Collings in his utility, standing up with his head through the roof, waving a huge Union Jack; then two of the FSP boys on motor cycles, John Gabriel on his bike and Charles Banbury in his tank, bowing and waving like the Queen Mother. The French were obviously elated, their morale high. French civilians less so, their hands raised in not-so-sure gestures of goodwill : they had seen this before. By contrast the Belgians were overwhelming in their welcome. Old people were crying, young people cheering, the roads lined with crowds applauding what they imagined – alas! – to be the advance guard of the BEF. Many of them had only just learnt (from the wireless or friends) that they were at war, and here we were already, their friends coming to their help. Sergeant Hodges said, 'They won't cheer so much when they see us going back.'

It was a beautiful day with a burning, persistent sun. In Mons I stopped behind to check the column and people showered flowers and cigarettes on me, asking if I were hungry or thirsty. A middle-aged woman looked at our light tanks roaring by and said, '*Oui, c'est beau mais c'est triste.*' A hugely fat woman with a moustache insisted on kissing me squarely on both cheeks – not too easy with my height and mass of equipment.

The column moved easily, and we found good cover with shade and green for halts underneath huge trees. Nivelles was the first sign of active warfare. They had bombed the aerodrome there with little effect : most of the machines had been flown across France early that morning, we were told. We moved fast.

One of our staff in Brussels – a consistently useless man – had plotted our first HQ at the side of an aerodrome without realising it.

The first echelon dismounted but had hardly lit their cigarettes when a squadron of German bombers roared down and dropped thirty or forty bombs on the ill-concealed Belgian fighters, setting most of them on fire. 'It was like the Hendon air pageant ,only more realistic,' said the Colonel.

We had hardly arrived at Mielen-sur-Aelat, our new HQ, when Hoppy had a job for John Collings and me. We went off to St Trond, about eight miles away, passing the bombed aerodrome on the way. A house was spread neatly over the road, some bedding set quite comfortably in the ditch, a cyclist off his bicycle, as motionless as the latter. It was the first corpse I had ever seen. The whole thing looked just like the pictures from Poland : all I missed was a dead child on the pavement with a trickle of blood flowing gently into the gutter.

Reaching St Trond, we found that the HQ was further north at Hasselt. A guide raced ahead up the long, straight road, averaging a really ferocious speed, and with considerable difficulty McGee and I managed to keep up. The road was thronged with refugees of all sorts and soldiers doing nothing in particular. We found the HQ. Dirty and dishevelled, John C. and I barged into the General's room. Whilst the latter reeled off his stuff quite calmly, I jotted it down roughly on a piece of paper.

The situation wasn't too good. The huge and powerful fort of Eben Enael, which commands the bridges west of Maastricht, had been put out of action at crack of dawn : apparently parachutists descended and stuck sticks into the main casement, blowing the whole thing – including themselves – sky high. The bridges at Vroonhoeven and Veldtwezeldt had not been blown up, and possibly another one at Eysden. Our job was to get some bombers over there as soon as possible and make things difficult for the Nazis. We shot back and I read the stuff to the Colonel over a crowded little table in the failing evening light. Map references were laboriously worked out and a code message carefully constructed and wired off to Mission HQ at about 8.30. The Hopkinson Mission was in action.

As we gobbled up an excellent supper of fried eggs and bread and tea, we listened to the welcome news that old Chamberlain had at last given in and handed over to Churchill, who was about to construct a cabinet of all parties which meant business. It was a cheering start to what looked like being a tough time.

Saturday, 11th May : Up at 5, not at all reluctantly. In a battle you feel that the Germans are busy the whole time and it's better not to rest or keep still any more than necessary. Also, the morning is fresh and clear.

Shortly after a scrap of breakfast I was sent off with a Guy Light-Wheeled Tank and a section of motor-cycles to investigate results of not blowing those bridges. We set off with the customary cheers of crowds still lining the roads, not knowing quite what was happening, but glad to see '*Les Anglais*'. A little way beyond St Trond we sighted some bombers coming over slowly in a bombing formation, and as there were trees we took cover. I was definitely scared hearing the bombs crashing down along the road, seeing an explosion 50 or 100 yards away, seeing the bombs dropping out of those big lazy Dornier 17s. In the tanks the chaps were pretty safe, locked down under a good steel casing. They were quite safe from the machine-gunning which had also started up as a side-show; but things weren't so rosy for the people on motor cycles. All we could do was fling ourselves into the ditch and wait.

I wirelessed back our progress. Meanwhile, some Belgian troops in lorries stopped just where we had pulled up for the fifth or sixth time and during the next lull I got some information from a sergeant. He said they had been under fire all yesterday and had at length been told to withdraw back to Louvain. I checked this later and wirelessed it back, then had just decided to go ahead with the tank into Tongres when they told us to withdraw. We had a feeling of futility and lack of achievement. Information was scanty and other accounts were misleading. Germans were variously seven, six, ten and fifteen miles away but all agreed that Tongres was being pretty heavily bombed.

On the way back I was impressed by the mess they'd made of Looz. Half an hour earlier it was clean; but by the time we'd come back several houses had been thrown half way across the street and the railway track and station had stopped a bomb or two. They'd scored a direct hit on the school, but someone must have miscalculated as there weren't any children there just then. I stopped at the hospital and talked to an officer in charge. He was miserable but calm : the hospital was full and he was trying to organise things for the surplus they expected. '*Où est le RAF?*' That was what they kept repeating and we felt guilty, almost personally responsible for its failure to put in an appearance. It is a tenable theory that a couple of squadrons of Hurricanes flying up and down the frontier for the first twenty-four hours would have so cheered up the Belgians that they might have stuck it out.

We changed HQ to an orchard at Neerlanden and then put down

some. lunch – bullybeef. McGee came in on the back of a lost Belgian sergeant's bike: his own had finally broken up after being chucked about all day in ditches. McGee (a quiet pleasant inoffensive chap – 'the embodiment of the Little Man', as Norman R. put it) had so far had 'more fun' (according to the Colonel) than anyone else; but he told me it was fun in retrospect, not at the time.* The Belgian was a useful man whose whole detachment had been wiped out. He seemed quite calm, but they both took a good swig at my cognac. The sergeant said the parachutists he had seen were all quite young, the oldest about eighteen: they wore Flying School badges and had been told they were going to France. Where, he wanted to know, was the RAF?

Later John Gabriel came back from Pirange. He'd chased the HQ over a ploughed field and when he caught them a Staff Major shouted that the Germans were just behind a hedge; but that wasn't so.

However, the Germans were advancing pretty comfortably west-wards, along the line Maastricht-Tongres-St Trond, and were making straight for Brussels. What the Colonel wanted to know was: Were they bothering about their flanks? Were they branching out south to Waremme, for instance? So in the afternoon I was sent off with Davis, an adenoidal D.R. who whistled the Pathetique Sonata rather too gaily when he cleaned the plugs of his bike. He looked and sounded like a village idiot but was really very sensible.

We went along steadily until I saw some refugees gaping into the sky, some of them already scrambling for cover in the ditch. Looking over my shoulder I saw a Junkers 87 – one of the dive-bombers which make such a row – streaking up that road at not more than telegraph-pole height. I must have set a new all time high getting into that ditch; but even then I hadn't got the drill taped – I couldn't help looking up to see what he was going to do. That Nazi didn't seem to think us worth his fire: anyway he zoomed up and about twenty seconds later let off a lot of lead into Waremme station and wounded about six civilians.

In Waremme, we found the HQ we wanted gathered in the Town Hall, a very disorderly show. I managed to get some sort of a situation out of a major, but it wasn't very helpful: only as I was leaving a captain mentioned quite casually that a counter-attack was going to be put through on the two roads running N and NE from the town. As we went away to the SW we saw this counter-attack assembling south of the town and I thought it as well to get further information from

---

* Lance-Corporal W. B. McGee was awarded the Military Medal for 'showing conspicuous bravery near St Trond on 11th May, 1940'.

the General, who was alleged to be sitting on the grass in front of a château down the road; but he wasn't there. Whilst I was waiting, a report came through that the Germans were in Waremme. I stayed put and took advantage of the Baron's offer of some food in the kitchen, then tried to get the latest information until 7, when I made off. Davis I had sent back with the information so I was on my own, threading through a gigantic convoy – a *mélange* of military and refugee cars.

Eventually I found the HQ and a very capable liaison officer from the 12th Lancers – one of the few ostensibly efficient cavalrymen I had seen in the British Army. He was very much interested in my news and took me to see General Altmeyer, who was settling down to a fine meal in the approved French manner. (That this section of the Army had been mechanized and no longer marched made no difference to the best-known Napoleonic dictum.) The General was a tall and efficient Alsatian and he too was very glad to get my information: with such experiences we began to learn how valuable information was; how scarce it was at all stages of the battle and how welcome Intelligence Officers with news were. (Later the General was promoted!)

I found the second HQ at Jauchelette, only to hear that we were moving north in about an hour. There was just time for a meal. Those meals were terrific. Quite plain, plus some good wine taken from the country or given to us.

We were soon off. The idea was to go up to the northern section near the Dutch border, in the sandy, fir-clad Campine: our HQ would be in front of the 12th Lancers who were the advanced recce force for the BEF. It was a long ride. We went at about 10 mph all the way. You weren't supposed to use lights at all, but occasionally we had to, in spite of a good moon and some parachute flares. You would make haste to catch up the man in front, and then suddenly he would loom out of the darkness and with difficulty you'd avoid him, only to have to jam on brakes in avoiding a crash with one of the cars. Then there was a lot of stopping and starting with engines overheating and people not being able to hear each other. In Louvain we had soldiers and pedestrians to contend with as well, apart from huge convoys coming from the opposite direction. Later we also had to deal with the dust and bumps and ruts of country lanes. All this with a load of equipment on yourself or your bike. No one enjoyed that ride.

We fetched up at a little village right out in the open: an eerie place, and we hadn't the faintest idea whether the Germans were in front, behind or at the side. We dossed down on the stone floor of a pub : this was about three in the morning and we'd been on the road since ten. The Colonel said very convincingly that stone was much better to sleep on than wood and we ought to be thankful we'd got that floor. We all believed him. We tried some Swiss-German with an *'Opgepaast den Schroeven'* * intonation on the pubkeeper and extracted some cushions and a few bottles of beer. Later John Collings surprised us all by breaking into fluent Flemish.

Sunday, 12 May : We had a good one and a half hours' sleep before it was decided that the Germans were too close for comfort. At about 4.30 a.m. we made off in the half-light. That dawn ride was entrancing. We were as tired as could be, but the freshness of morning raised our spirits high. The mist was thicker now but sunshine penetrated here and there, throwing long shadows. The countryside was all deep blue and green, like a water-colour by Paul Nash.

That mist concealed us. After easy riding along good roads we came to the Dyle 'line' of ditch and de Cointet obstacle : with a little explanation we got through, and the gates were closed quickly behind us. John Collings hadn't been so lucky. They'd taken him for a German in disguise and refused to let his car through, so he had to destroy it and all the intelligence documents. These included my list of HQs in which I had put Steenockerzeel, where the Archduke Otto lived. It was his mother, the sinister, intriguing Zia, about whom the old *Baronin* † used to begin, *'Man sagt . . .'* taking off her spectacles with a suggestive nod. I had toyed with the romantic notion of playing a Hapsburg piano in this House of Exile! However, we arrived to find a Belgian and a British Unit already installed at Steenockerzeel (and the Germans had bombed it consistently the day before), so we moved on towards the Forêt de Soignes.

At the crossroads before Tervueren there were wide spaces underneath huge beeches where we parked the vehicles; there were woods where the men could sleep and there was a pub. Here we ate a superb meal of ham and eggs, after a good washdown : the extent of cleansing was measured by inch-deep dirt on the towels. I have seldom spent time in a lavatory with such good results. Then we slept, or rather dozed fitfully, under the trees.

In the afternoon there was nothing to do because the Colonel, having hardly slept a wink for forty hours, went off on a motor cycle

* 'Beware of the Propellers' – a notice always studied by travellers waiting at Ostend for transport.

† Baroness von Aretin, a German cousin of C. M. C.'s mother.

with a tank troop to find out what was happening in the Louvain area. I asked to go up to Mission HQ near Antwerp to see Norman Reddaway and the rest of the 'bureaucratic boys'. They were hidden away in farm buildings in a little village just behind the fort which housed Belgian GHQ. I drank half a gallon of milk and gossiped with Norman about the war: he had me laughing the whole time with his meticulously exaggerated accounts of the campaign. We went over to examine the remains of a Blenheim, from which the pilot and a sergeant observer had escaped. Mission HQ were spending their spare time dismantling the valuable parts and old George Zech was rapidly availing himself of yet another W/T contraption. We went back through Brussels, which is neatly laid out and easy to find your way through.

The night wasn't too pleasant, though we attempted to induce sleep by eating a huge meal at the pub, a very good one too. Belgium is good for food if lousy for everything else. One or two parachutists had been landed in and around Brussels and it was believed that they were all over the place in the woods; thus we had to keep a double guard with two officers on duty all night. I watched more and more troops going up towards the Louvain line, and then slumped over the driving-wheel of one of the utilities and slept till breakfast-time.

The situation gradually became worse –
Sunday, 19th May: Later on, after a leisurely wash and shave, we had one of those 'creeping alarms' – not as a result of any direct order; it emanated rather from conversation on the return of one of the patrols. People began to collect their equipment and harness themselves, nerves on edge for Germans; but nothing happened and the rest of the morning was only punctuated by bursts of AA fire which greeted the German recce planes. We could not understand what function we were fulfilling in this position, and the same critical nervous feeling which had overcome us when waiting for decision at Argenteuil again took the upper hand. Only the Colonel gave an appearance of complete composure.

Then one of the motor cycles returned and in a few seconds the story went round. Trooper Hall had been left on a side-road to cover the flank of a recce patrol, and from the concealment of trees had fired a magazine of Bren into a hedge-hopping Heinkel. Hall was a good shot – he had shown that with the balloons at Le Touquet – and this bomber had apparently caught it all in the cockpit, for it turned over on its side and crumpled up in the next field – in a blaze and a bang!

We were cock-a-hoop. Trooper Hall had turned us in two seconds from worried retreating soldiers into giant-killers.

My bottom was getting rather sore from constant rough-riding over bad roads (and from lack of baths too, no doubt), so I asked the Colonel if when we moved I could go in a car. As he wanted my bike for his own use he agreed. In these small things he was the most reasonable of men, and was repaid in the morale of his men. In exchange he gave me his car with Higgins, the Cockney driver from the Old Kent Road, and a radio operator. He wanted me to go down to the HQ of the First French Army at Douai (where we used to attend the Corps Intelligence courses) and try to find John Collings, or alternately to get information.

We started comfortably along easy roads – I had in fact to restrain the speed-frenzy of Higgins, as the refugees seemed already nerve-racked and it seemed a pity to add imaginary scares to the legion of real dangers. We handed out spare food to some of the more miserable ones. Once we stopped when hundreds of retreating officerless Belgian soldiers swarmed across the road into a ditch. I encouraged in the approved manner, telling them that if we aimed straight we could bring down German bombers with our rifles. However, the necessity never arose, which was unfortunate as I am sure we could have emulated the feat of Trooper Hall.

These soldiers were tired creatures, but amiable and willing. They had at least the guts to march back into France and carry on the fight against the Nazis. '*En Belgique, officiers pas bons, pas bons du tout, M'sieur,*' one explained simply. '*Nous marchons en France . . . officers français beaucoup mieux . . . Nous cherchons officiers fançais.*'

We pressed on towards Douai. Tournai was blazing fiercely and a great deal of damage had been done to the houses. We managed to thread a way through debris and glass and craters and reached the outskirts of the city to the south. Here in what had been a football field was mounted an AA battery, the first I had actually seen. We were still looking round when a couple of roaring aeroplanes appeared from the south, making towards the emplacement. We drew in quickly and took cover with our arms behind a shrub – by now a well-drilled movement.

Suddenly one of the machines, a silver Messerschmitt 110, zoomed towards the field, chased at about 400 mph by a Hurricane holding onto its tail – 'Drrr . . . Drrr . . .. Drrr . . .' went the Hurricane machine-guns, and 'Popopopopop' replied the rear-gunner in the Nazi machine. We were just becoming enthralled in this terrific chase (which was the 'films plus') when only a few hundred yards to our right another battle broke out, this time a Hurricane eluding an Me110, which was in its turn being chased by another Hurricane. Bullets sprayed down the road to our right and into the field as the planes dived and zoomed and twisted and turned. Then the first 110 went bang into the ground with a great burst of smoke and flame, its pursuer rolling upwards and around to join in the other battles. One Me110 dived to about 50 feet only 300 yards away, and I decided to let off some Tommy-gun rounds at it, just for the 'heck' of it. I aimed excitedly and fired – one little round. I had forgotten to put the change lever over to automatic : but that silly little bullet satisfied me somehow – I felt a party to the destruction of those three 110s, Goering's pride, and not a mere spectator.

Everyone was thrilled to the marrow : from being depressed, re-treating men and women they had become elated heroes and heroines who had witnessed the destruction of hitherto all-powerful enemies. In lifting the morale of both soldiers and civilians there is nothing so powerful as a successful air-battle. We drove on satisfied, excited and happy.

Near the frontier – what an artificial boundary in such a tempest ! – the crowds of refugees began to agglomerate, swelling the road as they reached the barrier. There was nothing odd about them; but what gave us a shock, and puzzled us all the way down to Douai, was the position of the English guns. They were pointing the same way that we were heading.

At Douai I found Janel, whose forecasts had so far been so good, trying to conceal his fright by continually washing his hands. He moved round quietly in circles, occasionally asking how Oxford was and quoting – not ineptly – Kipling. I found Miles Reid, a charming and studious-looking somewhat dreamy gunner – in many ways the ideal liaison officer. I also found John Collings – in one of his dramatic moments. 'You know the situation, old boy? Where's that fellow McGee got to? You don't? The Germans are all round us ! We're all in the bag now ! I know he wants to, but it isn't safe to settle down that side of the Scarpe – they're going to blow up the bridges at any moment ! The Germans may be on the Scarpe now, old boy !'

John Collings marked out the position, looking serious and worried, while Miles Reid calmed the excited staff. We had not thought it possible for the Germans to be where we had pretended they were only a fortnight before, on the Canal du Nord. But the Germans were there, all right. Despairingly the Staff began to draw lines and encircle towns. Blue lines for the Allies, red for the Germans: the red pencils were thoroughly used up. That side of the Scarfe was definitely unsafe. John Collings told me to go to Hasnon and there to warn them to get ready to leave.

His melodrama was infecting me – I began to see things in terms of disaster. We were surrounded. We were in the bag. I sent McGee back to the Colonel with our news and swore at Higgins for having left the car for food: this seemed heartless as he was a fat chap and had been starving all day, according to his story.

Short of Denain we turned left to the north, along unknown roads, and on nearing the outskirts we sighted more bombers: this time they seemed so near that we decided to park close to a house and take cover and fire if they came low enough. A man came out of a house, a weeping woman staring at us from behind him. We asked them to take shelter until the raid was over; but they looked at us suspiciously. An unfriendly look from an ally is a nasty thing. The machines were circling round and the woman began to sob while the man remonstrated with her in vain. Then she became hysterical and clutched at my Tommy-gun to lower its muzzle, the husband intervening ineffectually.

'*Ne tirez-pas!*' she yelled. '*Ne tirez-pas! Hier à cette place un soldat a tiré sur des avions et ils sont revenus nous bombarder!*' 'What the hell's a soldier for if he isn't going to fire his gun?' I asked rhetorically; but it was impossible to fight the aeroplanes and the woman simultaneously, so I appeased the latter. We wouldn't fire, I said, glancing slyly at the departing Dorniers. It was my first experience of the effect casual bombing can have on civilian morale. I had a talk with the man afterwards and suggested that this hysteria was just what Hitler was aiming at – this slavery to emotion was playing his game for him? He agreed apologetically adding, '*Moi aussi j'étais soldat au front le dernière fois . . .*'

Friday 24th May: We remained in constant touch with 'MacForce' HQ * and realised the immense importance of accurate information. The Chief of Staff was Colonel Templer, head of FSP† with the BEF. He's a young man with black, untidy hair swept back like a Slav, and his face is fierce and neurotic, his eyes piercing. He is remarkably alert and intelligent, and I always imagine him sitting behind his police-desk, chain-smoking and asking hundreds of questions of obstinate

---

* So named from its Commander, General Mason-Macfarlane.
† Field Security Police.

prisoners. He would have scared any member of the Gestapo; but as an officer in charge of operations he seemed to inspire confidence. He is, I think, a rare type in the Army.

At the French HQ I used to speak to German prisoners whenever possible, and put an awkward question to them point-blank. 'Do you have orders to shoot and bomb women and children refugees on the roads?' They seemed terrified and implied that such an order would never be given; but I insisted, 'I have seen refugees mixed up with a few vehicles from a convoy being machine-gunned and bombed on the roads.'

'Well,' said a fair-haired young Pomeranian pilot, 'we have orders to bomb those tree-lined roads and sometimes, you know, it's difficult to see . . .' I felt the RAF would have taken greater care.

Our use in this area was ebbing out, and the Colonel decided we should be much more helpful as an additional news-service for GHQ. Accordingly we transferred to some comfortable farmhouses (with good lofts to sleep in and friendly farmfolk) near Prémesques. It was in a lonely stretch of country which in the last war had formed part of the German lines : two concrete machine-gun posts stood on either side of the road.

At GHQ I met an old friend who had stayed at Hatherop * and whom I'd last seen in Arras, Ulick Verney. He was assisting one Brigadier Sir Oliver Leese, Deputy Chief of the General Staff. These two invited me to help myself to a passable lunch and asked me for news, which I gave them. It surprised me that the nerve-centre of British operations should manifest such intense interest in information from a very junior subaltern, and the situation was rather comic. Here was I, hung with every kind of equipment and in shabby, dustfilled battledress, and there were the Generals in smart service dress, with red and gold emblazoned on lapels and caps, ribbons gleaming from their breasts. Leese tried to give me the impression that he was a consumate fool; and in this he was successful. He asked questions which some of my NCOs would have disdained to consider, and his general attitude was that of a good-natured and ignorant child.

I was surprised at the lack of stiffness and formality in this Holy of Holies. We were permitted to roam about where we pleased : into the 'I' Room, into the Operations Room. Fortunately there was none of the panic and excitement and passion of the First Army.

* Hatherop Castle, Gloucestershire.

Then on to Cassel.

We exchanged some food with the French and filled our hungry bellies with thick buttered crusts and the warm wine of Provençe. Every two or three minutes we would try to establish contact with the tanks. No reply. I had a short conversation with the Colonel who told me to continue until dark and then return. We continued sending and receiving but the only people we could pick up were some Germans giving locations and orders in code. '*Allo . . . Bartlos zweiundzwanzig Gesicht schmalles – Gesicht blaue Augen . . .*'

I listened to these locations for a bit to get the hang of their code and the pace of sending. The signaller tuned in with greater precision and then switched over to send. I started off in guttural German asking them for their exact position and giving mine in some phoney juxta-position of the features of the face. Someone replied giving a message in code which might well have indicated a position. I then told him to retire because of the weight of the enemy on their front. He went off the air. I tried the same game on another wave-length and drove this German off the air too. The hillside had been almost bare when we arrived; but now troops were thronging it like bees on a hive, British and French soldiers taking up positions and concealing their anti-tank weapons with great ingenuity.

The General was delighted with my story (though Colonel Templar appeared sceptical) and wanted to come and join in the fun on the radio. He knew most of the German words of command, which would have been helpful; but darkness was now setting in (and with it the expectation of an attack), so we ate and drank some more and began to pack up.

Sunday, 26th May: This morning Old Moore and I went off to the Corps for the last time. A day of dark ill-omen. It rained earlier and remained cloudy. From the south, a huge column of smoke from some burning oil lay across the sky. At Marchiennes there was little to report save that the Germans were making some headway with a bridgehead at Bouchain. Lieutenant Seyffert of the Deuxième Bureau (the Alsatian interpreter who always managed to get so much information from the Germans and shared it all with me) pointed out the situation. '*Voyons, mon ami . . . Qu'est-ce-que vous pensez? . . . Les Allemands ici . . . et ici . . . et ici . . . et par là . . . En effet, les Allemands partout! Comment pensez-vous que ça soit possible que nous nous sauvions d'une telle situation?*' He went off into spasms of nervous laughter.

I replied that the situation was not exactly *belle,* but maybe we could strike southwards if Weygand pushed northwards simultaneously. Alternatively we could evacuate ourselves by sea. It would be a bit of a crush at the port of course, I said, smiling philosophically. He went on with his work.

I had to find the III Corps as well. As I went down to Carvin, where there was much noise of battle and the smoke of burning oil, they seemed to be coming up. I found only some RASC men, rather annoyed that they hadn't had time to shave, and quite unmoved by the bombing and the apparent proximity of Germans There was no sign of the Corps, which had moved out earlier. When I left it was with a feeling of relief : already the eerie threat-charged atmosphere of no-man's land was beginning to creep into Carvin.

Wednesday, 29th May : Someone, an archetype of incompetence, gave us an overcomplicated route and told us to be ready at 3.30 yesterday morning. We snatched a few hours fitful sleep and then in the darkness yawned ourselves awake, packed our little kit into his car and gulped down some milk.

The Colonel was there to see us off. He wasn't the sort of man to say Goodbye in the evening and then go to bed. He worked very hard and only seldom – when something quite unnecessarily stupid or incompetent had happened – would he betray in a bitter sentence (repeated a little for emphasis) his lassitude. Throughout it has been a pleasure to work for him; and when you consider that many of us are cynical civilians with very pronounced views about the Army, that is saying a lot.

It was because we felt that our work would, in his hands, yield results; because we had seen his attractive and unorthodox methods meet with great success when others more true to tradition were failing; because at all times he had a ready smile to greet even the feeblest attempt at humour; because despite his heavily advertised blood-lust and love of danger he maintained a consistent regard for the safety of his men that we were always glad to work for him. 'Well,' he said, 'it's been a good show and you've all done very well. When we get back to England you can be sure that if there is anything going I will get you into it too.'

Heavily-laden we set off into the night. The roads north were crammed with every type of vehicle and the going was difficult, though not so bad as we had expected. As usual, our bikes were much better adapted than Mackenzie's car for this sort of thing, so when the traffic became really bad round Ypres (where they were massing for yet another battle) I got his permission for us to go ahead. Fisher, of course, had a puncture. We had to leave him behind, hoping for the best. Once I got entangled in some tramlines and came off twice; but I was more perturbed by what the men in the convoy would be thinking than by my injuries.

Towards the coast, convoys began to thin out, and already we witnessed the destruction of some of the larger lorries and less mobile material. A Scottish sergeant, appearing very lost and exhausted, asked my advice. He had got out of touch with his unit, and another officer had told him to destroy all his equipment, which included some useful trucks. We considered this order ridiculous and suggested that it was his duty to disobey it. This may sound unorthodox; but one of the more obscure and confusing Field Service Regulations tells you: 1) always obey an order; 2) disobey an order if you think you ought to.

Nearing the coast the sky became darker, for another great ladder of oily smoke from the Dunkirk direction straddled the fresh sky. The roads by this time were completely deserted and a strange feeling took me: I imagined that at any time German machine-gunners would open up on our queer little high-speed party, tearing along those flat Belgian roads.

Soon we arrived at the little villa which was Mission HQ. Familiar faces greeted us: George Zech, the wireless expert who had performed wonders with ticker machines salvaged from Bruges wreckage, and with a private line to London – it was good to hear his Glaswegian slang again; Breezy Bertie Woolcock, the Cambridge Soccer Blue, was keeping the men in good spirits and dealing with the cypher machine with great competence; Saunders the Stockbroker, smooth as usual but more irritable and with deep lines under his eyes; Bill Humphreys, as efficient as ever in his clerical way; Humphrey Symonds, the motoring expert. The Wing Commander had been working pretty continuously since 10th May and was utterly exhausted; but even so he managed to retain his composure and his temper at a time when there was ample excuse for any 'choler'. And then old Norman Reddaway, just the same, using the art of comic exaggeration to great effect.

Soon we had a good breakfast; but it was not yet clear whether we were to wait and fight it out (as John Collings suggested with gloomy drama) or whether we were to make a dash for England in whatever transport remained. We washed, slept and repacked our valises; and up in the top storey I discovered a queer, squeaking organ which I coaxed into life with some rather disjointed Handel. Overhead the

Belgian AA guns were active, the German aircraft more so. Bombs were dropping in the main road some 300 yards away. There was a small lake where Bertie spent his time fishing with little results, and there were a few acres of woods. Norman and I walked around there for an hour or so, discussing our experiences and reaching agreement on the incompetence of the Allies, and on the general efficiency of the Mission as well as the Germans. Norman had the capacity for being consistently funny, even when describing experiences necessarily obnoxious to himself, or when analysing a subject of impenetrable complexity. It was like this when we used to saunter round the dilapidated suburbs of Valenciennes: long canals and railways and the hovels which passed for working-class dwellings.

By the lake, after lunch, we slept again in the hot sun. Suddenly we were woken by frantic shouts – Mackenzie and John Collings were rushing around as we had got the order to go to Ostend.

Along the road people were still taking shelter from imaginary aircraft, and Ostend bore the appearance of recent raiding. The harbour and adjacent streets were practically deserted. Broken glass and tangled tram-cables lay about the streets. The station was blazing fiercely, causing the harbour to be covered with a pall of smoke. We were all sent off to look for two ships: the *Aboukir* and the *Marquis*. Presently I found them intact, though bereft of their masters at that moment.

The *Aboukir* was the larger and most comfortable; but the *Marquis*, a scruffy little coaster, had more storage room for our vehicles, which we had been ordered to load if possible. It was 3 p.m. and the ships were forbidden to sail until dark. We amused ourselves collecting the bullybeef, sardines and condensed milk which had been somewhat optimistically unloaded. Junkers 88s kept diving out of the clouds and delivering salvos of bombs into the basin behind us.

In the evening, a lorry-load of Belgian policemen drove up with a dozen Nazi prisoners, all airmen. We ventured to ask them a few questions, but surrounded by Belgians they would say nothing. Later we handed them beef and biscuits and sardines (so much, in fact, that we had to ask for some back for ourselves) and then they talked a lot. Their standard story 'that they had collided with each other' soon gave place to more credible accounts of their demise. We discovered that one of them came from a village near Chiemsee I had good cause to know, since the Aretins' BMW had once crashed near there and had taken several weeks to repair in Prien, under the dilatory hand of a vast, paunchy mechanic who came to be known as Herr Hardy. As

they were in a group it was a little difficult to get any opinions of
Nazidom; but in general they appeared to be the usual pleasant type of
young German : ostensibly pleasant and *anstaendig*; but when infected
with the virus of Hitlerism, capable of any bestiality.

Just before sundown the RAF lot arrived and boarded the *Aboukir*.
At 9 p.m. we (on the *Marquis*) moved slowly out of harbour astern of
the *Aboukir*, and almost immediately parachute-flares enclosed us in a
triangle. I thought little of this; but John Collings felt they were
sinister. Before we sailed, a bewildered youth carrying a bundle of
washing had arrived on the boat. He dropped the washing, which was
a parachute, and revealed the face of Michael Maxwell, whom I had
met at Oxford. He had enjoyed himself immensely up above until
suddenly lifted into the sky by what appeared to be an AA shell; and
finding the controls dead, decided to jump. As he fell he had been
rather puzzled to know which ring to pull, but fortunately, by trial and
error, he found the right one. Later, after much tea and bully beef, the
mad Captain [of the ship] invited John Gabriel, Michael Maxwell
and me to use his cabin. Some of us had to be on watch, others slept.
We slept.

At about midnight we were woken by the rattle of machine-gun
fire as well as oaths and commands and chatter. John Collings' sten-
torian voice was audible issuing contradictory orders above the din.
Next door the refugees muttered disapprovingly. Then came two loud
reports which shook the ship. We got ourselves and our pistols ready
for anything, and after another half-minute clambered over the
huddled refugees and made our way cautiously up to the deck.

John Collings was brandishing his machine-gun. 'Get down below,
for Christ's sake! They'll start again soon! My God! Can you see
them over there? They're trying to torpedo us! Christ! Why hasn't
that Lewis gun got going again! McGee! Tell that Lewis Gunner to
fire all he's got at that bloody German boat! Quick! Christ!' Mackenzie was ddd . . . ddd . . . ddd . . . ddding his Tommy-gun, McGee was
firing his rifle off into the dark (the first time of the whole war), and
others were optimistically discharging their pistols. I crept astern under
cover of the gunwhale (later I discovered that it had been neatly
punctured by armour-piercing bullets) and got next to the Lewis gun
which – as usual – had jammed. The MTB had been firing tracer,
which gave away her position; and we were replying with indiscrimin-
ate rifle shots and continuous machine-gun fire. Soon the German boat
was silent and drifted away astern. It had been a hectic five minutes.

John Collings explained that the MTB had fired a torpedo wide, which the *Marquis*'s Captain Morrison had avoided; and then another one which allegedly went under the hull. When the German prisoners heard it pass without exploding, they said, *'Gott sei dank!'*

Later we heard that the *Aboukir* had been torpedoed, and all the RAF staff and most of the refugees and crew went down. A few men were saved but only one officer, and this was Norman. For three or four hours he had collected bits of wreckage to make a raft (his days as a scout were bearing fruit) on which he sensibly sat, only his knees in the water. He was sick and cold. All around him men were becoming hysterical, then succumbing and sinking beneath the waves. A sensitive person, he found himself lacking in feeling. He abstained from wasting his breath by hailing aeroplanes and tried to keep Saunders, the stockbroker, afloat; but when a destroyer hove in sight, Saunders collapsed. The destroyer was the *Greyhound*, in which poor Charles Blennerhassett – who had so longed to fight in naval battles – had been killed some days before.

Off Deal we waited aimlessly. John Collings fell asleep, Mackenzie too. We wanted to land. Soon a doctor came and transported the wounded ashore. We proceeded to Dover through a battle between destroyers and bombers.

Dover looked grey and forbidding – the familiar greeting after beautiful and exciting times abroad. When we landed we encountered much red tape and officialdom. Numbers of soldiers watched us unload without helping. Presently it began to rain.

*

Christopher Cadogan returned to England and married Stella on 11th July 1940. Hopkinson had forbidden his young officers to marry, saying that the presence of women was a 'security risk'. Cadogan therefore left Phantom and joined SOE (Special Operations Executive). He was sent on a special mission to Turkey. On the way back, he travelled as a civilian on a Turkish ship (which was, of course, neutral). The ship was torpedoed near Cyprus. He was never seen again. He was twenty-four.

Like many others, Christopher Cadogan had left a farewell letter to be delivered in the event of his death. His letter said :

Do not grieve too much about my dying. I have done a little already in this life . . . but there is a huge amount still to be done. Remember that the world will get better if people behave in a decent Christian way to each other.

CHAPTER TWELVE

The Recollections of Light and Thompson

Harold Light, who eventually commanded the Training Unit, joined Phantom in 1940; previously he had been in a TA Artillery unit. He remembers most people clearly. He described Niven as having brought 'a fresh and exuberant spirit to his duties' and getting on well with everyone. Light remembers that at the concert arranged by Niven at Richmond there was a very beautiful Swedish film star who sang a song called 'I'm a Spy'. Her hobby was collecting badges so she went around removing badges from officers' tunics. She took Hopkinson's badge from his cap which was lying on a chair. He was not pleased when he realised what had happened. Until the lost badges were replaced the officers' uniforms looked somewhat unbalanced.

Light recalls introducing Second Lieutenant Mark, the future Sir Robert Mark, to the jeep. Unfortunately he forgot to explain that what looked like bottom gear on an American jeep was in fact reverse. Mark thereupon got in and drove off. To his surprise the vehicle hurtled backwards into the nose of the vehicle behind. Mark landed in France soon after D Day and served throughout the NW European campaign. Eventually he reached the rank of major. A modest account of his experiences with Phantom and the rest of his career is given in his book *In the Office of Constable*.

Other interesting personalities whom Light recalls include E. E. Rich and P. Hincks. Teddy Rich had been a Fellow of St Catharine's, Cambridge, where some time after the war he became Master. He was a distinguished oarsman. Appropriately he became Professor of Naval History at Cambridge. Peter Hincks was an enormous man who had earned fame as a shot-putter at Cambridge. After a period with Phantom, Hincks managed to transfer to the RAF. Another notable shot-putter was G. O'B. Power, who also played Rugby Football for Bedford.

Light also recalled a story which R. J. T. 'Reggie' Hills had told him. (Reggie Hills eventually became Lieutenant-Colonel R. C. T. Hills. He wrote several books including one entitled *Phantom was*

There (published in 1951). How, in 1950 – or earlier – he managed to obtain clearance for much of the material he put in that book and how, for that matter, he managed to write such a comprehensive account when none of the official histories had been published and there was little in the public records is both a mystery and a miracle. Hills had originally come to Phantom from the Life Guards as Quartermaster but later took a more active role, becoming a squadron commander: he was in the thick of operations throughout the NW Europe campaign including Arnhem.)

At the start of the First World War Hills had joined the army by the process of falsifying his age, which was approximately eighteen months younger than the statutory requirement. He had been made a waiter in the officer's mess. War or no war the Life Guards believed in proper standards and ceremonial so had taken a fairly complete mess to France, regimental silver and all. Wine was available in plenty but not port. For an evening when the Regimental Colonel was visiting Hills was told to obtain some bottles of port. He went to the NAAFI and came away with a bottle or two which bore the right description on the label and at the end of dinner appeared at the Regimental Colonel's elbow with the uncorked bottle. Just as he was about to pour the Colonel said, 'Wait, let me look at that bottle.' He inspected it. 'Good God,' he said, 'Take it away and bring me some brandy.' However the Colonel was staying a further night. Hills was therefore ordered to obtain some proper port but the NAAFI had no more and there was no supply locally. The Messing Sergeant said, 'Look, get hold of some decanters and fill those with the same stuff.' The next night when the Colonel saw the decanters he beamed. He poured out a glass and sipped it. 'Ah, good, my boy,' he said. 'That's the real thing.'

Years later Hills was at a dance given for the Life Guards and castle staff at Windsor Castle. It was all very democratic, and the drinks flowed freely, to the satisfaction of Hills. He found himself dancing with an aristocratic lady who said, 'I see you are in the Life Guards. Did you ever serve under my brother, the Earl of —?' Hills said, 'Yes,' and when questioned blurted out the story of the port. 'How marvellous,' said the lady. 'Now I've always thought he was a complete humbug and now you must tell him that story to prove it. Stay here while I go and find him.' She swept away.

Sobered by the awfulness of the moment, Hills quickly recovered his common sense. Like a flash he grabbed his greatcoat and disappeared from the dance. 'Went faster than Cinderella, I did,' he commented.

Frank Thompson, who was with H Squadron in the desert, was a dedicated Communist. His father was a poet, and novelist; his mother descended from a line of Americans. Frank Thompson had been born in Darjeeling but his parents came to Oxford in 1923 when he was three. They lived on Boars Hill where they were friends of Robert Bridges, John Masefield, Sir Arthur Evans (the archaeologist) among others. He was educated at Winchester, where he learnt Russian, and travelled widely abroad learning several languages, including modern Greek.

He wrote later (in 1943): 'The culture imbibed at Winchester was too nostalgic . . . Nostalgia, once it enters your being is difficult to eradicate. It muddies the well-springs of your thought and action.' In 1939 he went up to New College Oxford, already a convinced Socialist. In 1939 he joined the Communist party. He volunteered for the army at the outbreak of war, was commissioned into the Royal Artillery, and in May 1940 was appointed to Phantom.

His military qualities were appreciated by those around him. He was a brave, capable and compassionate officer. His political views caused some comment but the general verdict on him was that he was such a conscientious fellow one could overlook a few flights of fancy. That view did not appeal much to Thompson who felt that although the British army had taken the right step by engaging in this war against tyranny there were too many long-established practices which everyone realised were wrong but no one seemed disposed to alter; conditions on troopships was one. (Anyone wondering why soldiers voted enthusiastically for Socialism in 1945 should do some research on the division of space on liners converted to wartime 'troopers'.) Thompson believed that British officers were almost the best in the world; he suspected the Russians were better although he had not met any. He recorded his memories of the Sicily landings in his diary. July 10th was a calm day. 'Back on the hill slopes guns of some kind were flashing and their shells were dropping into the water off the beaches sending up fountains. There was nothing in these graceful water-spouts to suggest hostility or death'.

They were late coming in, then : 'Two mortar shells landed on the rear gun mounting about fifteen paces behind us, killed the crew outright and set the whole stern of the ship ablaze. The gang planks were lowered with a splash and the disembarkation proceeded with very little ceremony. I seized one of the ropes of the sea-barrow and got the unwieldy apparatus lumbering down the starboard gangway. It must have taken us three minutes, at the outside five, to drag that heavy barrow across the soft sand and into the cover of the ravine but it seemed like a quarter of an hour . . .

'The mortar shells continued to fall fairly regularly, most accurately. I remember noting one tall lance-corporal striding past me on the left. Just as he overtook me he reeled, his trousers suddenly turned bright red, and a couple of comrades helped him into cover . . . Half a minute later the same thing happened to a fellow a few paces in front of us. His trousers turned bright red, he limped forward groaning for a yard or two then fell on his face. Sam, who observes these things with a more anatomical and analytical eye than I do, afterwards told me this chap had an arm and a leg pretty well torn off. I can't honestly say I was frightened during all this – nothing much as frightened as I have been on other occasions. I had too much to think about.'

In September 1943 he left Phantom, but with some sadness. 'Out here with home far away, one takes more responsibility for the men and comes to feel for them a strong comradeship which is part brotherly but more paternal – I found it a tough job saying good-bye.' *

From Phantom he went on a parachute course and in July 1944 was dropped in South Serbia. The aim was to assist the Bulgarian resistance, 'The Fatherland Front'. Their immediate task was to establish dropping zones on Yugoslav soil and later in Bulgaria itself. In March they were surrounded by Bulgarian Government troops and suffered casualties, but Thompson escaped. In May his luck ran out. After a battle he was captured, put on trial with various Bulgarian partisan leaders, and then shot. He gave a short talk to his companions before he faced his executioners with complete calm. With seventy others he lies in a common grave. It is marked by a headstone bearing all the names, and a hammer and sickle at the side.

* *There is a Spirit in Europe: A Memoir of Frank Thompson* by T. J. T. and E. P. T., Gollancz, 1947. Reproduced by kind permission of Dr Edward Thompson.

CHAPTER THIRTEEN

The Scene on Many Fronts

For a small regiment Phantom attracted an amazing variety of officers who would distinguish themselves later; some had already done so. There would be two privy councillors, three life Peers, six hereditary peers, one Master of a Cambridge College, four professors, one actor playwright, one film-star, one Law Lord, one leader writer, one ambassador, one Steward of the Jockey Club and one Commissioner of the Metropolitan Police. There was also a sprinkling of athletes of various sorts; an international hurdler, a notable Ruby footballer. The saddest story was that of Peter Baker who became an MP, was involved in a dubious business venture, went to prison, had a mental breakdown and died while still young.

A typical recruit was Michael Oakeshott, later to be Professor of Political Science at London University: 'I joined the army on the fall of France, recruited and given a shilling by a retired Indian Army Artillery Colonel, who lived in my village and had a more or less private AA Battery at Duxford, and it was there I spent the Battle of Britain. Later I went to an OTC and had a gun (Bofors) somewhere near Barnet. It was pretty dull and I looked out for a move. I was turned down for a drop into Germany, the last thing I wanted was Bletchley, and somehow (I forget how) I got in touch with Tom Reddaway (an old Cambridge friend) who was then Adjutant of Phantom – and was admitted to his charmed circle. Tom soon left; I hoped to be given a patrol and sent to Greece or Turkey but was considered too old and I knocked about in HQ Richmond for some time, doing nothing much but learning to signal with the Morse code. When Tomkinson (a highly efficient accountant) became Adjutant I was made his assistant and sat in the office which was very boring.

Then, nearer the Day, the regiment was organized into squadrons, each with an administrative officer, and I was made the admin officer of B Squadron under Peter Pattrick and John Dalby and achieved the rank of captain. And that was where I stayed. We moved out of

Richmond – to Scotland, to East Anglia and finally to Reigate and so
to France. But I suppose I must have spent the best part of a couple
of years at HQ and knew most of the chaps well. It wasn't the war I
had hoped for : I wanted to know what it was like to be a soldier but,
of course, except for the few professionals, none of us was quite a
soldier – except for learning to be patient and to remain awake when
nothing was happening on the North-West Frontier. There were
moments when one (or at least I) could imagine myself to be under
the command of Wallenstein, but they were all too few. And, of course,
nothing like Arnhem came my way.'

At one time Oakeshott had tried to join SOE to be parachuted into
Germany. He was already thirty-nine. He was told that his knowledge
of German was adequate but that his appearance was so unmistakably
English that he would not last a day. Soon after he joined Phantom he
was told to become an expert on pigeons, and put in charge of them.
He read every possible book about pigeons and conferred with the
experts. The pigeons were then taken up by aircraft to mid-Channel
and released to fly home. This exercise was to enable the pigeons to
observe the French countryside so that they would not lose their
bearings if they had to fly over it after a future landing on the
Continent.

David Niven is so well known as a film actor and amusing author
that it is difficult for many of his admirers to realise that he was also a
dedicated and very professional soldier. He had been at Sandhurst
and had held a commission in the Highland Light Infantry from
1929–1932. In Phantom he commanded A Squadron which, according to his own account, was a colourful group of men, including stock-
brokers, burglars, and poachers. According to them he was even more
colourful. In spite of a cheerful happy-go-lucky disposition, he was
very keen to get on with the war and on one occasion volunteered his
squadron to assist the Navy in some of their more hazardous coastal
protection work. His own version of this is typically modest.

'When A Squadron was doing intensive training around Dartmoor
I did answer an SOS from the Navy who were trying to handle E-
boats which had twin Oerlikons pooping off from an armour-plated
bridge and all they had was 3-pounder salute guns off, I suppose, the
Victory or something like that with which to cope. Anyway, they had
their eyes on our anti-tank rifles so I called for volunteers hoping
nobody would suggest that I went too but unfortunately everybody
wanted to have a few nights at sea so off we went but, thank God,
apart from endemic sea-sickness and the squadron's cook losing his

teeth overboard nothing happened. No E-boats showed up or if they did, thank God nobody noticed them.

'The other saga was the pigeon. Hoppy gave us baskets of these foul beasts to carry messages when all else failed. I think General Paget was the Commander-in-Chief Home Forces and an elaborate loft was constructed outside his headquarters in St James's Park. Hoppy told him with great pride that messages would soon be arriving from the far-flung squadrons. Paget waited expectantly and at last a bird slapped in through the intake box. It was from A Squadron. A massive exercise was in progress all over southern England and the message was ripped off the poor bird's leg and read in an expectant hush as follows: "That beast Major Niven sent me away because he said I had farted in the nest". I understand there was not much happy laughter in St James's Park !

'I have forgotten the name of the Scandinavian actress I brought to the Richmond party who pinched everybody's cap badges but I do remember organizing a concert in Richmond for the entire outfit which included Flannigan and Allen, Nervo and Nox, Frances Day, which included Flanagan and Allen, Nervo and Nox, Frances Day, Naunton Wayne, Arthur Riscoe, Leslie Henson and Debroy Sommers and his entire band. I believe the show was a hit though as master of ceremonies I was too drunk to be able to assess it properly and afterwards, in the officers mess, one of the Crazy Gang asked Hoppy what the sandwiches had inside them. Hoppy pointed to a flag on the pile marked "sardine". Whereupon Jimmy Nervo ate the flag, brushed the sardine sandwiches to the floor and broke the plate on Hoppy's head.

'They were wonderful days which I would not have missed for anything.'

The Dieppe operation has been described, but there now follows the personal account of Corporal Masterson who was taken prisoner. His hands were kept in chains for a year afterwards.

Corporal Masterson:

The Phantom patrol attached to 3 Commando consisted of Lieutenant Hillerns, Corporal Masterson, Lance-Corporal Craggs and Driver Richardson. The patrol joined the Commando at Seaford on 11th August 1942 and there did W/T with the Commando Signals. On the 16th August all personnel were confined to barracks and given a series of lectures on the coming operation. One thing stressed on all concerned was, 'Should only one boat get through, it must land'. All were confident of success as many had taken part in several other raids.

Our part of No 3 Commando was due to land at Green Beach I, and after final orders all were confined to barracks again. On the morning of 18th August each man was given his landing craft number, and then all stood by at a moment's notice. At 1700 hrs 18th August all personnel taking part in the operation were taken to Newhaven Harbour in covered trucks, and there embarked on their respective craft. By 1900 hrs all craft were ready and we moved out of New haven Harbour escorted by MGB and destroyers. The Phantom patrol were on the second wave, and other troops in the same boat consisted of a Commando officer, an RSM, three ORs and five French Commandos, whose job was to calm the French civilians in the sector chosen for the task.

The force proceeded in the direction of the French coast at about four knots. Each craft carried sufficient petrol in the tanks and around the gunwales for the trip across, and back to England. By 2300 hrs the escorting force had left us, and the landing craft closed in to tighter formation. All was quiet for the next few hours, but about 0100 hrs 19th August Very lights were fired and a running fight began between the Commando force and German E boats. Several of the Commando boats blew up, owing, in my opinion, to the spare petrol tanks being hit. The fight continued with our boat zigzagging in different directions, until we were clear of the engagement. This had taken us until about 0400. At first light we could not see any craft in sight. As we were to land at 0500 hrs, the Commando officer ordered full speed for the appointed beach.

On the way two more of our boats joined us and as we approached the French coast we fell in with another two boats. These were sinking fast, and Commando troops were steering them in shore. About one mile from the shore a British ML came abreast with the Second-in-Command, 3 Commando aboard. He directed us in, leaving us as the water was too shallow for his boat to approach nearer. The beach where we landed was quite sandy and the cliffs about 20 yards ahead. These cliffs were about 150 feet or more in height, and contained two gulleys which we were to proceed along. The task of the 3 Commando was to destroy the heavy guns about two miles inland or to engage the crews in action, so preventing them from firing on the main Canadian force which was to land at Dieppe.

The Commando force was rather depleted by the naval fight and only around sixty men landed on our beach. These were without the mortar sections, which were to have played an important part in the operations. As we landed we were met by MG fire and snipers, which prevented the Phantom patrol from setting up station immediately. The two gulleys up which we had to proceed were mined and 15 yards of barbed wire was also placed along them. We reached the cliff tops however, with only slight casualties, and opened up station about 200 yards inland at 0645 hrs. The patrol attached to No 4 Commando was heard passing messages. Lance-Corporal Craggs endeavoured to get through, and thought he had finally passed a message which stated how hard pressed we were.

We then moved further inland with the small HQ which had been formed until we were in sight of the enemy gun positions. At this point we were receiving a good deal of heavy MG fire, to which we replied with our Brens and rifles. In the meantime Lance-Corporal Craggs was trying to get through on the wireless. By that time the frequency had changed and before he could make contact on the new frequency we were ordered to withdraw. Smoke bombs were put down to give us some cover as we made a dash for the gulley we had come up. On the way back to the gulley a MG opened fire on us, killing of our patrol Lance-Corporal Craggs and wounding Driver Richardson and myself. We then managed to get into a garden which gave us some cover. Lieutenant Hillerns at this period took off his uniform and, having civilian clothes on underneath, said he was making a break for it. When the remains of the force arrived back at the beach the time was then about 1000 hrs. No boats were in sight, and we were being subjected to snipers' fire from the cliffs, so we took shelter in several caves, hoping to hold out until boats arrived or darkness came. Shortly after this Lieutenant Hillerns arrived at the beach and taking his suit off, entered the sea and started swimming out to a boat which was drifting by. A MG fired at him from the cliffs and after shouting 'Help' twice he sank in the sea and did not appear again. After being in the caves until 1500 hrs and having no more amunition, the senior officer ordered us to break our weapons and surrender, as there were then more wounded.

A German patrol took us over and all wounded were dressed and taken to Rouen Hospital by train, where we were sorted out and sent to different POW camps. One thing of interest in Stalag VIII B, which I reached ten days after being captured : the Germans posted on the notice board a copy of the Dieppe Operational Plan with the part underlined that any emergency messages were to be passed by Phantom communications. This order was put up in order to explain why we were put in chains. This was the German reprisal for the Canadian order that German POW's hands were to be tied in the temporary camp on the beach before embarkation to England.

The Dieppe prisoners' and the RAF prisoners' hands were kept in chains officially for eighteen months but after the first twelve months this order was not rigidly enforced.

*

Victor Stump had an active war. He summarised the early years but kept a full diary from D Day onwards. Here we have the summary and extracts from the diary.

Victor Stump:

1940: We were a group of some twenty-five troopers sent, after training at Warminster, as reinforcements for the 4th Battalion RTR. In France we picked up Mk 2 Matildas and set off to joint the 4th. But we never ever got there. The 4th by then had been cut to pieces and Dunkirk was fast approaching. We were ordered to dump our tanks in Nancy and eventually got on a boat at Cherbourg.

After some leave (and here my mind is a bit hazy), we were each interviewed by a senior Phantom Officer. Anyway to cut a long story short, I landed up in Phantom.

1941: I met Denys Hart for the first time (he was then a Rifleman) and we were both sent on an NCO's course. We both emerged as lance-corporals. Denys eventually went off to OCTU and I lost sight of him for nearly two years.

1941: Great excitement in January. Our squadron was issued with tropical kit – but we handed it back a week later!

I was then driving our Daimler Scout for Major Jakie Astor. During this time, we had to give a demo of the car to some senior officers. To demonstrate its reversing abilities I drove in backwards at 50 mph; it frightened the life out of Major Astor (and me!). Bless him, he billeted us at his home at Cliveden and introduced us to his mother, the Rt Hon Lady A.

1942: This was a year of intensive training on Schemes ranging from Cornwall to Scotland. I think the highlights were :
1. A visit to the Daimler factory in Coventry, where they were making our Scout cars. We were able to discuss the pro's and con's of the vehicle with management and chaps on the shop floor.
2. In June our patrol had the privilege of visiting the Pye factory in

Cambridge, where they were manufacturing the new 22-sets. We were billeted in St Catharine's College and right royally treated – the lads were very impressed. We ate in the Masters' Dining Room and were waited on hand and foot – from steak to strawberries and cream. We carried out various tests using single and double end-fed aerials beamed on our HQ at Richmond. All were very successful.

3. In August, our patrol did an exercise with the Airborne Division. We managed to get a glider flight, weather was shocking and our pilot was recalled by a Very Light. It was a hairy landing, across a ditch, across a road and then on to the landing field.

4. Two of us managed to scrounge a night flight in a Beaufighter. It was great; they were using equipment which they referred to as 'Granny'. It was of course a new advanced form of radar.

1943: Action at last. Fifteen of us including Lieutenants Lart and Brawn sailed in convoy on 22nd January and landed Algiers 1st February. Eventually met up with Denys Hart again on 5th May. After many patrols we reached the Tunis area on 11th May and drove straight on to Cap Bon. We went to the POW cage, containing 25,000 prisoners. It was an incredible sight, they were driving themselves in, truck load after truck load. We went to a rest camp and then did various exercises, assault courses and rock climbing. The highlights of this period were the Victory Parade in Tunis on 20th May and 1st June when Winston Churchill spoke to us in the Amphitheatre at Carthage.

Eventually, we boarded the cruiser *Aurora on* 11th September and, with our jeeps lashed to the deck, sailed on the night of 12th September. She went like a bat out of hell, and we reached Taranto on the morning of 13th September. There were mines in the harbour, two ships had already been sunk, so we offloaded onto pontoons. We pushed off and entered Bari on 14th September.

On 19th September we heard that the Germans had threatened to take 120 hostages in Trani and the Bishop who helped us to escape had offered his life in exchange. My diary notes that during this period we worked with Popski and the SAS.

Our squadron was now HQ'd in Trani and I had to take over 'Q' work. So, while the chaps were relaxing 'Joe Soap' was down in Bari bargaining for fresh fish and then up into the mountains to buy carboys of Marsala from a monastery. On 9th October Captain Hart went to see the King of Italy and the Bishop who helped us to escape was decorated. It was filmed by Paramount News.

After many rumours, we sailed from Taranto on 22nd November and eventually reached Bizerta on 28th November. Then by train to Romba, about 25 kilometres outside Algiers, arriving 5th December.

Well, it was getting close to Christmas and, since it was rumoured that we may be sailing about 25th December, we made plans for an early Christmas dinner for the squadron. Life was getting boring and was delighted to get permission to go off on a two day egg hunt. So on 9th December I set off in a jeep with one of the lads. We headed for some of the remote villages in the Atlas mountains. The procedure was that my navigator would guard the jeep while I sought out the Headman of the village. We would squat on the floor of his tent or hut and commence bartering; this was for cigarettes, blankets or French francs. Having agreed on terms, he would send his minions off to get *des oeufs*. Well, on the two day trip we got 1,770 eggs and 10 turkeys. I went off alone on 16th December for a one day foray and got 405 eggs.

We had our Christmas dinner on 20th December, then prepared for our departure to Algiers. After the usual cock-ups we eventually boarded SS *Molapa* at 2300 hours on 25th December – what a Christmas Day! We sailed at 1500 on 26th December.

On the trip back Major Fraser interviewed some of the senior NCO's and asked us whether we would like our names put forward for OCTU. I asked him what the chances were of getting back to Phantom. He said pretty slim at this stage in the war – 'You will probably end up in the Infantry.' I decided to stay with Phantom.

We eventually landed back in the UK on 4th February 1944. After leave and various exercises we eventually went into the so called 'sealed camps' in preparation for D Day. My diary records the events of No 5 Patrol from D Day onwards:

Diary of V. A. Stump, No 5 Patrol A Squadron
    5th June: Sailed from Gosport in LCT 372.
    6th June: D Day. After a fairly rough passage we landed at 1330 hrs on Queen – Red, between Ouistreham and Lion-sur-Mer. Contacted Div HQ at Hermanville-sur-Mer. Shelling and sniping here, several bullets quite close to us. Bridgehead secure, but progress slow. Closed down 0300 hrs. Patrol working well. Moved with Division at 1930 hrs to Colleville-sur-Mer. Saw the Air Landing Brigade coming in.
    7th June: Colleville. Little progress, enemy opposition increasing.

Enemy paratroops dropped about two miles from us. We're getting a lot of trouble from snipers; three were shot in the village this morning. Defence Platoon Sergeant reckons he 'cut one of 'em in 'alf with 13 mm bullets'. Next of kin message passed to say landed safely and all well. Weather fine. Air cover splendid. Could do with some sleep.

8th June: No progress on this front, but they are advancing on our right flank. Bayeux has fallen. Major Russell visited us. Canal bridge at Bénouville bombed. Went to inspect with Captain Hart, also looked round the Air Landing gliders.

9th June: The patrol receives a personal message from GSOI Second Army HQ, quote, 'Congratulations your splendid work. Keep it up.' Lieutenant Mackenzie, 12 Patrol officer, called in on his way up to join 6th Airborne Division. Later he had difficulty with his wireless so I went on a bike to Airborne to collect a sitrep from him. A few minutes after my arrival they were heavily shelled, including mortars and rocket projectors. Enemy then attacked and got within 200 yards of perimeter. I left with notes – just after crossing bridges at Bénouville, got blown off bike by shell, hitch-hiked remainder of journey. Heard later that enemy had infiltrated through to bridges, just after I had crossed. Captain Hart went to salvage bike at 2300 hrs. While he was away Divisional HQ bombed, three killed, seventeen wounded. Two ammo trucks set on fire.

10th June: Very noisy last night, enemy dropped a lot of anti-personnel bombs – very unpleasant. Quiet day. Started digging in with a vengeance.

11th June: Monty visited this HQ. Things quiet again. Started re-organizing and getting things straightened up. Message from RHQ from Chief-of-Staff 21 Army Group as follows, quote, 'To all ranks Phantom. Deep appreciation your work.' One enemy aircraft got through today, dropped his bomb about 500 yards away.

12th June: Squadron HQ took over control in France at 2000 hrs. We rigged up Captain Hart's portable bath, and the whole patrol had one. Also changed underwear and did washing. Captain Tomkinson arrived here with 600 very welcome cigarettes. Another air attack on this HQ about 2359 hrs. Vehicle park and two store sheds burnt. Some killed and casualties. DR runs started.

13th June: Closed down wireless today to rest. Divisional Commander wounded by mine near Cambes.

14th June: Quiet day. 2nd Panzer Division has now arrived on our front. That makes 21st and 2nd Panzer Divisions, 12th SS Division and 346 Infantry Division (it's piling up).

20th June : Quiet day. Nine Me109's over 153 Brigade area dropping leaflets about new secret weapon saying 'Is London in flames?' So, this an attempt to break our morale! What a hope! Wonderful news from all American fronts, now shelling Cherbourg.

22nd June: A sad day which brought the first Phantom casualties. Usher was killed at Rear Army by shell burst. Direct hit on tent. Two others seriously wounded. LCT loaded with ammo hit on beach this morning. Also 6th Airborne ammo dump.

27th June: Moved at first light and caught up with 29 TAC HQ. Had difficult time getting there, we were given wrong bearings and landed up in St Mauvieu, held only by a handful of infantry. Saw a couple of lads whom I thought to be asleep on side of road – they were dead. Enemy SP air burst shells close in morning. Moved in afternoon to Cheux. God, what a mess! The heap of rubble, mud, blood, and dead typified the horrors of war. Dug in outside of Cheux in a tight laager. Stuff is flying in all directions now as the Spearhead goes forward, it comes from front, rear and flanks.

10th July: Bulldozers working like hell to clear the routes into Caen. This afternoon went into town with Captain Hart and another. Town a shambles, 2,000 living in Cathedral and 5,000 in school next door, both buildings undamaged by some amazing miracle. Those civilians really wonderful. Canadians taking over this area. Recalled to Squadron HQ this evening. Had to tow White all way from Bretteville with Jeep, arrived SHQ 0100 hrs.

19th September: Left Squadron HQ with new Command 9 Set, and a special job. To get up as far as possible to contact the Airborne pockets. Crossed Dutch frontier and reached Valkenswaard at 1400 hrs. Then pushed on and reached Eindhoven. Stopped by civilians in centre of town, they reported enemy tanks advancing on outskirts of town. So we put vehicles on side road and took up defence positions. Then at 2000 hrs large number of enemy aircraft attacked centre of town. Thought we'd had it, but patrol and vehicles all safe. All routes out of the town were now blocked by blazing ammo and petrol trucks. Civilians took it well, but there's urgent need for bandages etc – having emptied patrol first-aid box. Eventually moved patrol to a field on immediate outskirts of town. There opened wireless and sent a priority request message for ambulances.

25th–27th February 1945: Operation Blockbuster started 0330 hrs yesterday morning (24th). Preceded by the usual terrific artillery barrage, the Canadians got on well followed by 4th Canadian Armoured Division who made a dash for the Hochwald gap and breached it, but not without loss. Op Grenade. The town of Erkelenz has fallen and 5th Armoured and 84th Division have broken through. This afternoon they reached Weidniel and so outflanked the important industrial town of Munchen-Gladbach.

28th March: We made the crossing at 0530 hrs this morning. Followed by 22nd Armoured Brigade, who are passing straight through to make the 'break-out'. Centre Borken captured, then pushed on to Gemen and Heiden. In Gemen we recaptured forty-five British wounded in a hospital. Opposition unco-ordinated, but stubborn in places.

5th April: Division reached Diepholtz and pushed eastwards to Wagenfeld. Since crossing the Rhine we have moved every day with Division, sometimes twice a day. It's hard going because of bad weather we're getting now, I can think of a lot of easier things to do than erecting wet canvas. We are passing on an average 50–75 'J' messages and about 15 Phantom messages per day. However, the patrol is working like clockwork. Enemy aircraft have been profiting by the greatly increased distance that we are now from our airfields, and the bad weather which is 'unsuitable for flying' according to *Englische Luftwaffe* standards. The Ruhr pocket has been considerably reduced by pressure from the First and Ninth American armies. Yesterday we crossed the Dortmund-Ems canal of RAF fame.

7th April: Today 22nd Armoured Brigade made long advances to reach the River Weser in the Bucken and Hoya areas. Total POWs now claimed by this Division since crossing the Rhine is 57 officers and 3,583 men. Today our Armoured cars in the Bassum area, encountered Hitler Youth aged eight to twelve armed with rifles. Yesterday I went out and 'acquired' a 4-cylinder Mercedes Benz saloon, as a replacement for our trailer.

10th April: The ancient capitals of Königsberg and Hanover have fallen. Russians are in Vienna. General Patton within fifty miles of Czechoslovakia. In Italy the Eighth Army has started a new offensive. 53rd (W) Division has established a bridgehead over the Weser at Hoya and have reached Rethem.

11th April: We are now in Lemke, east of the Weser, opposite Niemburg. Division now advancing north towards Bremen. *Technique!*

Dedication on a girl's photograph found amongst the papers of POW Obergefreiter Karl Schagg of 115 Panzer Battalion : '*Du kannst es so nett und so lange*' (You do it so lovely and long).

29th April: Today we joined 8th US Infantry Division for the crossing of the Elbe. Their intention is to reach the Baltic coast and contact the Russians. Apparently we are the first British troops they've ever had attached to them – so they're making a little fuss of us. We're located eight miles from Velzen.

8th May: Quiet day today. There's a lot of firing, shouting and singing going on. They're firing everything from ack ack guns to pistols, it's not safe to be out.

CHAPTER FOURTEEN

Working with the SAS

Phantom supplied the signals to various SAS operations in France. Here follows the report by Lieutenant-Colonel Brian Franks, MC, who, as we saw earlier, had once been a member of Phantom but was now commanding the 2nd SAS Regiment. It is followed by Captain Greville-Bell's report and then by Lieutenant C. R. Moore's. Lieutenant Moore was later awarded the MC.

The officer commanding F Squadron was Major the Hon J. J. Astor.

Like his brother Michael, 'Jakie' Astor had joined Phantom in 1940 but their subsequent experiences had been very different. Jakie had been in the Dieppe Raid, had subsequently trained with Special Forces in Commando tactics and had then been invited to volunteer for the SAS. Service with the SAS meant parachuting into France and taking part in various activities behind the German lines. The Phantom service met all the SAS requirements adequately. After France had been liberated Jakie Astor's squadron was engaged in Germany in advanced reconnaissance with the SAS.

Michael Astor wrote of his experiences with Phantom in a book entitled *Tribal Feeling*. The book contains much interesting, modestly told, information about the remarkable Astor family. Michael Astor had a gentle, slightly cynical, sense of humour. After D Day he was with the 2nd Canadian Armoured Brigade, 21st Army Group and American Third Army. Colonel Franks who had earlier been with Phantom was now commanding SAS.

Lieutenant-Colonel Brian Franks, MC: Report on Operation Loyton

1st September 1944: My party left Fairford aerodrome shortly after midnight in two Stirling aircraft. The trip was uneventful and the sticks from both planes dropped successfully on the DZ at V 320850 near Veney. A few of the party dropped on trees, however, and all had difficulty with their leg bags. The party collected quickly round the lights on the DZ. Containers were dropped at the same time, one of which exploded and caught fire on the ground. I was met on the DZ by Captain Druce and also by a large number of Frenchmen making an almost unbelievable noise. Captain Druce, however, appeared to have the situation under control and the removal of containers, etc, from the DZ was, to start with, well organised. However, after we had been there about an hour and a half there was considerable shouting and shooting and I was told that the Germans had attacked, which news did not surprise me in view of the noise made by the French.

Lieutenant Dill and I, with a small party, moved round on the flank of the firing to see of we could assist or discover what was going on but found nothing there at all, and the firing had by then ceased. After searching around for some time we left to lie up for the day in the woods to the south, during which time we heard distant firing and some shelling over our heads which we afterwards discovered to have been directed at a Maquis camp evacuated the day before.

Towards the evening Lieutenant Dill went off to make a recce and returned with the news that the Maquis leaders were in a farmhouse at V 312848 not far away. They were anxious for me to go there. I reached the farm after dark and met Captain Marks and Captain Barreaux (Jedburgh).* Captain Gough (Jedburgh) had been with me all day. Food was found at the farm at which were the Maquis and some of my party. It was not known to what area the others had disappeared. It appeared that the firing on the DZ had been caused by some Russian members of the Maquis who spoke only German and were mistaken for enemy. Also, one Russian had eaten a stick of plastic and died noisily, which added to the confusion.

*

Captain Greville-Bell, DSO (half of whose patrol of six were Phantom members): Report on Operation Dunhill

Left Fairford night 2/3rd August 44, at 23.45 hrs, and arrived over the DZ at about 02.00 hrs. We saw some lights but they disappeared after the second or third run in. We jumped blind and landed in thick woods, seven kilos from the planned DZ. I collected the party and we lay up near the DZ.

3rd August: We contacted the French Resistance and heard that American patrols were in the area. We decided to find them and dis-

* Three-men Jedburgh teams were intelligence-gathering units directed by SOE

cover the situation. The only definite US location was Planches, map ref M9746 (Sheet 14) so I borrowed a civilian car and drove there via Châteaubriant with Sergeant Hodgson. The Resistance were killing stray Germans along this road. We entered Fougeray at 18.00 hrs, ten minutes after the Germans had left. We had a very pleasant reception. We put out lights for the second party, who dropped at 23.59 hrs approximately three kilometres from lights. They lost two leg bags.

4th August: US tanks arrived in Messac. I commandeered the village fire engine and contacted them. We organised the Resistance there and gave them orders to patrol the roads Messac–Guichen, Messac–Planches, and sent recces south as far as Fougeray, which had been re-occupied by Germans. Gave US tanks infantry protection during the night 4th/5th. At dusk two German recce cars attempted to break through the village. One car succeeded. The other was knocked out and one man killed. There were no casualties on our side. The reported attack on the village did not materialise.

5th August. Germans started to dig in east of Messac and their troops on foot approached from St Malo, map ref M8828, and Fougeray. I moved north to a farm near Loheac which I decided to hold as a strong point while I found cars.

[This shows the type of work, i.e. reporting exact position of Allied spearheads and German troops.]

*

Lieutenant C. R. Moore, of Phantom: Account of Operation Hounds-worth:

10th June: Two sticks, each of ten men, were to be dropped in Morvan as recce party for A Squadron, 1 SAS. One party under command of Major Fraser, MC, the other under command Lieutenant Cooper, MM. Both parties arrived on Fairford airfield at 2130 hrs. The stick consisted of :

1 SAS	*2 Patrol SAS Phantom*
Major Fraser, MC	Lieut Moore
Tprs Marson	Cpl Wood
Furness	Rfm Rolli
Babington	Tpr Harris
Kennedy	Pte Brinton

Special Forces: Lieutenant-Colonel Hasting with Canadian Sergeant. Took off in Stirling at 2230 hrs, passed over bridgehead and was able to see the craft formed up below. Some flak but a good trip, nobody being sick.

11th June: Presumed pilot could not see ground as we received order 25 minutes to go, and so on until 4, 3, 2, 1 minute 'GO' by Sergeant Thompson, the despatcher. The aircraft did not look for DZ but made straight run in. Very high drop above clouds and I saw lights a good distance away when I came through the cloud. I had great difficulty in releasing my kitbag and the rope tore and burnt my hands. Soft landing on side of steep hill, in a bush which tore my trousers from bottom nearly to the top.

I contacted the stick in following order: Rolli, Wood, Brinton, Lieutenant-Colonel Hastings, Canadian Sergeant, Harris, Furness, Babington in tree, Marson. Searched for Major Fraser and Kennedy until 0730 hrs. Lieutenant-Colonel Hastings had injured ankle so moved party and kit to wood. The men were very tired so they slept during the morning whilst I tried to find our location, without success. Sent off pigeon and reported situation on WT. Sergeant tried to locate containers with out kit and SF wireless, but was unsuccessful. Phantom carried two Jedburgh sets in preference to personal kit in rucksacks in their kitbags and both sets were in good condition. There were also three 24-hr ration packs per man. We buried our 'chutes and decided to move south until we could find out our location. We were near a main road and town and so expected search parties to be sent out to look for us. Before leaving search parties went out to look for Major Fraser and Kennedy, but had no success. At 1400 hrs moved off by compass through thick wood. The going was slow owing to Lieutenant-Colonel Hastings' bad leg. We slept during the night.

12th June: Continued to move south in heavy rain. Came out of wood and found our location to be N115530, so we must have landed west of Lormes which was approximately 25 miles away from the DZ. Reported on WT. WT crew were working in a clearing 75 yards from road when two Gendarmes came along on bicycles, stopped at the clearing and appeared to look straight at the crew, who remained still. They either thought our men were Germans or the camouflaged smocks were so good that they were concealed. Traffic on the road was considerable all the morning. We received pre-arranged RV N 296527 from Lieutenant-Colonel Hastings. It was decided that Lieutenant-Colonel Hastings and Sergeant would leave us to contact Maquis, which was their task, and I would proceed with the rest of the party to the RV. We agreed that if we did not contact each other within a week we would be at the RV at 0200 hrs on every even day. I gave

Lieutenant-Colonel Hastings a Jedburgh set and some rations. We parted in the afternoon. We proceeded very cautiously because we had heard MG, rifle and pistol firing all day in our wood. We thought it was parties out searching for us but afterwards learnt that it was a battle between Germans and a group of Maquis. Our plan was to follow the railway marked on map to the west.

13th June: After searching for the railway it was discovered that the rails had been taken away years ago and the track had disappeared in most places, so we marched through woods on compass. Arrived at Sommes N151530. Received a message stating Lieutenant Cooper and party at N3346 so decided to join them. Moved south and slept in wood N1351.

14th June: In morning moved to N132513 and then to N126496. Corporal Wood and I made recce of open country intending to move west during night. Received message in evening to say Cooper would pick us up with MT so gave RV N132513 on WT because of shortage of water in present location, and moved to this RV in the evening.

15th June: Rations were getting short and the French had so far approached had received us coldly. Either they thought we were Germans dressed as British or else it was not a Maquis area. Nobody in the party could speak French. Babington, Marson and Furness made recce for food and returned with seed potatoes which had been planted. No transport arrived. We received message in the afternoon to contact Cooper that evening twenty-five miles away. We replied we could not get there.

16th June: Still no transport so we decided to move west at 2100 hrs and advised base. Rained hard and very dark. We saw Very lights and flares so rested in field until dawn.

17th June: Moved at 0430 hrs to N2052. Rained hard. Patrol rested in wood whilst I made recce of village. Went up to sign post in centre of village and the inhabitants who saw me went on as though I was not there. Rolli and I then proceeded to an isolated farm about $1\frac{1}{2}$ miles away, for food. We were made very welcome when the farmer was once certain that we were British. A Jew and his mother were then brought in, having previously left by the back door before we had been allowed in, as they thought we were Germans. He could speak English and was hiding in the farm. His father had been killed by the Germans. He told us it would be safe to move on the roads during the night and the farmer gave us good rations and produced some wine. On our return to the wood we found the rest of our party drinking wine with three farmers who had found them in the wood.

They promised to bring us a meal at 2000 hrs so I decided to stay and move by road during the night. At 2000 hrs a farmer arrived with Maquis truck and BSA combination, and took us to Maquis Jean where we met Lieutenant-Colonel Hastings and Major Fraser. We then marched to Major Fraser's HQ at N2659, arriving at 0010 hrs.

18th June : Still raining and everybody soaked. Cooper and party had also arrived at HQ so both recce parties were safe. Danger, Harrison, Jackson 202 wireless channel were there but were not having a great success. We formed into one station and made contact. We always put our aerial in direction of base station with set nearest base. Whether this is theoretically correct or not we do not know, but in practice it has proved correct because we always obtained contact and immediately the aerial was changed on this site we had good contact. We built shelters or wood and leaves for cover.

19th June: During this period 2 Patrol SAS Phantom 102 link was with Major Fraser to 5th September and A Squadron SAS HQ, so that all our movements will be in his report. On 10th July 202 channel Corporal Danger, Harrison, Jackson went with Captain Wiseman's troop to Dijon area and worked with him until recalled. Corporal Danger was recalled on 11th August to go with Lieutenant-Colonel Mayne and Major Melot to bring in C Squadron. Corporal Danger is still with C Squadron. During period 10th/12th August Rolli took a Jed set with Lieutenant-Colonel Hastings and Lieutenant McCready to recce LG for Dakota.

During the operation the Phantom Patrol maintained its objective, i.e. continuous communications with base. 102 link sent the following number of messages :

June	64	
July	169	No record of messages received kept.
August	199	
September	35	

In addition the patrol manned the Eureka and organised the DZs in A Squadron HQ area.

6th September: The great move home started. The convoy consisted of eighteen civilian cars, two German heavy trucks and six jeeps as protection. We expected to meet German convoys moving east but got through to Joigny without any mishap. Base wanted a WT set to go with Lieutenant McCready to Auxerre airfield for Dakota landings, so 2 patrol remained with him and the rest of A Squadron went on to Orleans under command of Captain Wiseman. The patrol had two cars and spent the night in Joigny.

7th September: Returned to Auxerre with Lieutenant McCready. Received great welcome as we were the first British troops to arrive there. Inspected airfield. There were several FW190s in hangars and at edge of airfield which had been damaged by the Germans before they left. The barracks were not badly damaged. I brought back a map of the airfield and handed it in to the 'I' office at Moor Park.

8th September: Went to airfield intending to stay the night to bring in Dakota but operation was cancelled. Met Englishwoman who was hiding on Polish farm. She said the Germans had treated her better than the French. Received orders to return to base, so set off in the cars and reached Sens where we spent the night.

9th September: Two Peugeots running well. Spent night in Le Mans with Americans who looked after us very well.

10th September: Reached No 60 Transit Camp near Bonyeaux. Received very prompt attention and extra rations because we were SAS troops. Whoever organised the reception of SAS troops in this camp should be complimented.

11th September: We were not allowed to bring cars over so gave them away. Left France in LCI at 1630 hrs, very rough trip.

12th September: Arrived Newhaven 0600 hrs and proceeded to Moor Park where I received the first real shock, i.e. that I had to write a report before going on leave.

CHAPTER FIFTEEN

The Experiences of Denys Brook-Hart, 1939–1945

The most continuous narrative of Phantom experiences came from Captain Denys Brook-Hart.

The events of which I write took place some forty years ago and these notes are based on my memory which may well be at fault in some details. However, if there are errors, at least the overall outline is likely to be substantially correct.

When Mr Neville Chamberlain returned from Munich to wave that little piece of paper I was one who cheered the words 'Peace for our time'. I was twenty-two years old and had a job in the City. There was a good deal of patriotic feeling amongst the young men who were my friends (words like 'duty' and 'loyalty' were not yet debased as they were after the war) and we vied with each other in joining Territorial units or the RNVR – in spite of Mr Chamberlain's soothing attitude, which was belied daily by accelerating events in Europe.

The Queen Victoria's Rifles appealed to my sense of adventure, as that unit described itself as a *corps d'élite* and said that its role would be forward reconnaissance on motor bicycles. So I joined the 2nd Battalion headquarters in Grosvenor Square, spent two annual camps marching across country in Hampshire and many evenings struggling with morse lamps in the Square. John Morgan, then a subaltern, taught the morse lamp.

When war came, I was called up with everyone else and, as an ordinary rifleman, found myself equipped with a very old Lee Enfield .303, and a decrepit laundry van (instead of a gleaming motor bike). Our various duties included 'guarding' the headquarters of Coastal Command at Northwood (against what, I now wonder – especially as we had no ammunition). Eventually in the winter of 1939 I found myself 'guarding' a large heap of coal in the London docks against the advent of German parachutists. It was bitterly cold and the coal heap diminished quite rapidly as we burnt it on fires which roasted our fronts whilst our behinds froze.

One particularly cold night, I was called in front of the Colonel and asked whether I would like to volunteer to join a special unit which would embark on a secret mission to France. Six friends in my company were similarly propositioned, and needless to say we 'volunteered' as a far better alternative to coal dump duties. (I have no idea why I was chosen, as I had not up to this time displayed any visible signs of intelligence.)

We arrived at a Crimean War barracks in Aldershot, I think in January 1940. When assembled I think that the special unit totalled about sixty or eighty officers, NCOs and other ranks, comprising about thirty men from the QVRs, and a similar number from the 12th Lancers, the RN and RAF. We were fairly soon equipped with some Norton motor-cycles and sidecars and Norton solo machines. I was made a Bren-gunner (although I had never before set eyes on the weapon) and this gun was installed on a Motley mounting in a sidecar. Subsequently, I was called up to the War Office one day to take a cup of tea and demonstrate the mounting to Colonel Motley, its inventor. He was a very kind man who was rather disconcerted when I pointed out that it was almost impossible to traverse the gun without knocking off my driver's head – and firing it would be an operation more hazardous to us than the Germans.

At Aldershot, the secret was revealed to us: we were to be the reconnaissance unit for the British Air Striking Force in France, commanded by Air Marshal Barratt (and any other intelligence tasks which seemed appropriate). We were to be based on the Belgian frontier ready to cross and advance through Belgium immediately the cold war unfroze and radio back information about suitable targets for air bombing. If my recollection is chronologically correct, this indicates that a German strike through the Low Countries was anticipated as a possibility at that time. Certainly, the unpreparedness of the French and our politicians now seems strange in view of the role we were preparing to take.

Our CO was Lieutenant-Colonel G. F. Hopkinson, MC ('Hoppy') a small, wiry man, forthright and energetic. He was totally without fear both in Whitehall and in battle. I believe he was employed in the intelligence service before the war and had, I think, been in Persia and Russia. He seemed to be able to get us equipment and privileges at very short notice. He told us that the name of our unit was 'The Hopkinson Mission', code-named 'Phantom'. We proudly sewed the badge – a white 'P' on a black square – on to our right sleeves, and were told not to reveal what it meant, which appeared to be a somewhat paradoxical injunction.

The officers I remember at this time were: Tony Warre, Lord (Charles) Banbury, and John Morgan who was in charge of the QVR element. There was an excellent sergeant whose name I cannot remember; he was a good organiser, fair disciplinarian, and a very civilised man, who more or less held the unit together. (Another strange quirk of memory is that I cannot remember the name of my sidecar driver, although his face and personality remain vividly with me.)

We embarked for France, probably in February, and on arrival in Calais or Dieppe, were astonished to see the dockside piled high with smashed army transport vehicles – the result of amateur army drivers on the then frozen roads of France.

Phantom was stationed in barracks which we shared with some French cavalry at Valenciennes, near the Belgian frontier. The French cavalrymen took little notice of us or we of them.

I cannot remember any training that might have led later to intelligence operations. One preoccupation seemed to be to get the Hopkinson Mission marching in step and at the same rate – the problem being that the QVRs were used to a fast rifleman's pace whilst the navy and air force were hardly used to any pace at all. Apart from vehicle maintenance, I remember a sort of night endurance exercise in the Forêt de Mormal and on frozen roads, one consequence of which was that two of my friends, Riflemen Andrews and Dutta, lost one leg each in motorcycle accidents.

Although the atmosphere in Phantom in those early days was a happy one, the ethics were presumably those of the prewar regular army; for instance, other ranks had no direct communication with the officers and could address them only via an NCO. The officers (with the singular exception of Hoppy) were amateurs, as were the ORs. This period was in direct contrast to the later development of Phantom which, after Dunkirk, grew into a large and highly professional intelligence organisation whose officers and other ranks lived and worked together in closely knit units ('Patrols') or seven or ten men.

Spring came, and the magnolia trees blossomed in the park at Valenciennes. Although we were some way from the area occupied by the BEF, Gracie Fields paid us a visit and sang some of her famous songs. Afterwards, she was photographed with a few of us grouped around a motorcycle (why I was thus honoured is a puzzle, as I had no special qualification). There was some coming and going by officers in civilian clothes between us and the British Embassy in Brussels.

A vivid memory is of a motorcycle trial. I had long had an ambition to be a despatch rider, and in an attempt to prove my ability I wangled the use of a solo machine in a very gruelling endurance test through woods, up the sides of cliffs, through a sea of mud, etc., over a course of some twenty miles. (I remember Hoppy riding like a bat out of hell through the sea of mud.) To my surprise and the amazement of all the others, I came in first – but even after this I was still firmly kept in my job as a Bren-gunner!

Into action: the invasion of Belgium

During the night of 9th/10th May, the Luftwaffe bombed parts of the town and at first light we moved from full alert to frenzied activity. As an impressive and noisy motorized column we crossed the Belgian frontier at about 7 a.m., the first British to do so, I believe. No problems with the Customs – and to begin with, flowers and cheers from the Belgian populace all along the route. Soon the civilians disappeared, and we saw airfields strewn with burnt-out aircraft, bombed during the night.

Phantom's activities during the next three weeks seem in recollection like a series of small sepia-tinted photographs. As I have said, our principal task was supposed to be to locate suitable enemy targets for the RAF and radio their whereabouts. Since, as a matter of history, the German panzer divisions swept through the Low Countries and the Luftwaffe dive-bombed and strafed the roads and refugees continuously, I doubt whether we contributed much information which was not already apparent. In any case, I don't remember setting eyes on a British aircraft. (Indeed, we saw none when we were on the beaches near Dunkirk and this was a source of great bitterness amongst the men – although I now understand that our criticism was misplaced and that the RAF were fighting desperately in areas unseen by us.)

However, I believe that we did handle a lot of information about British troop movements, etc., which proved of great value to the HQ of the BEF in the chaotic conditions of that short campaign.

I remember advancing to the Albert Canal; going out on some individual reconnaissances with the sergeant, or sometimes just with another motorcyclist, to see if bridges were blown; finding a main line of anti-tank obstacles completely deserted (a tarpaulin lay beside the road and when I lifted one corner I found two bodies beneath it);

sheltering in woods with not much idea where the Germans were coming from; going to Cassel (?), 'the hill of cats', in order to escort Lord Gort from his HQ to a safer location (the enemy was supposed to be coming up the road). Lying behind a hedge with my Bren gun and John Morgan and seeing little enemy figures running in the distant fields. The bombing was continuous, and from one farmhouse bivouac I loosed off a couple of magazines in pure frustration at a German aircraft – only to get a ticking off from Tony Warre for wasting ammunition. I expect he was right – and at least he crossed the communication barrier between officer and rifleman!

Finally, we started to draw back to the beaches, my motorcycle combination towing another broken-down one by means of two or three rifle slings. As the Norton sidecars – fully laden with two men, Bren gun, ammunition and our kits – could only do a maximum of 20 mph flat out on level ground, the progress of our towing party was between 5 and 10 mph.

During the week before Dunkirk, Hoppy was busy volunteering Phantom for the special forces hastily thrown together to try to stem the German onslaught; 'Petforce', 'Macforce', etc. I cannot remember much positive action in all the chaos, but his spirit remained undaunted. He broke his wrist or forearm, but continued to ride either pillion or a solo motorcycle with one hand – he was an outstandingly tough and courageous man.

One day I went foraging for food with my driver and we came across an abandoned truck stacked high with mail. One of the first parcels I saw was addressed to me and contained a birthday cake (for 1st June). This perhaps must be one of the tallest coincidence stories of the war.

Eventually we arrived on the beaches at La Panne. We were set to guarding road approaches and turning away stragglers and units of the French army – a tricky task. A bomb fell straight through a building where I was on cross-road duty, and arrived unexploded in the basement from whence a Belgian rushed out with half his dinner plate, which he said the bomb had smashed!

Hoppy then volunteered Phantom for rearguard duties, which offer was not accepted (to the relief of many of us). On 30th May we took all our vehicles and ammunition a few miles eastwards along the coast and dumped nearly everything. Some shots were fired into petrol tanks, but the dump was not set on fire. For some reason my sidecar outfit was spared, and we had a last drive along the beach, first towards the Germans and then back to La Panne.

We sat amongst the sand dunes being bombed, and I remember a Bofors gun firing until its barrel glowed. A pier of vehicles was built into into the sea, but proved ineffective.

During the afternoon and night of 31st May we were told to look after ourselves and 'make our own way home'. There were only wrecked boats in the water, and not much chance of swimming out to off-lying destroyers. However, at about 2300 hrs, another rifleman and I and Charles Banbury found a small swamped dinghy and we paddled off shore. Charles Banbury urged me to bale out with my tin hat – request I ignored as I had stored two bars of chocolate on my head underneath the helmet.

We were picked up by the destroyer *London* (?) and amongst a crammed mass of other rescued men were landed at about 1100 hours on 1st June at Dover harbour. Smartly turned-out NCOs on the dock-side regarded us ragged tramps with hostile disdain and told us to throw our weapons on to a great pile which had already formed.

We were loaded into a train which wandered over southern England until it reached Shrivenham. En route, at every stop, we were plied with tea and buns by kind ladies who evidently regarded us as young heroes (to our genuine surprise).

From Shrivenham, we were sent home on a week's leave.

We were called back to Lechdale and Hoppy had arranged for us to become a mobile column with the 'Ironsiders' – supposedly to repel the imminent German cross-channel invasion. I achieved my ambition of becoming a despatch rider and was given a new solo machine. Two of my DR friends and I were sent off to take supposedly urgent des-patches to some destination near Chatham. Naturally, we rode at top speeds – 70 mph around some corners, with sparks striking from our exhausts scraping the road surface as we leaned into the bends. (Like many volunteers to the QVRs, my two companions had been fanatic peacetime motor cycle fans and trials riders.)

Not far short of our destination, I hit a slewed tank at about 60 mph and spent the next six months in Chatham Hospital. The first choice was to take my leg off, but fortunately a Canadian ortho-paedic surgeon became interested, and after some three or four opera-tions at monthly intervals my leg was saved. However, the effects and pain have remained with me all my life, and certainly had some bear-ing on my subsequent service career – obviously I would not have been much good either as an infantryman or a parachutist.

The 'new' Phantom

My return to Phantom must have been about December 1940 or January 1941. They were headquartered on Richmond Hill and I found a very different organisation to the one I had left. The new Phantom was much enlarged, organised into three squadrons, each squadron sub-divided into four patrols. A patrol consisted of an officer, a sergeant or corporal radio operator, another radio operator, two drivers and two or three despatch riders. Vehicles were an armoured scout car, a 15 cwt truck and motor cycles. I think we had two radios – one in the scout car and one in the truck, but I may be mistaken.

The new organisation, called No 1 GHQ Reconnaissance Unit, was entirely drawn from army units ranging over the Guards, the Cavalry, the Royal Armoured Corps, the county infantry regiments, etc. There was also a large section of Royal Signallers ('Siggies'), and a REME section. New Phantom was from this time onwards a highly efficient and professional intelligence service, whose function was to supply detailed and specific information to army commanders, the Chiefs of Staff, or the War Cabinet, as appropriate in different circumstances. Later, special squadrons were developed for special tasks such as working with the French Maquis, assault, and combined operations. Some patrols also worked with SOE or the SAS. The new organisation must have been impressive, because the Duke of Kent arrived one day in Richmond Park to inspect us – another of Hoppy's achievements.

My squadron, commanded by Miles Reid, was sent off to Greece, where most of them were either killed or captured. Due to my limping disability (and it is a fair question to ask why I had not been discharged unfit from the army) I was left behind.

Since the QVRs were supposed to be an officer-producing regiment, I found that some of my riflemen friends had departed for OCTUs whilst others were spread far and wide in the field. I had been very happy as an ordinary rifleman, but now decided that I had better start climbing a bit higher. I got on to an NCOs course run by Havard Gunn and emerged as a lance-corporal. The taste of petty power enddowed by one stripe must have gone to my head and in the following four months I went through every rank until I reached the dizzy position of Squadron Sergeant Major.

For some reason, at that time we had an RSM (RSM Mickie, from the Life Guards) and he and I used to visit his friends in the Knightsbridge barracks and at Windsor Castle. I don't think he had many duties in an organisation like Phantom and I believe he left after a fairly short period of time.

We established a training camp in the Maidenhead area near Cliveden, the Astor residence. Major Reggie Hills was keen that we should get some exercise (as we were usually driving around in our vehicles) and I remember some marches through country lanes with Reggie leading the column in a small pick-up van from the back of which stirring marches were played at us through a loudspeaker.

At Richmond, the operations room was in the charge of Captain John Wrightson, who took the job quite seriously. One day I entered the operations room after knocking on the door and hearing no reply. The room appeared to be empty, until Wrightson sprang from behind the door.

'Sergeant, why the hell didn't you salute?'

'Sorry, sir, I thought the room was empty.'

'Well, bloody well salute the room in future!'

For a week after that, sergeants would be seen saluting rooms and corridors, to the mystification of those officers who caught sight of them.

For a few months I was David Niven's squadron sergeant when he had his squadron based on Stourhead House in Wiltshire. Niven's personality was one which attracted and created amusing and unusual incidents. I remember several, one of which concerned pigeons. Phantom kept a pigeon loft in St James's Park, just near the War Office, under the command of Corporal Starr (later to become Colonel Starr, DSO, MC, Croix de Guerre, etc. – a most distinguished intelligence officer). We had some carrier pigeons at Stourhead and one day Niven wrote out a message and sent a bird winging for London. It so happened that a lady member of the Royal family had been invited to inspect our carrier pigeon facilities and she and Niven's bird arrived at St James's much at the same time. This was thought to be a lucky demonstration of our efficiency. The capsule was removed from the bird's leg and handed to HRH who opened it and read out the following message in Niven's hand: 'I have been a very naughty girl and so Daddy has sent me straight home!'

Life was very pleasant in the sergeants' mess and out on exercises. However, someone said I'd better be an officer, so off I went to OCTU, first in Wales and then on to an assault course in Scotland – perhaps the worst six months in my life for misery and endurance.

At the first OCTU at Barmouth in Wales, the cadets were treated with contempt and iron discipline. Having survived some three months of this, the OCTU closed down – because there was no fighting going on, the OCTUs had produced a surplus of officers. So we started all over again at Dunbar in Scotland. Here we were badgered from dawn to dusk by little men in kilts, made to swim half frozen rivers and struggle up snow-covered mountains with live ammunition being fired at us (one instructor blew his hand off with a grenade). I found myself able to cope with all this in spite of my gammy leg, which took some concealing; however, the most important part of our training appeared to be rifle drill and square bashing – and here my leg gave me problems. Stamping my feet invariably made me a split second later than my companions and the sergeant major got fed up with me. One day he called me out of the ranks for an eyeball confrontation.

'For Christ's sake, sir, can't you stamp your feet like everyone else?'

'No, Sergeant Major.'

'Why the hell not, Sir?'

I explained the matter briefly. The Sergeant Major's face turned purple and his eyes bulged horribly. After a few moments whilst he breathed heavily and stared at me, he said: 'You'd better get back into the ranks, Sir.' I hoped he meant the place I'd just vacated in the front rank of the parade. Anyway, from then on he turned a blind eye to my imperfect drilling.

When the time approached for 'passing out' some officer asked which regiment I wanted to join. I wanted to re-join Phantom, but as they refused to believe such an organisation existed they told me not to be stupid and to name a regiment. I said 'The East Surreys' as my home happened to be in Surrey at that time. I put up the rather decorative badges of the East Surreys and there was some surprise at my OCTU when a War Office telegram arrived saying that I was promoted 1st Lieutenant and posted wef immediately to the now re-named GHQ Liaison Regiment (Phantom) at Richmond.

I spent some months in Richmond (which brings my narrative up to about the autumn of 1941) and remember that the Phantom duty officer was the final link, amongst other responsibilities, for giving the code word to set off the 'London docks on fire' simulation display in the park to entice the German bombers to drop their loads there rather than on London. In consequence, Richmond had rather more than its share of incendiary bombs that winter.

Another recollection I have of Richmond was the day I was told to march the whole unit, several hundred officers and men, down Richmond Hill to the cinema at the bottom to see a film called *Bachelor Mother* starring Ginger Rogers and David Niven. Niven, of course, had arranged this treat. Presumably I was detailed for this chore under the illusion that I was a drill expert, having recently come from OCTU. We arrived at the bottom of the hill and I decided to take Phantom by a short cut round to the back of the cinema. Unfortunately, I didn't know that the short cut ended in a six-foot brick wall – so we had the classic situation of the men in front being pressed on to the wall whilst those behind marched merrily on.

Phantom in Northern Ireland

Soon, I was sent to join a squadron stationed at Lisburn in Northern Ireland. The CO was, I think, Major Terry Watt. Wearing my East Surrey badges (with a beret) I waited in a Belfast bar to rendezvous with one of the Phantom officers. Unfortunately, the East Surreys were then stationed not far away and a keen-eyed officer in the bar soon addressed some questions to me which I obviously could not answer. Result : escorted to the battalion HQ where I was interrogated by the Adjutant for several hours until telephone calls eventually established that I was not an impostor or a spy, and I was then allowed to go on to Lisburn – feeling under something of a cloud for wearing the badges of a regiment I had never served in.

I cannot remember what we were supposed to be doing in Northern Ireland apart from some horse riding. Whatever it was did not last very long, and I think the squadron was disbanded.

At Winchester

My next memory is of joining the squadron commanded by 'Washy' Hibbert, a very fine officer whose only vice was to rise at 6 a.m. daily, leap over two or three coils of barbed wire and run several miles before breakfast – an activity which the officers were supposed to follow. He didn't drink or smoke, but always became jollier than any of the drinkers at a mess party.

Phantom then consisted of six squadrons, each commanded by a major with a captain as second-in-command. The squadrons usually consisted of six patrols, each patrol having one first lieutenant, a sergeant or corporal, and four or five other ranks with specialist duties. On active service, one squadron was allocated to an army; the squadron HQ usually being located at or near Army HQ and the patrols sent out on specific tasks or to specific areas or divisions. My own role was as a patrol officer and I remained one until the end of the war, retaining more or less the same men with me, taking my patrol in situ to another squadron when required, and working almost continuously out in the field. Thus, I am qualified only to talk about Phantom operations in the field – an absorbing but often lonely task. Colonel

Hopkinson went away to become brigadier, commanding one of the first air landing brigades. After Hoppy, COs seemed (to me) to be unnecessary in Phantom – they were rarely seen or heard of by patrol officers, anyway, and the squadron COs seemed sufficient in themselves.

The patrols by now had exchanged the small armoured scout car for a 'White' armoured car – a lumbering vehicle which housed the main radio; not much use for reconnaissance, and I invariably used the jeep. My sergeant and No 1 radio operator was Vic Stump – with me for most of the real war. The No 2 radio operator was Trooper Parris, 'White' armoured car driver: Trooper Whiting. Dispatch riders: Rifleman Metcalf and Trooper Matthews (known as the heavenly twins) – old friends of mine from the QVR days. I can't remember the name of my jeep driver, but I do remember his capacity for driving at high speed into every pothole in sight. As a close-knit little group we worked well together, free from over-irksome discipline and free in the field from the control of anyone except the requirements sent to us by our squadron HQ. I think Hoppy had originally arranged that Phantom was 'responsible' to MI9 – I'm not sure about the MI number – and thus could gain many privileges and equipment whilst remaining uncommitted to any army formation.

'Washy' Hibbert's squadron was located at Headbourne Worthy, just north of Winchester. The second-in-command was John Dulley.

Working with airborne forces

During this time the squadron cooperated in a number of exercises on Salisbury Plain with Hoppy's air landing brigade. We also spent some time in Whitley bombers and taking patrols up in small gliders. I think the small glider was called a Horsa. It appeared to consist mainly of plywood and wire. My men sat, packed in, side by side in the fuselage, whilst I sat next to the pilot who appeared to operate the machine with a broom handle. Landings consisted of skidding along the grass until friction overcame the speed. In action, the men were supposed to smash their way out through the side of the fuselage. Lord Halifax came to watch us, the rain poured down, and a glider slightly out of control skidded madly past him and stopped just short of a hangar wall.

Hopkinson also arranged a demonstration of an airborne assault. Troops were dropped from Whitleys at a very low level (some parachutes had no time to open, others became entangled with each other). My patrol was located on a hill top near Hopkinson and a party of

VIPs as the drop took place – then a low level attack by aircraft dropping phosphorus bombs put us and the VIPs flat on our faces. Hoppy loved the smell of danger and always thought everyone else would like a whiff of it.

In the autumn and winter of 1942 we were based at Penn Wood, Buckinghamshire, and it was here that I became interested in training my patrol as an assault patrol, i.e. for use in combined operations roles, or for landings.

Whilst we were exercising with 6th Airborne Division, the ill-fated Dieppe raid took place. Four Phantom patrols took part in this operation and established the value of our particular brand of intelligence work in an assault role.

By this time (the autumn of 1942) the Desert War had been taken over by General Montgomery and Operation Torch was in the offing. Monty refused to use Phantom in the desert – probably because we had the ability to radio directly to the UK and therefore information could have gone directly from the battlefield to London: a notion which would be contrary to Monty's policy. Instead he used the J and Y Services fairly extensively and effectively, and he was also supplied with some key information from the Enigma operation.

To North Africa

Torch took place and E Squadron, under Mervyn Vernon of the Life Guards (2nd i/c Hugh Fraser), was operating with First Army in North Africa. In January 1943, Vernon sent a request for two more patrols and Pat Brawn's and mine were selected to go. On arrival in Algiers we found no arrangements for us to join the squadron. We eventually made our way to Army HQ where Robin Baring was in charge of our 'Anchor' operations. At the beginning of February my patrol moved up into the mountains and I spent my time training them in unusual radio exercises, the use of explosives, etc. (One Sunday whilst the local army unit was at Church Service, we blew up the village manure heap with gun cotton charges. A messy demonstration which was not popular – but it showed the extent of my frustration by then.)

Although Mervyn Vernon had specifically asked for us, he apparently made no attempt to use us when we arrived. (Early in March we heard that K Squadron, commanded by Tony Warre, had arrived in Algiers – but I cannot remember whether the squadron was actively deployed.) In due course, by pestering, I got a bit nearer the action and found myself helping Hugh Fraser at 18 Army Group HQ. I was there for about four weeks but it was not really my idea of active service. Besides which I had all my kit stolen in my sleep by an Arab, including my revolver (attached to my wrist by a lanyard) and special security pass. I told Hugh that I was fed up with not being up front and early in May I was despatched with a patrol to join the 5th Indian Division.

We arrived, after a top speed journey, at 4th Indian Division Advance HQ the afternoon before the final assault on Tunis. As I retported to the G1 I caught a glimpse of myself in a shaving mirror in his caravan – coated with grey-white dust with two staring eyes peering out.

The 4th Indian Division had its HQ in front of their own front line – which seemed rather unusual – and in the low hills and dunes just behind us were some 400 25-pounder guns. At 2200 hours they started their barrage. The noise was so great that it was impossible to think or hear anything except this thundering, tearing sound. The Gurkhas advanced behind the barrage with their gleaming knives handy – and I was assured they would be busy cutting German throats.

The main attack started at 0500 hours. The battle went well (all objectives were taken) and I was very pleased to find my patrol functioning efficiently and smoothly after so many years of preparatory training. The information went back in a steady stream – whether anybody used it effectively was a question I never really asked myself at any time until after the war.

We advanced through burning tanks and abandoned enemy trenches. The sun beat down and I remember seeing what I thought was the shadow of a man spreadeagled on the flattened desert – in fact it was a German soldier who had been run over by so many vehicles that his body was like a cardboard cutout.

I stopped my patrol by the side of a track where I could observe the battle on the plain before Tunis. Presently, General Tuker, commanding 4th Indian Division, came along in his jeep. He stopped and got out.

'Well, young man, what do you think is going to happen now – what's your appreciation?' (He'd been told by the G1 that I was an intelligence officer.)

I said I thought the Germans would retreat into the Cap Bon peninsula and try to evacuate as many of their troops as possible.

'Well, I'm afraid you're wrong,' said the General. 'They're going to hold Tunis and that will be the next battle.' Well, it so happened that Tunis fell the next day and the Germans retreated into the Cap Bon peninsula. The next time I saw General Tuker was at the Victory Parade in Tunis, but he didn't speak to me.

The 4th Indian Division had completed their task and I was ordered to join the 1st Armoured Division, Eighth Army. It was not clear to me, for some reason, that to reach them necessitated a journey through German-held territory (the enemy still held the ground between the two divisions). Anyway, my patrol entered the 1st Armoured area via their forward outposts! I find it difficult to understand why I did not have this information at my fingertips; perhaps I thought the long route round would be too long.

There was a lot of useful information we were able to send back from the Cap Bon peninsula when my patrol got amongst the surrendering Germans, and I felt elated to at last be in active operations and taking part in a major victory.

Fighting ceased in North Africa on 13th May 1943.

Winston Churchill at Carthage

After the defeat of the German army at Tunis, Mervyn Vernon's E Squadron (and Tony Warre's K Squadron) assembled in the grounds of a large house overlooking the blue Mediterranean at a peacetime millionaire's resort called Sidi bou Said. Here we were supposed to rest and reorganise. There was also a Court of Enquiry into my stolen security pass, but I cannot remember the outcome. From here one day we all trooped to the nearby ruins of Carthage and watched an aircraft circle in the sky, land at the airfield and deliver to us Winston Churchill accompanied by Anthony Eden. Churchill told the assembled troops that they had just won a great victory, but that this was only the beginning, etc. He thanked the soldiers and made a great impression with his famous 'V' sign and big cigar.

After some weeks at Sidi bou Said, the squadron went off to camp at Bugeaud, in a cork forest about 3,000 feet up in the mountains west of Bizerta. From this period I remember Hugh ('Tam') Williams, Mickey Meade and Mark Mainwaring – very fine officers who became great friends of mine – Johnny Mackintosh, Percy Pennant, Norman Reddaway (Adjutant), Harmar Bagnall and Hugh Fraser. Apart from training, a certain boredom set in and much backgammon was played, often for high stakes. There was an old casino on the mountain top which sheltered a few WRNS who were resting. One night Hugh Fraser decided to resuscitate the casino and run the roulette table. Unfortunately, he worked out the odds incorrectly – so that it was impossible for the punters to lose, and word quickly got around so that the table was soon surrounded with joyful winners.

In mid-June King George VI passed by on the coast road, with General Anderson sitting beside him. Percy Pennant made a 'V' and 'G.R.' in wild flowers and displayed it on a mound of rubble. I'm not sure whether the king saw this tribute.

The Italian episode

The 6th Airborne Division invaded Sicily and in the evening of 9th September 1943 E Squadron received a message from Major-General Hopkinson saying our services were urgently needed. Hoppy never forgot Phantom and always set a high store by the information we could provide.

We packed up and made haste to Bizerta. We were to embark on the cruiser *Aurora* and it turned out that only a limited number of vehicles could go with us. This meant that patrols had to be 'canibalised' and utilise less vehicles than hitherto.

We steamed full speed out of Bizerta harbour at sunset. As I watched the sun touching the North African mountains I said to myself, 'That's one place I don't want to see again!' The dust, the flies, the boredom and the generally derelict atmosphere of the villages were not romantic and were insufficiently offset by the sea and mountains. The so-called Arabs of these parts, too, were a miserable lot.

Our flat-out cruise brought up to Taranto which had been surrendered by the Italians – who had by now capitulated to the Allies and were technically with us rather than against us. A perimeter north of Taranto was lightly held by our airborne forces, but the main German forces were facing westwards towards our principal invasion army and in consequence we were coming in 'behind them'. We were landed in the dark on 12th September and assembled in an olive grove.

My next recollection is of entering the town of Bari – quite an important port – and finding the HQ of the Italian 19th Corps. Since they had only just that minute stopped being our enemies, the atmosphere was a strange one, to say the least. I was received by a nervous general who assured me that there were many German Tiger tanks just down the road – what were the strength of my forces to hold them off? I skated over the fact that I had only five or six men outside the building and assured him that a large column of British tanks was on its way (which of course was entirely untrue). Then there was some sort of a signing ceremony and I have a feeling that I accepted responsibility for the City of Bari on behalf of King George VI. I don't suppose it mattered.

Hugh Fraser was now commanding our Phantom force (Mervyn Vernon had flown to the UK for some purpose). He set up a headquarters in a vineyard a few miles south of Bari and from there we conducted our reconnaissance and intelligence operations behind the German lines.

We would go carefully through the countryside, chiefly on small roads, gleaning information from villages and expecting to encounter Germans at any cross roads. A railway ran through the vineyards and I found the men in the signal boxes and small stations a great help – they could phone through to colleagues up the line and find out much about German strengths and dispositions. I also located a sub-telephone exchange belonging to the Italian water company, and we were able to obtain useful telephone reports from quite a wide area.

The ambush at Trani had a strange aftermath.* Elements of the Eighth Army were landed on this coast and my patrol joined 5th Recce Unit in a normal Phantom role. We were thus engaged from about 22nd September until 3rd October, when our advance became bogged down before Termoli in rain and mud. On 3rd October, the Special Services Brigade landed at Termoli (a Phantom patrol under Tony Crawley-Boevey with them) and I went back to SHQ near Trani.

Meanwhile, as I discovered later, the Germans had not believed it possible that a British patrol could have penetrated to Trani in September and they accused the Italians of killing their men – in spite of the fact that we had abandoned two motorcycles, two tommy guns and some small kit, which they must have found. As a result, 200 civilians were taken as hostages to the German headquarters at Barletta and . were to be shot. The Archbishop of Trani, Seigneur Francesco Petronelli, took the gold cross from his cathedral and walked bare-footed with it the twenty miles to Barletta to see the German commandant. The Archbishop offered his own life in exchange for the hostages. The German commandant was convinced by the sincerity of the Archbishop and released the hostages and allowed the Archbishop to go free.

Of course, I knew nothing of this until I went on 8th October to the cemetery north of Trani to thank the Italian priest who had saved our lives. He told me that the King of Italy was arriving next day to decorate the Archbishop for his bravery. The following day I attended the ceremony and afterwards went to the Archbishop's palace to give him my thanks and receive his blessing.

* See pages 74–5.

During this brief Italian foray by Phantom, we also worked with the PPA (Popski's Private Army) and the SAS who were operating in that area.

Towards mid-October, the Eighth Army wanted Phantom 'out' and the J Service 'in', rather to Hugh Fraser's dismay. Hugh asked me if I would like to spent the winter up in the mountains with the partisans, but I don't like cold climates and saw little purpose to this proposal. In any case I wanted to take part in the invasion of Northern France, which was now in the offing.

On 21st October, Mickey Meade and Tam Williams were blown up on a mine en route to Naples. They had a lucky escape, but Corporal Rose, their driver, was killed. I got permission from Hugh to join K Squadron, and at dawn on 22nd October I hitched a lift in a Dakota to Tunis and thence on to Bizerta and Bone. Julian Fane was then OC K Squadron, and on arrival he promoted me to captain.

K Squadron left North Africa at the end of November 1943, and we were at home for Christmas.

Overlord: the invasion of France

The Allied campaign in north-west Europe, which culminated in the defeat of the German armies, was the period of the war in which Phantom played its most important role. We had about 150 intelligence officers and 1,500 other ranks deployed, covering the entire operations from the Normandy landings until the enemy surrendered.

During this time, my patrol was in more or less continuous operation from D Day, and through France, Belgium, Holland and Germany until we met the Russians in the Baltic near Schwein. Our final wartime task was in Denmark in connection with the surrender of the enemy forces in that country.

In consequence, my patrol was involved in a large number of events a description of which would be too lengthy in these notes. I have therefore selected a few from a patrol 'War Diary' which I have recently found amongst some old papers, and these are dealt with as briefly as possible.

In January 1944 I joined F Squadron (OC Jakie Astor) at Frimley near Camberley. Training was now started to fit us for the forthcoming invasion. About March, the squadron was given the task of parachuting into France to help the resistance movement there. As I had serious doubts about my ability to perform in parachuting operations with my dud leg, I asked that my patrol should be transferred to a D Day assault role, which was my ambition at that time in any case. I therefore went with my patrol to A Squadron, commanded by Dennis Russell – probably the most efficient and outstanding squadron commander of those days.

The 3rd British Division was ordered to carry out the assault at the eastern end of the Normandy beaches, and the 6th Airborne Division was to land on their extreme east (left) flank in the area of the river Orne and the Caen canal during the night of 5th/6th June.

The Phantom intention was for my patrol to land as close to H Hour on D Day as possible, and radio information back to SHQ Dover for direct transmission by secure land line to Invasion HQ at Portsmouth.

The first problem I had to overcome was that Woodrow Wyatt,* i/c loading LCTs, 3rd British Division, did not see why an odd collection such as us, who did not belong to his division, should be given priority to get ashore. After some pressure had been brought to bear, we secured our place on LCT 372 (commanded by Lieutenant Victor Newton) together with two secret weapon tanks with excessively long barrels intended, I think, to blast strongpoints.

We set off across the Channel on the night of 5th June, the advanced forces of 6th Airborne passing overhead. Radio silence was imposed until H Hour: 0730 hrs 6th June. We opened a listening watch 2½ hrs before H hour, by which time we were lying off the beaches. We picked up our first message at H+18 minutes, followed by a further six intercepts by 0832 hrs. At 0845 hrs I got my first message back to SHQ Dover, and I believe this was the first information received at Invasion HQ direct from the beaches.

Unfortunately, 6th Airborne Division was not heard all day; their radios were not working effectively and in any case they were engaged in desperate fighting.

Due to intense enemy fire, much of it from the Merville battery which was not yet out of action, my LCT found difficulty in getting into the beach. Also, many of the obstacles had not been cleared. We also had a last minute hitch when a rating got sliced up in the gear for dropping the bows. Anyway, we got ashore at 1250 hrs and my last glimpse of the LCT showed her on fire and drifting on to some obstacles.

(I remember the deafening noise from all sorts of gunfire and bombs, and the performance of our two radio operators both on this

* Later a prominent Labour MP.

and many other occasions deserved very high commendation. Very often during this campaign the operators had to decipher high-speed morse through a mass of static interference in addition to extreme physical discomfort and excessive external noise, and often at night with only a very dim light to work by.)

Our landing point was between Ouistreham and Lion-sur-mer (code-named Queen, Red). The houses along the beach were on fire (no sign of the beach marshals with flags who had directed us in the dress-rehearsal in England). We moved inland through a minefield being cleared by flails, along an open road where my armoured car ran over some bicycles belonging to infantry sheltering in the ditch from machine gun fire, and reached advanced HQ 3rd Division in a wood at 1600 hrs.

On 7th June, due to lack of communications with 6th Airborne, I went by jeep to Ranville, passing on the way a truck with a few Germans – who were as startled as I was. (A large cast-iron Crucifix at the fork road to Ranville was blown to pieces just as we passed. When I returned to this spot some years after the war, I found the pieces carefully laid at the foot of a new wooden Cross.)

I found Major General Gale, impeccably dressed and cool as a cucumber, and he gave me a clear and complete exposition of his situation.

Due to difficulties with the 6th Airborne radio, my patrol kept up a shuttle service between them and advanced 3rd British HQ (a distance of about ten miles) until John Mackenzie was sent to Ranville with a Phantom patrol. Mackenzie's radio was then not heard by our control, so I sent Vic Stump to tell him I would pick up and re-transmit his messages. Vic was blown off his motor cycle by a shell near the Bénouville bridge but hitch-hiked the rest of the way. When I went myself at 2300 hrs to 6th Airborne, I found that John Mackenzie had burnt his code-books, because the Germans had attacked to within 200 yards of his HQ and he expected to be over-run. I mention these incidents to illustrate the problems of effective communication in an assault operation.

In spite of the physical difficulties around us, the whole Phantom network operated with amazing efficiency and the value of our information was soon appreciated by the commanders in the field. On 11th June we received this message: 'From Chief of Staff 21 Army Group to all ranks Phantom. Deep appreciation your work.'

On the same day, the 3rd Division Intelligence Summary included the following items: 'Disappointment has naturally been felt at the

BBC's failure to mention this division as being in the forefront of the assault . . . (however) the division has been specially mentioned in another connection. The Phantom officer at this HQ has been congratulated from Army HQ on the speed and accuracy of the reports he has sent back.'

Thus, it seemed that many years of training were well vindicated.

I have already mentioned the coolness and competence of our radio operators, upon whom the effectiveness of a Phantom patrol's work finally depended. It is worth noting that in the first six days of 'Overlord' my two operators handled 251 messages, of which 87 were 'inwards' to us and 64 were 'outwards' from my patrol. In the following three weeks we handled approximately 130 messages a week, which was about the average thereafter. All inward messages had to be decoded and all outward messages encoded – in itself a tedious task requiring meticulous attention in order to achieve accuracy. Coding was done from a one-time numerical pad – said to produce an unbreakable cipher. Our first week's out messages alone required over 4,000 groups of four digits each – and if this figure is multiplied by the number of Phantoms in the field, the magnitude of morse and code traffic at our HQ can be imagined.

In addition to our radio reports, when SHQ was within a reasonable distance, i.e. not more than forty or fifty miles away, we would send a DR at least once at the end of each day with a complete written report on the situation in our area.

It may also be seen that one's time was fairly well occupied for about eighteen hours in every twenty-four. Apart from information gathering and personal reconnaissance, intelligence messages had to be prepared and coded almost on an hourly basis; in addition, after breaking out of the bridgehead we were almost constantly on the move.

Our reconnaissance during the campaign in the bridgehead included observation of the Merville battery from the top of the Ouistreham lighthouse and, after the mass air bombing of Caen, a visit to the 600 women and children sheltering in the cathedral there.

The lack of effective signals communication from 6th Airborne Division must have pointed up the value of Phantom in those early days. For instance, on 7th June (D+1) my patrol received an urgent request from G1 Army asking for information about Airborne locations and which bridges over the river Dives were still intact. This request was made at 1025 hours. At 1415 hours I was able to send a full report from General Gale, having visited him and obtained a complete picture.

According to the Patrol War Diary, a 'quiet day' (on 22nd June) included: '6th Airborne Division ammunition dump hit hard by shellfire', 'LCT loaded with ammunition exploded on beach' and, most sadly, one Phantom killed and two others badly injured by shellfire at SHQ.

On 24th I complained in the War Diary about the difficulty in obtaining lead pencils, as nobody would take the responsibility to supply them!

About 26th June we moved to 29th Armoured Brigade for an attempted breakout from the bridgehead. On 7th July we joined 185 Brigade for the assault on Caen, which was preceded by a bombardment by 600 Flying Fortresses. On 15th July we moved to 277 Brigade for the attack on Evrecy.

At the beginning of August we jointed 53rd Division for the battle of Falaise. A J Section under Geoffrey Lucas was added to my patrol and the first bonus arising from this was that we were able to stop our own gunners firing on 7th Armoured Division who had advanced rapidly and were out of touch with their flanks.

By 1st September we had crossed the river Seine near Rouen (French and American troops had entered Paris on 24th August). Operations were so fluid that at the request of the divisional G1 (POS) I took a spotter plane and flew back to Army HQ to get a clear picture of surrounding formations. By 8th September we reached Antwerp and in the following days I was able to liaise with the White Army (the Belgian resistance movement) who provided much valuable information.

Operation Market Garden: Arnhem

On 15th September the 101st and 82nd US and 1st British Airborne Divisions were dropped by parachute into Holland for Operation Market Garden (later known as the Battle of Arnhem). There was a big flap at Phantom RHQ as the Colonel had promised to let Queen Wilhelmina know the first firm news of this operation so that she could call upon the Dutch people to rise.

On 16th September the Nijmegen bridge was secured intact but the situation at Arnhem was reported obscure and not so good. I was asked by Dennis Russell if I would like to take my patrol up to Arnhem to find out what was going on. (Neville Hay, Phantom, had dropped with 1st Airborne Division and Reggie Hills was with Air Corps HQ, but information was not coming through satisfactorily due to obvious difficulties.)

My patrol left SHQ on the morning of 19th September equipped with a new Canadian No 9 transmitter. The Guards Armoured Division was making a drive towards Eindhoven in Holland and our progress was slow at first. By 1700 hrs my patrol had reached the centre of Eindhoven when we were stopped by Dutch civilians who told us that German tanks were coming down the road. We pulled into a side street and the patrol took up defensive positions whilst I went forward on a motorcycle to reconnoitre. I could not get further than the outskirts of the town and therefore returned to the patrol and we immediately came under continuous air attack from 2000 to 2100 hours. The house behind which we were sheltering was hit and the streets were blocked by burning petrol and ammunition lorries. We went back through the town trying to find ambulances for the wounded, and we turned back a further convoy of ammunition and petrol wagons attempting to enter the burning town.

We went into a field on the edge of a wood and were told by SHQ to withdraw south. This was not possible, so we stayed where we were and next day made a dash for 101st Airborne Division, eluding the Germans en route and arriving at 2130 hours.

On 22nd September we reached I Airborne Corps at Nijmegen (Reggie Hills assisted by Springett Demetriadi). At this time, the Phantom radio link with Neville Hay was the only contact with 1st Airborne Division at Arnhem.

On 23rd September, I took a jeep and motorcycle across the Nijmegen bridge which was intact but under accurate shellfire. By getting off the road and driving along the tops of dykes we were able to reach the Polish Parachute Brigade at Driel. We found the situation of the 1st Parachute Brigade to be desperate. The enemy were in strength at Elat, nearly behind us, and firing everything including 88 mm guns. We eventually got back to Nijmegen to report. On the following day we returned to Driel. By this time rain was pouring down. There was a lot of noise and the Poles were concentrating on defending themselves against great odds. We transmitted from a waterlogged ditch, but after a time our radio packed up and my operator collapsed from shellshock.

We went back to Nijmegen once more, replaced both the set and the operator and returned under cover of darkness to Homoet where we set ourselves up in a barn. From here we established radio contact with Neville Hay on the other side of the river Rhine and from the night of 24th to 26th were able to report the evacuation of survivors from the Arnhem side of the river.

In the various post-war accounts of the Arnhem operation, there has been much criticism concerning the lack of effective signals communication between the units involved, the unsuitability and ineffectiveness of the radio sets provided, etc. Indeed it was said in Christopher Hibbert's book *The Battle of Arnhem* (page 137) that: 'The only sets which had any sort of link with the outside world were the BBC war correspondents' set and the set operated by the Independent (sic) Phantom reporting unit.' * Certainly, during the evacuation operations, I am fairly certain that Neville Hay and my patrol provided the only communication from both sides of the river bank to General 'Boy' Browning at 1st Airborne Corps. Between us we passed back General Urquhart's now famous message of the night of 24th September in which he said that it was unlikely that his forces could hold out any longer and that they would break out (of the perimeter of the north bank) rather than surrender.

Awards and ranks in Phantom

At the end of September, my patrol joined our old friends 3rd British Division on the river Maas. The J Sections were split up into separate units and one unit was attached to my patrol under my command. We were now in a static mud-bound position in heavy rain, so I was able to link outselves to SHQ by a land line, which relieved the pressure on the radio operators. On 23rd November, Dennis Russell came through on this line to say that I had been given an immediate award of the Military Cross for my part in the Arnhem operations. Vic Stump was to be promoted from corporal to sergeant. In fact, awards were very difficult to come by in Phantom – perhaps we were not included in normal army considerations. I was sorry that Vic Stump and Matthews, my DR, had not been individually recognised. Matthews in particular deserved an award for his part in continuously riding over long distances in very hazardous conditions, both by day and night, to deliver urgent and important reports. (By the same token, the rank of Phantom patrol officers was inconsistent with their responsibilities, and on at least one occasion I recommended that it would be more appropriate to forgo our special staff and intelligence allowances and have the basic rank of Major, which would have helped us with the G(OPS) staffs at most formations.)

On the general subject of recognition, it seems surprising that so few awards were made to the 150 Phantom officers and 1,500 other ranks

* Batsford, 1962.

over a period of some five years. Phantom personnel were engaged in the majority of wartime operations, except in the Western Desert, and many of them had worked in dangerous conditions for long periods. As far as I know, the only other Phantom officers who were awarded the Military Cross were Neville Hay, Tom Moore and Bill Mackintosh-Reid. There were about twenty Mentions in Despatches (of which I received two, but I don't know what for – the last one was delivered by the postman after I was demobbed.) I believe there were one or two MBEs given out at the end of hostilities, and I think John Morgan was given one.

Winter in Holland

The army became somewhat bogged down in the mud on the west side of the river Maas although there were some local advances and behind us the port of Antwerp was being cleared of enemy. As far as my patrol was concerned, we spent a lot of time pulling our vehicles out of the mud and ditches. I got a bit of shrapnel in my hand, which became poisoned, and after having it operated on at a FAP, I spent several days of welcome rest in bed at a village schoolmaster's house with his daughter looking after me.

At the beginning of October, I sent a Top Secret report on all divisional dispositions and intentions by SHQ DR to Corps HQ. The DR, in a jeep, took two left-hand instead of two right-hand turns on leaving us and drove straight into the German lines. Some flap ensued.

At Christmas, the Germans were issued with half a bottle of Schnapps and one Christmas tree per bunker. By midnight on Christmas Eve they had become rowdy and the noise of their singing and shouting drifted across the river.

Up to the Baltic

The spring offensive has left only disjointed memories in my mind. I remember crossing the Rhine (probably with 7th Armoured Division) and in April was with the 8th US Airborne Infantry Division. The General commanding this division led his troops from the front, and so my patrol found itself accompanying his jeep in a dash towards the Baltic coast. He used to sit in his jeep with a sub-machine gun, loosing off at various targets as we drove along.

I have a recollection of driving over the north German plains and seeing a low grey cloud on the horizon. As we approached, the cloud turned into a solid mass of thousands of German soldiers, intent on surrendering to the Americans or British rather than the Russians. Also a very strange coincidence : some Allied POW camps have been overrun and the liberated prisoners were making their way westwards. One little group straggling along the ditches included some old friends of mine from the QVRs, captured at Calais in 1940.

We eventually arrived at Schwerin where we were halted on orders from higher command. The Patrol was established in the house of a German Baron (still in residence) and I made my way forward to meet the Russians some miles east of Schwerin. The first meeting on this front between the British (represented by me) and the mighty Soviet armies (represented by a rather scruffy Cossack-type officer who spat on the ground after morosely accepting my handshake) was a strange and lonely affair. I drove our jeep several miles into Russian-held territory, despite the protests of the Russian officer, and turned back when our allies, the Soviet soldiers, began to look increasingly suspicious and hostile. The troops I saw looked like bandits and seemed to be equipped with civilian cars and lorries – but so fearsome was their reputation that the Germans had fled before them.

At Schwerin, I arrested Thomas Heller Cooper, a leading member of the so-called British Free Corps, together with five of his colleagues. The operation was tricky, in so far as the Americans would not give me any help although they were responsible for this area. Their intelligence colonel took the attitude that as Heller Cooper and his party were British subjects, the Americans had no jurisdiction. The story of Cooper's apprehension and arrest is a long and strange one, on which I was subsequently asked to report by MI5.

Cooper was taken to England some months later (by another long arm of coincidence, his plane and the one in which I was travelling for another purpose, landed at Croydon airport much at the same time, and I saw him being escorted away). He was charged with treason, tried at the Old Bailey and found guilty.

In Denmark

In May, 1945 (I think) my patrol rejoined 7th Armoured Division who fought their way up to Hamburg and thereafter were supervising the surrender of the German armies in the area of Schleswig-Holstein. From here, perhaps in June and July, the patrol was sent into Denmark to report on the disbandment of the German army and their installations in Jutland and the Copenhagen area.

We were located in the house of the Chief of Forests in Haderslev. His family name, Dalgas, is famous in Jutland for its ancestors' reclamation of the lands from the sea. His children had helped the local Danish Resistance movement, and his family became friends with whom we have exchanged correspondence and Christmas cards to this day.

Touring the German camps in my jeep provided many strange experiences. I remember the Dalgas children leading me to a large radar station on the coast, still manned by the Germans who seemed reluctant to give up and were very hostile.

Towards the autumn I helped to establish a German POW camp just north of Hamburg. At this time, I got kicked on the head by a German cavalry horse from which I was thrown whilst riding it. Ironically, I was very well operated on by German doctors in a local hospital, although the concussion gave me some trouble later.

From the hospital, I was ordered to return to RHQ at Bad Oeynhausen which was also the HQ either of SHAEF or 21st Army Group (I forget which). On arrival I was told that I was to be Adjutant – a position not much to my liking, as I preferred life out in the field. This was not a happy period, because the drive and excitement were superseded by an air of uncertainty – the area was a dreary one and most people were impatient to be demobilised and return to civilian life.

I think I took over from Tom Reddaway, who had been Adjutant for some years. The duties were fairly depressing and included some civilian investigations with the FSP and a court-martial. Also, at this time, many psychological problems must have set in amongst the soldiers, and one of our Phantom officers and an OR shot themselves (for what reasons, I don't know).

We had a succession of COs, due to the demobilisation programme. I think Colonel Sandy McIntosh left Phantom from Bad Oeynhausen. There were, after this, Colonel Smyly and Colonel Stuart French, and although I have some papers signed by them I cannot in fact remember them.

After I had been Adjutant for a few months, there was talk of forming a new Phantom Regiment and training it at Richmond for service in India. I cannot remember what its function would be – perhaps it was intended for use in providing intelligence information in the move towards India's independence. I was asked whether I would like to command this new regiment but although the idea of sudden promotion to lieutenant-colonel might have seemed attractive at first glance, the possibility of a return to civilian life seemed far more attractive at that time.

Thus, Demob day arrived and so my career in Phantom ended – 'not with a bang but with a whimper'. It was the same for all of us, I think – we were eager to leave the Service, and yet it all seemed rather an anti-climax when the time came.

Epilogue

Although by 1945 Phantom was a very different unit from the one originally conceived by Lieutenant-Colonel Hopkinson it was entirely in accord with his ideas on flexibility. Norman Reddaway, who observed Hoppy over a long period, commented:

'From the beginning Hoppy realised that the set-front pattern of World War I was unlikely to be repeated. In a future mobile war he felt that the set-front signals system would be inadequate and that it was therefore essential to find a substitute relying on radio and reconnaissance. His single-mindedness was completely dedicated to this idea. He was only interested in the future.' He never asked Reddaway about the shipwreck in which most of his close associates had perished.

But he fully understood how to get the best out of men. He insisted that officers should do all the things which the men did: ride motor cycles, become expert wireless operators, and be constantly busy. He would not have wives at Richmond, saying that their chatter would lead to breaches of security. The idea of making cavalry officers skilled wireless operators in 1940 was a revolutionary idea but he made it work by making them practice incessantly.

When he was killed in Italy his death was a greater loss to the British Army than was realised at the time. In the time he had been with 6th Airborne he had already impressed them by his complete grasp of essentials.

Phantom has now disappeared from the Army, made superfluous, it is believed, by technical advances. But from the Stone Age to the Nuclear Age the principles of war have remained constant. One of them requires that the commander should know what is happening everywhere on the battlefield. Perhaps modern methods have found an adequate substitute for men with enquiring minds who can obtain unbiased information from harassed staff officers. Until it is proved that they have, the experience of Phantom should not be set aside.

Further Reading

Last on the List Miles Reid, MBE, MC, DL, Leo Cooper, London 1974
In the Office of Constable Robert Mark Collins, London 1978
Confession of Faith Peter Baker, MC Falcon Press, London 1946
Tribal Feeling Michael Astor John Murray, London 1963
Phantom was There R. G. T. Hills Arnold London 1951
The Enemy Within John Watney Hodder, London 1946
There is a Spirit in Europe : *A Memoir of Frank Thompson,*
T. J. T. and E. P. T. Gollancz, London 1947

APPENDIX I

Five Months after VE Day

GHQ LIAISON REGIMENT (PHANTOM)
DISTRIBUTION OF OFFICERS
List No. 15 (4th September, 1945)

BAOR REGIMENT (WEs XIV/1236/2 & III/304/1)
Regimental Headquarters, "A" and "L" Squadrons in Germany

Lieut-Colonel J. A. T. Morgan
Major Lord Cullen of Ashbourne, MBE
Major T. F. Reddaway
Major J. M. Hannay
Major J. A. Darwall-Smith
Major T. H. Lambert
Major W. R. Tomkinson
Capt W. Adam
Capt B. A. Amswych
Capt A. F. C. Barnwell
Capt R. W. Baring
Capt A. L. F. Borman
Capt N. C. Bridge
Capt G. F. Castle
Capt A. M. S. Clark
Capt M. F. Cleghorn
Capt J. F. Colliver
Capt F. M. Cumberlege
Capt J. N. Currie
Capt S. S. Demetriadi
Capt (QM) A. T. E. Driskell
Capt J. W. Gray
Capt F. L. G. Griffith-Jones
Capt D. Brook-Hart, MC
Capt N. A. Hay

Capt H. R. M. Langley-Webb
Capt G. P. H. Lucas
Capt R. MacFarquhar
Capt W. S. McIntosh-Reid, MC
Capt A. C. Mackinlay
Capt F. A. de Marwicz
Capt T. A. S. O. Mathieson
Capt J. A. Meade
Capt D. J. Owen, MBE
Capt P. V. R. Pennant
Capt T. J. Potter
Capt K. W. Salter
Capt A. Speed-Andrews

Capt R. M. Weston
Capt E. B. Ware
Lt A. J. Richards

'B' Squadron attd 1 Canadian Army in Europe

Attached : Capt F. S. Lamb
Capt R. G. Rennie

Major J. E. Dulley
Capt C. G. Brain
Capt R. V. Brunsdon
Capt B. G. Coward
Capt P. H. L. Ling
Capt I. M. P. Millar
Capt P. S. Newall
Capt Earl of Rosslyn
Capt C. N. F. Webb
Capt H. McK. Butcher
Lt P. G. Worsthorne

'F' Squadron

Major Hon. J. J. Astor, MBE
Capt B. E. Hutton-Williams, MBE
Capt J. L. Hislop
Capt C. R. Moore
Capt P. D. Pattrick, MBE
Capt D. L. Russell, MBE
Lt K. J. Brookes

SEAC REGIMENT (WE XV/1/1)
Reforming in Germany for SEA

Lieut-Colonel J. C. de F. Sleeman, OBE
Major G. S. B. Cohen
Capt I. V. Balfour-Paul
Capt B. F. L. Bateman
Capt J. A. Beaumont
Capt P. B. Blamey
Capt R. A. Bryce
Capt A. S. Davies
Capt J. W. Jackson
Capt P. B. Johnson
Capt A. W. Laurie
Capt P. M. Luttman-Johnson
Capt I. R. Mackrill
Capt A. A. MacLaren

Capt M. B. Ramage
Capt J. C. T. Waring
Lt F. M. Cassavetti
Lt P. G. G. Chapell
Lt S. G. Davenport
Lt G. J. Davis
Lt P. J. M. Hill
Lt C. McDevitt
Lt A. J. Major-Stevenson
Lt A. H. Pettigrew
Lt E. Phillips
Lt D. A. Rogers
Lt K. V. Rose
Lt C. J. Skinner
Lt I. S. P. Sedgwick

Capt D. G. R. Oldham
Capt R. W. Pannell
Capt R. Perret
Capt J. T. D. Probyn

Lt J. H. Webbe
Lt N. R. Wooldridge

Training & Holding Unit, GHQ Liaison Regiment
(WE V/1200/1)
at Regimental HQ at Richmond Park in Surrey

Major H. L. Light
Capt J. B. L. Fitzwilliams
Capt C. H. F. Catt
Capt H. Averill, DCM
Capt R. W. Burgess
Capt D. K. H. Bell

Capt A. S. Foster
Capt A. H. Carter
Lt S. D. Player
Lt W. R. Watson-Smyth
Lt P. L. M. Hill
Lt A. H. English

APPENDIX II

Phantom British Airborne Div. Log

1. From Phantom Airborne Corps	Source 1 Airborne Corps 0815 hrs. No information or contact with 1 Airborne Div. TOO 181305 THI 181345
2. From Phantom Airborne Corps	Source 1 British Airborne Div 1315 hrs. Line of rly area E7178 held by enemy of unknown strength. ARNHEM E7678 held by approx three coys SS troops. TOO 181815 THI 181850
3. From Phantom 1 Airborne Div	Source G1 British Airborne Div 0700 hrs. Br E7577 occupied by enemy but NOT demolished. TOO 190700 THI 190825
4. From Phantom 1 Airborne Div	Source G2 Ops 0200 hrs. Locations own tps. 1 Para Bde HQ area 739776 with second bn in same area. Third bn 717777. Air Ldg Bde HQ E6878. 7 KOSB area wood 7079. 2 S Staffs area E 7177. Div HQ E6978. TOO 190725 THI 191121
5. From Phantom 1 Airborne Div	Source G2 1 Airborne Div 2155 hrs. Rly br E7076 demolished. TOO 190830 THI 191020
6. From Phantom Airborne Corps	Source 1 Br Airborne Div. Correct location 3 Para Bn is E716727 TOO 191200 THI 191245
7. From Phantom 1 Airborne Div	Air Support request. a. Max bombing effort on Flak posns outside Bomb line and especially at 716762 – 725774 – 744767 – 748755 b. before Z hr c. Bomb line NORTH bank NEDER RLJN to 743770 to 735795 to 718810 to 670784 river bank at 673763 TOO About 191000 Passed to Second Army
8. From Phantom to 1 Airborne Div	Attack on NIJMEGEN held up by strong point SOUTH of town. 5 Gds Bde half way

in town. Br intact but held by enemy. Intention attack at 1300 hrs to-day – details follow.

TOO 200820 (From Second Army)

9. From Phantom
1 Airborne Div

Source Patrol, Officer Airborne Div. SITREP at 191530 hrs. Elts senior formation still in vicinity NORTH end of main bridge but not in touch and unable re-supply. Part of 2 Bn now being concentrated SOUTH of DERBRINCK E7277. Next senior and junior formations now being reorganised to hold rd and rly crossing 699799 Pt 635 and 687785 – x-rds 688793. Third lift very hvy oppsn by Flak. ARNHEM entirely in enemy hands. Request all possible steps taken expedite relief. Fighting intense and oppsn extremely strong. Posn not too good.

TOO Not stated.   THI 201105

10. From Phantom
Airborne Corps

To 1 Airborne Div. Gds Armd Div coming within range this afternoon. Give targets in order of priority.

TOO 201000 (Intercept)   THI 201110

11. From Phantom
1 Airborne Div

Source G3 Airborne Div. Situation confused. Enemy made local gains to NORTH. Div HQ being mortared. No air spt. BUFFS.

TOO 201130   THI 201359

12. From Phantom
Second Army to
Airborne Div

At 0930 hrs 508 Regt on general line of road WYLER E7857 to NIJMEGEN with patrols to river line 770637. At 1113 hrs 5 Gds Bde fighting in NIJMEGEN 7162 and trying to rush bridge. 504 Regt will attempt assault crossing at 1400 hrs.

TOO 201143   THI 201421

13. From Phantom
1 Airborne Div

Targets in priority :—

   a. 743763
   b. 751777
   c. 713774
   d. 706762

TOO 201145   THI 201440

14. From Phantom
Second Army to
1 Airborne Div

From G Air to 1 Airborne Div. Cover is being flown. Close support will be given shortly.

TOO 201315   THI 201459

15. From Phantom
1 Airborne Div

Source G2 Ops 1555 hrs. Div HQ E694784. Some infiltration has taken place and enemy are attacking from EAST.

TOO 201602   THI 210212

16. From Phantom
1 Airborne Div

Source GSO1 Ops 1845 hrs. EAST flank of Div box held by KOSB who are being heavily mortared. G1 states speedy advance of Gds Armd Div essential.

TOO 201900   THI 210038

17. From Phantom 1 Airborne Div	Source GSO2 Ops 1 Airborne Div 1555 hrs. Div area now from E697791 to 703782 to 704774 to 688773 to rd junc 685784 to 688788.

TOO 201930   THI 202250

18. From Phantom Second Army to 1 Airborne Div	For BGS 1 Airborne Div. Intention Gds Armd Div morning 21 Sep. At first light to go all out for bridges at ARNHEM. 5 Gds Bde leading for rd bridge. 32 Gds Bde for rly bridge.

TOO 202358   THI 210100

19. From Phantom	Intercept Gds Armd Div – 1 Airborne Div. Source Gds Armd G Ops 202255 hrs. Br at 7163 captured intact and firmly held but otherwise situation confused and enemy still strong NORTH of river. To-morrow contact 1 Airborne Div will be first priority but do not expect any advance possible before 1200 hrs.

TOO 210045   THI 211033

20. From Phantom 1 Airborne Div	Own tps holding NORTH of Ferry at ARNHEM have been withdrawn.

TOO 210515   THI 211415

21. From Phantom 1 Airborne Div	Further to 201900. 1 Airborne Div HQ 694784 Some enemy infiltration has taken place and enemy are attacking from EAST.

TOO 210720   THI 211030

22. From Phantom Main	For inf timed 0545 hrs. From 1 Airborne Div to AIRTPS. Bomb line as dictated by G1. Pass through to right authority. Following area clear of own tps any action taken. Area WEST of Grid line 68. NORTH of Grid line 83 as far EAST as rd junc 710800. Thence EAST of Grnd 71 as far SOUTH as rly cutting 710783. Then rly to junc 758777. Enemy pioneers flood (-?) and gun defences on SOUTH approaches to main brs. Suggest close co-operation tks and air.

TOO 210950   THI 211320

23. From Phantom Airborne Corps	To 1 Airborne Div. Source BGS 0845 hrs. Part HCR directed on Ferry 685768 to pass ammunition.

TOO 210958   THI 211105

24. From Phantom 1 Airborne Div	Being intensely mortared and shelled from high ground WEST of ARNHEM. Request max air

effort.

TOO 211015   THI 211105

25. From Phantom

Intercept net Airborne Corps – 1 Airborne Div. From 1 Airborne Div 211150 hrs. Can you confirm civilian report NIJMEGEN retaken by enemy. Reply 211300 hrs.

            Your 211150 hrs.   Report untrue.

TOO 211400   THI 211405

26. From Phantom
     1 Airborne Div

Source GSO3 Ops 1615 hrs. 1 Polish Para Bde dropped area SOUTH end of Ferry at ARNHEM. Re-supply this afternoon only partly successful.

TOO 211730   THI 211947

27. From Phantom
     1 Airborne Div

- - - - situation serious Div conc area - - - - MG fire continuous on left flank of posn. - - - - Para Bn has given ground.

TOO 211905   THI 212330

28. From Phantom
     1 Airborne Div

Source G2 Ops 1900 hrs. KOSB holding NORTH edge of perimeter E696789 heavily attacked and nearly over-run.

TOO 211950   THI 212240

29. From Phantom
     1 Airborne Div

At 212230 hrs. Situation quiet. Some enemy penetration along road E6877. Own tps E695792 693789 – 690772 NORTH through woods to 687783 to 686784. Enemy very strong with MG and SP guns. Much concentrated mortar fire. Casualties very high.

TOO 220145   THI 221115

30. From Phantom
     1 Airborne Div

From 1 Br Airborne Dv to Airborne Corps. Ref 30 Corps 2 Army Secret GO 33 of 22 Sep. Movement no longer possible.

TOO 220830   THI 221052

31. From Phantom
     1 Airborne Div

Movement no longer possible. Ferry not held. Relief column should be directed on railway between 705785 and 688797 – centre Div resistance being HARTESTEIN 694786. Are doing our best.

TOO 220830   THI 221207

32. From Phantom
     Second Army

To 1 Airborne Div. Intention. 129 Bde right 214 Bde left to attack ARNHEM 1000 hrs to join up with you. Patrol 2 HCR contacted Poles at 675745 – attacking enemy 0900 hrs.

TOO 221017   THI 221056

33. From Phantom
     1 Airborne Div

EAST, SOUTH and WEST sides of perimeter as now held : E696784 – 696774 – then WEST to 688774 and NORTH to 688785.

TOO 221045   THI 221425

34. From Phantom
    1 Airborne Div

Max air support requested. 3 areas indicated by these cardinal positions :—
one. 675772 – 682769 – 679866 – 674769
two. 678783 – 680775 – 674774 – 672782
three. 715880 – 712774 – 708781
B.   As soon as possible.
C.   As per last SITREP
D.   Nil.

TOO 221130   THI 221307

35. From Phantom
    1 Airborne Div

For information. From 1 Airborne Div to Airborne Corps. Ferry not held. Relieving troops should be directed on rly between E705785 – 688799. Centre Airborne resistance 694786.

TOO 220931   THI 221630

36. From Phantom
    Second Army

To 1 British Airborne Div. Reference Phantom Tac HQ 21 Army Group message 221307. Army states that after most careful examination regret owing to storm unable accept. Will accept as soon as weather improves.

NOTE : Above refers to air support demand
       by 1 Airborne Div.

TOO 221325   THI 221713

37. From Phantom
    1 Airborne Div

Nothing to report 1409 hrs.

TOO 221409   THI 221620

38. From Phantom
    Second Army

Source Airborne Corps 1300 hrs. Civilian report by telephone from ARNHEM at 1200 hrs. Many British PW being marched back on road going NE. British being pushed back later direction of HEELSUM 6477.

TOO 221555   THI 221815

39. From Phantom
    1 Airborne Div

Source G2 Airborne Div 2100 hrs. Perimeter remains unchanged except slight penetration to SOUTH. Enemy attacks weaker with less MG fire but heavy mortaring continuing.

TOO 222110   THI 230215

40. From Phantom
    Second Army

To 1 Airborne Div. Source G1 Ops 43 Div 0815 hrs. Div will now cross NEDER RIJN WEST of ARNHEM and NOT at ARNHEM as previously intended.

TOO 230830   THI 231020

41. From Phantom
    1 Airborne Div

Source G1 Ops 0845 hrs. Some Poles ferried over river to thicken our defences last night. Heavy mortar fire over whole area continues.

42. From Phantom
1 Airborne Div

TOO 230845   THI 231110
Second part of above message. Enemy attacking from EAST and WEST. Remaining span of rly br blown by enemy. Food and ammunition being ferried across river by Poles.

43. From Phantom
1 Airborne Div

TOO 230847   THI 231730
Source GSO 3 Ops 1000 hrs. 2 Borders beat off enemy attack with tanks and infantry. Vehs with supplies only arrived this morning.

44. From Phantom
1 Airborne Div

TOO 231015   THI 231815
Enemy infantry strength unknown with 2 tanks attacking 2 Borders area 686734. Being dealt with by arty.

45. From Phantom
Second Army

TOO 231126   THI 231930
Source G Ops 43 Div 1100 hrs. NO repeat NO supplies reached 1 Airborne Div last night as DUKWs cannot cross. 130 head of column at 7061 have boats with them to use to supply 1 Airborne Div.

46. From Phantom
1 Airborne Div

TOO 231315   THI 231440
Source GOC 1325 hrs. Intention. As soon as DCLI are across capture high ground overlooking Ferry to help crossing of armour. Attack NOT likely to begin before first light tomorrow.

47. From Phantom
Second Army

TOO 231330   THI 232015
To 1 Airborne Div. Source G Ops 43 Div 1815 hrs. 214 Bde attacked 1700 hrs to clear ELST. 129 Bde held up by enemy – no change in locations. Intention. 130 Bde will assault river during night in area 6876. RE will then build Class 40 brdge. 129 Bde on relief by 69 Bde under command Gds Armd Div will cross into bridgehead established by 130 Bde in area 6876. 214 Bde will clear and hold rt flk from 7070 to 7076.

48. From Phantom
1 Airborne Div

TOO 231820   THI 232200
Source GSo2 Ops 1845 hrs. Situation unchanged except for slight infiltration in NE. NO supplies across river to-day. Mortar and shelling increasing over whole area. Supplies dropped to-day unsatisfactory.

49. From Phantom
Second Army

TOO 231846   THI 232020
Source BGS Airborne Corps 0900 hrs. Approx 200 Polish troops crossed river during night and

joined 1 Airborne Div with some supplies.
TOO 241040   THI 241122

50. From Phantom
Airborne Corps

To 1 Airborne Div. Source G2 Ops. At 1200 hrs latest positions 43 Div. 129 Bde preparing to move NORTH from NIJMEGEN. 214 Bde less one bn hold ELST. 130 Bde bns 707763 – 693762 – 675747 – 612755. One bn D (.)6475 – 668750. One bn with Polish Bde in general area 6875. One bn 214 Bde 6874.
TOO 241220   THI 241552

51. From Phantom
1 Airborne Div

Source G Ops 1330 hrs. Enemy continues to attack in small parties with SP guns in support. Small numbers of Pz Kw IV area 694788. Mortar fire continues. Poles who crossed last night now fighting area 698782.
TOO 241330   THI 241945

52. From Phantom
1 Airborne Div

Source G Ops 0845 hrs. Only 300 Polish over last night. Water and food and ammunition short. Shelling and mortaring continues and intense.
TOO 241630   THI 241805

53. From Phantom
1 Airborne Div

Perimeter very weak and casualties mounting. Essential relieving troops make contact immediately on crossing. Enemy attacks made with SP guns or tanks and following infantry were NOT formidable. Heavy shelling and mortaring continues.
TOO 242205   THI 242330

54. From Phantom
1 Airborne Div

URQUHART TO BROWNING. MUST WARN YOU UNLESS PHYSICAL CONTACT IS MADE WITH US EARLY 25 SEP CONSIDER IT UNLIKELY WE CAN HOLD OUT LONG ENOUGH. ALL RANKS NOW EXHAUSTED. LACK OF RATIONS, WATER AMMUNITION AND WEAPONS WITH HIGH OFFICER CASUALTY RATE. EVEN SLIGHT ENEMY OFFENSIVE ACTION MAY CAUSE COMPLETE DISINTEGRATION. IF THIS HAPPENS ALL WILL BE ORDERED TO BREAK TOWARD BRIDGEHEAD IF ANYTHING RATHER THAN SURRENDER. ANY MOVEMENT AT PRESENT IN FACE OF ENEMY POSSIBLE. HAVE ATTEMPTED OUR BEST AND WILL DO SO AS LONG

AS POSSIBLE.
TOO 250830   THI 251040

55. From Phantom
     1 Airborne Div

Source G2 Ops 1330 hrs. Perimeter still holding though situation so fluid impossible state exact locations.
TOO 251345   THI 252035

56. From Phantom
     1 Airborne Div

Extract from 1 Airborne Div SITREP 242145 hrs. MDS in enemy hand-s and casualties being evacuated to ARNHEM 7577.
TOO 251400   THI 251444

57. From Phantom
     1 Airborne Div

Source Div G Ops 1530 hrs. Intention. 4 Dorset and 1 Airborne Div will be evacuated SOUTH to-night crossing in area 6876 covered by arty fire and smoke screen if operation continues after first light.
TOO 251550   THI 251825

58. From Phantom
     1 Airborne Div

Source G2 Ops 1545 hrs. Contact made with LO Dorsets only – NO repeat NO contact between tps on ground.
TOO 251550   THI 251948

59. From Phantom
     Airborne Corps

Airborne Corps Patrol now out of contact with 1 Airborne Div.
TOO 251915   THI 252100

60. From Phantom
     Airborne Corps

Source BM 130 Bde 2100 hrs. 130 Bde plan for withdrawing force SOUTH of river.

2100 hrs Arty barrage
2140 hrs First boats reach NORTH side to collect 1 Airborne Div
0200 hrs 4 Dorset start withdrawing to SOUTH side of river
0400 hrs Heavy smoke screen
0600 hrs Operations stop.
TOO 252130   THI 260130

61. From Phantom
     Airborne Corps

Source G2 Airborne Corps 0015 hrs. Elements 1 Airborne Div have reached SOUTH side of river.
TOO 260025   THI 260200

62. From Phantom
     Second Army

Source OC Evacuation Collecting Point who reported at 0530 hrs that of the 1200 men passed through his hands at that time 99% were 1 Airborne Div men and 1% Polish. About 1700 men in all it was believed had got SOUTH of the river by that time.
TOO 260550   THI 261120

63. From Phantom

Source 43 Div 0925 hrs. General URQUHART

Second Army | here during night. He estimated 2500 men to be evacuated. There are still approx 200 men on NORTH bank of river moving EAST.

TOO 261030   THI 261120

64. From Phantom Second Army | Source 43 Div 0845 hrs. Number of men evacuated 2800 repeat 2800. Operation stopped 0830 hrs.

NOTE : The Phantom Patrol Officer with 43 Div believed this included POLISH Paratps.

TOO 260925   THI 261035.

Index

Index

Note: The ranks given in this Index are not necessarily the highest ultimately attained by the people concerned.